How to Think Straight About Psychology

NINTH EDITION

Keith E. Stanovich

University of Toronto

Boston   Columbus   Indianapolis   New York   San Francisco
Upper Saddle River   Amsterdam   Cape Town   Dubai   London   Madrid
Milan   Munich   Paris   Montreal   Toronto   Delhi   Mexico City
Sao Paulo   Sydney   Hong Kong   Seoul   Singapore   Taipei   Tokyo

Executive Editor: Stephen Frail
Editorial Assistant: Kerri Hart-Morris
Executive Marketing Manager: Jeanette Koskinas
Production Editor: Maggie Brobeck
Editorial Production Service: Integra Software Services, Ltd.
Manufacturing Buyer: Frances Russello
Electronic Composition: Integra Software Services, Ltd.

If you purchased this book within the United States or Canada you should be aware that it has been wrongfully imported without the approval of the Publisher or the Author.

Copyright © 2010, 2007, 2004, Keith E. Stanovich

Published by Pearson Education, Inc., publishing as Allyn & Bacon, 75 Arlington Street, Suite 300, Boston, MA 02116. All rights reserved. Manufactured in the United States of America. This publication is protected by Copyright, and permission should be obtained from the publisher prior to any prohibited reproduction, storage in a retrieval system, or transmission in any form or by any means, electronic, mechanical, photocopying, recording, or likewise. To obtain permission(s) to use material from this work, please submit a written request to Pearson Higher Education, Rights and Contracts Department, 501 Boylston Street, Suite 900, Boston, MA 02116, or fax your request to 617-671-3447.

Many of the designations by manufacturers and sellers to distinguish their products are claimed as trademarks. Where those designations appear in this book, and the publisher was aware of a trademark claim, the designations have been printed in initial caps or all caps.

10 9 8 7 6 5 4 3 2 1—CRS—13 12 11 10 09

ISBN-10:   0-205-76092-9
ISBN-13: 978-0-205-76092-3

To Paula, who taught me how to think straight about life

Contents

Preface

There exists a body of knowledge that is unknown to most people. This information concerns human behavior and consciousness in their various forms. It can be used to explain, predict, and control human actions. Those who have access to this knowledge use it to gain an understanding of other human beings. They have a more complete and accurate conception of what determines the behavior and thoughts of other individuals than do those who do not have this knowledge.

Surprisingly enough, this unknown body of knowledge is the discipline of psychology.

What can I possibly mean when I say that the discipline of psychology is unknown? Surely, you may be thinking, this statement was not meant to be taken literally. Bookstores contain large sections full of titles dealing with psychology. Television and radio talk shows regularly feature psychological topics. Magazine articles quote people called psychologists talking about a variety of topics. Nevertheless, there is an important sense in which the *field* of psychology is unknown.

Despite much seeming media attention, the discipline of psychology remains for the most part hidden from the public. The transfer of "psychological" knowledge that is taking place via the media is largely an illusion. Few people are aware that the majority of the books they see in the psychology sections of many bookstores are written by individuals with absolutely no standing in the psychological community. Few are aware that many of the people to whom television applies the label *psychologist* would not be considered so by the American Psychological Association or the Association for Psychological Science. Few are aware that many of the most visible psychological "experts" have contributed no information to the fund of knowledge in the discipline of psychology.

The flurry of media attention paid to "psychological" topics has done more than simply present inaccurate information. It has also obscured the very real and growing knowledge base in the field of psychology. The general public is unsure about what is and is not psychology and is unable to independently evaluate claims about human behavior. Adding to the problem is the fact that many people have a vested interest in a public that is either without evaluative skills or that believes there is no way to evaluate psychological claims. The latter view, sometimes called the "anything goes" attitude, is one of the fallacies discussed in this book, and it is particularly costly to the public. Many pseudosciences are multimillion-dollar industries that depend on the lack of public awareness that claims about human behavior can be tested. The general public is also unaware that many of the claims made by these pseudosciences (for example, astrology, psychic surgery, speed reading, biorhythms, therapeutic touch, subliminal self-help tapes, and psychic detectives) have been tested and proved false. The existence of the pseudoscience industry, which is discussed in this book, increases the media's tendency toward sensationalistic reporting of science. This tendency is worse in psychology than in other sciences, and understanding the reasons why this is so is an important part of learning how to think straight about psychology.

This book, then, is directed not at potential researchers in psychology but at a much larger group: the consumers of psychological information. The target audience is the beginning psychology student and the general reader who have encountered information on psychological issues in the general media and have wondered how to go about evaluating its validity.

This book is not a standard introductory psychology text. It does not outline a list of facts that psychological research has uncovered. Indeed, telling everyone to take an introductory psychology course at a university is probably not the ultimate solution to the inaccurate portrayal of psychology in the media. There are many laypeople with a legitimate interest in psychology who do not have the time, money, or access to a university to pursue formal study. More importantly, as a teacher of university-level psychology courses, I am forced to admit that my colleagues and I often fail to give our beginning students a true understanding of the science of psychology. The reason is that lower-level courses often do not teach the critical analytical skills that are the focus of this book. As instructors, we often become obsessed with "content"—with "covering material." Every time we stray a little from the syllabus to discuss issues such as psychology in the media, we feel a little guilty and begin to worry that we may not cover all the topics before the end of the term.

Consider the average introductory psychology textbook. Many now contain between 600 and 800 multicolumned pages and reference literally hundreds of studies in the published literature. Of course, there is nothing wrong with such books containing so much material. It simply reflects the increasing knowledge base in psychology. There are, however, some unfortunate side effects. Instructors are often so busy trying to cram their students full of dozens of theories, facts, and experiments that they fail to deal with some of the fundamental questions and misconceptions that students bring with them to the study of psychology. Rather than dealing directly with these misconceptions, the instructors (and the introductory textbook authors) often hope that if students are exposed to enough of the empirical content of psychology, they will simply *induce* the answers to their questions. In short, the instructors hope that students will recognize the implicit answers to these questions in the discussions of empirical research in several content areas. All too often this hope is frustrated. In a final review session—or in office hours at the end of the term—instructors are often shocked and discouraged by questions and comments that might have been expected on the first day of the course but not after 14 weeks: "But psychology experiments aren't real life; what can they tell us?"; "Psychology just can't be a *real* science like chemistry, can it?"; "But I heard a therapist on TV say the opposite of what our textbook said"; "I think this theory is stupid—my brother behaves just the opposite of what it says"; "Psychology is nothing more than common sense, isn't it?"; "Everyone knows what anxiety is—why bother defining it?" For many students, such questions are not implicitly answered merely by a consideration of the content of psychology. In this book, I deal explicitly with the confusions that underlie questions and comments such as these.

Unfortunately, research has shown that the average introductory psychology course does surprisingly little to correct some of entering students' misconceptions about the discipline (Keith & Beins, 2008; Standing & Huber, 2003; Taylor & Kowalski, 2004). This unfortunate fact provides the rationale for this book. Psychology, probably more than any other science, requires critical thinking skills that enable students to separate the wheat from the chaff that accumulates around all sciences. These are the critical thinking skills that students will need to become independent evaluators of psychological information.

Years after students have forgotten the content of an introductory psychology course, they will still use the fundamental principles covered in this book to evaluate psychological claims. Long after Erikson's stages of development have been forgotten, students will be using the thinking tools introduced in this text to evaluate new psychological information encountered in the media. Once acquired, these skills will serve as lifelong tools that will aid in the evaluation of knowledge claims. First, they provide the ability to conduct an initial gross assessment of plausibility. Second, these skills provide some criteria for assessing the reliability of "expert" opinion. Because the need to rely on expert opinion can never be eliminated in a complex society, the evaluation of an expert's credibility becomes essential to knowledge acquisition. Although these critical thinking skills can be applied to any discipline or body of knowledge, they are particularly important in the area of psychology because the field is so often misrepresented in the general media.

Many psychologists are pessimistic about any effort to stem the tide of misinformation about their discipline. Although this pessimism is, unfortunately, often justified, this "consumer's guide" to psychology was motivated by the idea that psychologists must not let this problem become a self-fulfilling prophecy.

Although I have welcomed the opportunity to prepare several editions of *How to Think Straight About Psychology*, it is unfortunately true that the reasons for the book's existence are just as applicable today as they were when I wrote the first edition. Media presentations of psychology are just as misleading as they ever were, and students in introductory psychology courses enter with as many misconceptions as they ever did. Thus, the goals of all subsequent editions have remained the same. These goals are shared by an increasing number of psychology instructors. Stanford University psychologist Roger Shepard (1983) echoed all the concerns that motivated the writing of the first edition of this text: "Although most undergraduate psychology students may not go on to scientific careers, one hopes that they acquire some facility for the critical evaluation of the incomplete, naive, confused, or exaggerated reports of social science 'findings' to which they will continue to be exposed by the popular media. . . . Widespread notions that human behavior and mental phenomena can be adequately understood through unaided common sense or, worse, by reference to non-empirical pseudosciences, such as astrology, present us with a continuing challenge" (p. 855).

The goal of this book is to present a short introduction to the critical thinking skills that will help students to better understand the subject matter of psychology and better understand events in the world in which they live.

New to the Ninth Edition

The ninth edition of *How to Think Straight About Psychology* has no major structural revisions because a chapter reorganization occurred in a previous edition. The content and order of the chapters remain the same. At the request of reviewers and users, this edition remains at the same length as the eighth edition. Readers and users have not wanted the book to lengthen and, indeed, it has not. I have continued to update and revise the examples that are used in the book (while keeping those that are reader favorites). Some dated examples have been replaced with more contemporary studies and issues. I have made a major effort to use contemporary citations that are relevant to the various concepts and experimental effects that are mentioned. A large number of new citations appear in this edition (190 new citations, to be exact!), so that the reader continues to have up-to-date references on all of the examples and concepts.

The goal of the book remains what it always was—to present a short introduction to the critical thinking skills that will help the student to better understand the subject matter of psychology. During the past decade and a half there has been an increased emphasis on the teaching of critical thinking in universities (Abrami et al., 2008; Sternberg, Roediger, & Halpern, 2006). Indeed, some state university systems have instituted curricular changes mandating an emphasis on critical thinking skills. At the same time, however, other educational scholars were arguing that critical thinking skills should not be isolated from specific factual content. *How to Think Straight About Psychology* combines these two trends. It is designed to provide the instructor with the opportunity to teach critical thinking within the rich content of modern psychology.

Readers are encouraged to send me comments by corresponding with me at the following address: Keith E. Stanovich, Department of Human Development and Applied Psychology, University of Toronto, 252 Bloor St. W., Toronto, Ontario, Canada, M5S 1V6. Email: KStanovich@oise.utoronto.ca.

Acknowledgments

Many of the individuals I have acknowledged in earlier editions continue to contribute ideas for the book. However, I must single out Richard West of James Madison University, who has been a most valuable continuing contributor to the book's evolution. A humane scholar and a true friend, his intellectual and emotional support is much appreciated.

Several other scholars have provided valuable feedback on this and earlier editions. These include Wayne Bartz, American River College; Christopher Bauer, University of New Hampshire; Ludy Benjamin, Texas A&M University; Angela M. Birkhead-Flight, University of Cincinnati; Virginia Blankenship, University of Northern Arizona; Edward C. Chang, Northern Kentucky University; Michael Choban, West Virginia Wesleyan University; James Clark, University of Winnipeg; Jim Coan, University of Arizona; Ellen Cole, Alaska Pacific University; Ellen Cotter, Georgia Southwestern State University; Anne Cunningham, University of California, Berkeley; Ian Deary, University of Edinburgh; Julie Deisinger, Saint Xavier University; David DiBattista, Brock University; Wallace Dixon, Heidelberg College; Mark Fineman, Southern Connecticut State University; Herbert Fink, SUNY–Brockport; Heinz Fischer, Long Beach City College; Ronald Gandelman, Rutgers University; Michael Gasser, University of Northern Iowa; Traci A. Giuliano, Southwestern University; William Graziano, Purdue University; Nancy J. Gussett, Baldwin-Wallace College; Gordon Hammerle, Adrian College; Randy Hansen, Oakland University; William L. Hathaway, Regent University; George Heise, Indiana University; Albert Heldt, Grand Rapids Junior College; Dori Henderson, Metropolitan State University;

George Howard, University of Notre Dame; Barry Kendall; Bernie Koenig, Fanshawe College; Victor Koop, Goshen College; P. A. Lamal, University of North Carolina, Charlotte; Stephen Louisell, Kalamazoo Community College; Gwen Lupfer-Johnson, University of Alaska, Anchorage; Margaret Matlin, State University of New York-Geneseo; Douglas Mook, University of Virginia; Timothy Moore, York University; Edward Morris, University of Kansas; Joseph E. Morrow, California State University at Sacramento; Michael O'Boyle, Iowa State University; Blaine Peden, University of Wisconsin, Eau Claire; John F. Pfister, Dartmouth College; Sam Rakover, University of Haifa; Richard Redding, Hahneman University; Michael Ross, University of Waterloo; John Ruscio, Elizabethtown College; Walter Sa, Grand Valley State University; Allen Salo, University of Maine at Presque Isle; Frank Schieber, University of South Dakota; Marjorie Semonick, University of Minnesota; David Share, University of Haifa; Jeffrey Sherman, Northwestern University; Linda Siegel, University of British Columbia; Norman Silverman, University of Illinois, Chicago; Frank Smoll, University of Washington; Paul Solomon, Williams College; Mike Stadler, University of Missouri; Maggie Toplak, York University; Larry Vandervert, Spokane Falls Community College; John Vokey, University of Lethbridge; Carol Wade, College of Marin; Marty Wall, University of Toronto; Barbara Wanchisen, Baldwin-Wallace College; Toni G. Wegner, University of Virginia; Edward Wisniewski, Northwestern University; Murray S. Work, California State University at Sacramento; and Edward Zuckerman, Guilford Press.

The insights from many discussions about teaching methodology with Ted Landau, Larry Lilliston, and Dean Purcell, all of Oakland University, were incorporated into the book. Reviewers of recent editions who were particularly helpful include: Steven Isonio, Golden West College; Cindy Sifonis, Oakland University; Michael Tagler, Nebraska Wesleyan University; and Chris Ward, Stonehill College.

My editor at Pearson, Stephen Frail, has provided guidance, enthusiasm, and support for the book, as has his editorial assistant, Kerri Hart-Morris. Robyn Macpherson is thanked for her diligent library and reference assistance on several editions prior to this one.

Finally, I wish to thank Paula J. Stanovich for more than just the emotional support that is routinely alluded to in acknowledgments. Her concern for all human beings, particularly those less fortunate, is an inspiration to all who know her. A view we both share is that all human beings should have the opportunity to utilize their full potential. This book attests to the fact that I have had such an opportunity. Paula works to speed the day when this opportunity will be fully extended to all individuals with disabilities.

CHAPTER 1

Psychology Is Alive and Well (and Doing Fine Among the Sciences)

The Freud Problem

Stop 100 people on the street and ask them to name a psychologist, either living or dead. Record the responses. Of course, Dr. Phil, Wayne Dyer, and other "media psychologists" would certainly be named. If we leave out the media and pop psychologists, however, and consider only those who have made a recognized contribution to psychological knowledge, there would be no question about the outcome of this informal survey. Sigmund Freud would be the winner hands down. B. F. Skinner would probably finish a distant second. No other psychologist would get enough recognition even to bother about. Thus, Freud, along with the pop psychology presented in the media, largely defines psychology in the public mind.

The notoriety of Freud has greatly affected the general public's conceptions about the field of psychology and has contributed to many misunderstandings. For example, many introductory psychology students are surprised to learn that, if all the members of the American Psychological Association (APA) who were concerned with Freudian psychoanalysis were collected, they would make up less than 10 percent of the membership. In another major psychological association, the Association for Psychological Science, they would make up considerably less than 5 percent. One popular introductory psychology textbook (Wade & Tavris, 2008) is over 700 pages long, yet contains only 15 pages on which either Freud or psychoanalysis is mentioned—and these 15 pages often contain criticism ("most Freudian concepts were, and still are, rejected by most empirically oriented psychologists," p. 19).

In short, modern psychology is not obsessed with the ideas of Sigmund Freud (as are the media and some humanities disciplines), nor is it largely defined by them. Freud's work is an extremely small part of the varied set of issues, data, and theories that are the concern of modern psychologists. This larger body of research and theory encompasses the work of five recent Nobel Prize winners (David Hubel, Daniel Kahneman, Herbert Simon, Roger Sperry, and Torsten Wiesel) and a former director of the National Science Foundation (Richard Atkinson), all of whom are virtually unknown to the public.

It is bad enough that Freud's importance to modern psychology is vastly exaggerated. What makes the situation worse is that Freud's methods of investigation are completely unrepresentative of how modern psychologists conduct their research (recall that Freud began his work over a hundred years ago). In fact, the study of Freud's methods gives an utterly misleading impression of psychological research. For example, Freud did not use controlled experimentation, which, as we shall see in Chapter 6, is the most potent weapon in the modern psychologist's arsenal of methods. Freud thought that case studies could establish the truth or falsity of theories. We shall see in Chapter 4 why this idea is mistaken. Finally, a critical problem with Freud's work concerns the connection between theory and behavioral data. As we shall see in Chapter 2, for a theory to be considered scientific, the link between the theory and behavioral data must meet some minimal requirements. Freud's theories do not meet these criteria (Dufresne, 2007; Hines, 2003; Macmillan, 1997; McCullough, 2001). To make a long story short, Freud built an elaborate theory on a database (case studies and introspection) that was not substantial enough to support it. Freud concentrated on building complicated theoretical structures, but he did not, as modern psychologists do, ensure that they would rest on a database of reliable, replicable behavioral relationships. In summary, familiarity with Freud's style of work can be a significant impediment to the understanding of modern psychology.

In this chapter, we shall deal with the Freud problem in two ways. First, when we illustrate the diversity of modern psychology, the rather minor position occupied by Freud will become clear (see Haggbloom et al., 2002; Robins, Gosling, & Craik, 1999, 2000). Second, we shall discuss what features are common to psychological investigations across a wide variety of domains. A passing knowledge of Freud's work has obscured from the general public what is the only unifying characteristic of modern psychology: the quest to understand behavior by using the methods of science.

The Diversity of Modern Psychology

There is, in fact, a great diversity of content and perspectives in modern psychology. This diversity drastically reduces the coherence of psychology as a discipline. Henry Gleitman (1981), winner of the American Psychological

Foundation's Distinguished Teaching Award, characterized psychology as "a loosely federated intellectual empire that stretches from the domains of the biological sciences on one border to those of the social sciences on the other" (p. 774). Commentators outside of psychology have criticized this diversity. For example, anthropologist Clifford Geertz (2000) has complained that "from the outside, at least, it does not look like a single field, divided into schools and specialties in the usual way. It looks like an assortment of disparate and disconnected inquiries classed together because they all make reference in some way or other to something or other called mental functioning" (p. 187).

Understanding that psychology is composed of an incredibly wide and diverse set of investigations is critical to an appreciation of the nature of the discipline. Simply presenting some of the concrete indications of this diversity will illustrate the point. The APA has 54 different divisions, each representing either a particular area of research and study or a particular area of practice (see Table 1.1). From the table, you can see the range of subjects studied by psychologists, the range of settings involved, and the different aspects of behavior studied. The other large organization of psychologists—the Association for Psychological Science—is just as diverse. Actually, Table 1.1 understates the diversity within the field of psychology because it gives the impression that each division is a specific specialty area. In fact, each of the 54 divisions listed in the table is a broad area of study that contains a wide variety of subdivisions! In short, it is difficult to exaggerate the diversity of the topics that fall within the field of psychology.

Implications of Diversity

Many people come to the study of psychology hoping to learn the one grand psychological theory that unifies and explains all aspects of human behavior. Such hopes are often disappointed, because psychology contains not one grand theory, but many different theories, each covering a limited aspect of behavior (Benjamin, 2001; Griggs, Proctor, & Bujak-Johnson, 2002). The diversity of psychology guarantees that the task of theoretical unification will be immensely difficult. Indeed, many psychologists would argue that such a unification is impossible. Others, however, are searching for greater unification within the field (Cacioppo, 2007a, b; Gray, 2008; Henriques, 2004, 2005; Kenrick, 2001; Sternberg, 2005). For example, the coherence of psychology as a discipline has increased over the last decade due to the theoretical efforts of evolutionary psychologists. These researchers have tried to bring unification to our conceptualization of human psychological processes by viewing them as mechanisms serving critical evolutionary functions such as kinship recognition, mate selection, cooperation, social exchange, and child rearing (Barrett, Dunbar, & Lycett, 2002; Buss, 2005, 2007; Cartwright, 2008; Ellis & Bjorklund, 2005; Geary, 2005, 2008; Pinker, 2002). Likewise, Cacioppo (2007b) points to subfields such as social cognitive neuroscience as tying together numerous

TABLE 1.1 *Divisions of the American Psychological Association*

1. General Psychology
2. Teaching of Psychology
3. Experimental Psychology
5. Evaluation, Measurement, and Statistics
6. Behavioral Neuroscience and Comparative Psychology
7. Developmental Psychology
8. Personality and Social Psychology
9. Psychological Study of Social Issues
10. Psychology of Aesthetics, Creativity, and the Arts
12. Clinical Psychology
13. Consulting Psychology
14. Industrial and Organizational Psychology
15. Educational Psychology
16. School Psychology
17. Counseling Psychology
18. Psychologists in Public Service
19. Military Psychology
20. Adult Development and Aging
21. Applied Experimental and Engineering Psychology
22. Rehabilitation Psychology
23. Consumer Psychology
24. Theoretical and Philosophical Psychology
25. Behavior Analysis
26. History of Psychology
27. Community Psychology
28. Psychopharmacology and Substance Abuse
29. Psychotherapy
30. Psychological Hypnosis
31. State Psychological Association Affairs
32. Humanistic Psychology
33. Intellectual and Developmental Disabilities
34. Population and Environmental Psychology
35. Psychology of Women
36. Psychology of Religion
37. Child and Family Policy and Practice
38. Health Psychology
39. Psychoanalysis
40. Clinical Neuropsychology
41. Psychology and Law
42. Psychologists in Independent Practice
43. Family Psychology
44. Psychological Study of Lesbian, Gay, and Bisexual Issues
45. Psychological Study of Ethnic Minority Issues
46. Media Psychology
47. Exercise and Sport Psychology
48. Peace Psychology

TABLE 1.1 *Divisions of the American Psychological Association (continued)*

49. Group Psychology and Group Psychotherapy
50. Addictions
51. Psychological Study of Men and Masculinity
52. International Psychology
53. Clinical Child and Adolescent Psychology
54. Pediatric Psychology
55. Pharmacotherapy
56. Trauma Psychology

Note: There is no Division 4 or 11.

specialty areas within psychology—in this case, cognitive psychology, social psychology, and neuropsychology.

Some researchers see the diversity of psychology as reflecting an underlying strength of the discipline (Cacioppo, 2007a; Gray, 2008). For example, Cacioppo (2007a) views psychology as a so-called hub discipline—a science whose findings have unusually wide implications for other fields. He cites evidence indicating that, compared with other sciences, psychological findings have quite broad implications for other sciences.

No matter what their position on the issue of the coherence of the subject matter of psychology, all psychologists agree that theoretical unification will be an extremely difficult task. The lack of theoretical integration leads some critics of psychology to denigrate the scientific progress that psychology has made. Such criticism often arises from the mistaken notion that all true sciences must have a grand, unifying theory. It is a mistaken notion because many other sciences also lack a unifying conceptualization. Harvard psychologist William Estes (1979) has emphasized this point:

> The situation in which the experimental psychologists find themselves is not novel, to be sure, nor peculiar to psychology. Physics during the early twentieth century subdivided even at the level of undergraduate teaching into separate disciplines. Thus I was introduced to that science through separate university courses in mechanics, heat, optics, acoustics, and electricity. Similarly, chemistry has branched out, evidently irreversibly, into inorganic, organic, physical, and biochemical specialties, among which there may be no more communication than among some of the current subdisciplines of psychology. In both cases, unity has reemerged only at the level of abstract mathematical theory. Medicine has similarly fragmented into specialties, but is like psychology in that there has been no appearance of a new unity. (pp. 661–662)

Once we acknowledge the implications of the social and historical factors that determine the structure of disciplines, we can recognize that it is illogical to demand that all fields be unified. Indeed, it has been suggested that the term *psychological studies*, rather than *psychology*, would more accurately reflect the diversity of the discipline. The use of this new term would also make it less surprising to the student that the different areas within the discipline have been characterized by vastly different rates of scientific progress. Some have made impressive progress in the explanation and prediction of behavior, while others have progressed much more slowly. The term *psychology* does not convey this state of affairs. Instead, it implies a coherence of subject matter that is not characteristic of the discipline.

One way to find more unity in the field of psychology is to look at the *methods* that psychologists use to advance knowledge. Here is where we can hope to find more unity of purpose among investigators. But here, in the domain of the methods that psychologists use to advance knowledge, is where we also find some of the greatest misunderstandings of the discipline.

Unity in Science

Simply to say that psychology is concerned with human behavior does not distinguish it from other disciplines. Many other professional groups and disciplines—including economists, novelists, the law, sociology, history, political science, anthropology, and literary studies—are, in part, concerned with human behavior. Psychology is not unique in this respect.

Practical applications do not establish any uniqueness for the discipline of psychology either. For example, many university students decide to major in psychology because they have the laudable goal of wanting to "help people." But helping people is an applied part of an incredibly large number of fields, including social work, education, nursing, occupational therapy, physical therapy, police science, human resources, and speech therapy. Similarly, helping people by counseling them is an established part of the fields of education, social work, police work, nursing, pastoral work, occupational therapy, and many others. The goal of training applied specialists to help people by counseling them does not demand that we have a discipline called psychology.

It is easy to argue that there are really *only* two things that justify psychology as an independent discipline. The first is that psychology studies the full range of human and nonhuman behavior with the techniques of science. The second is that the applications that derive from this knowledge are *scientifically* based. Were this not true, there would be no reason for psychology to exist.

Psychology is different from other behavioral fields in that it attempts to give the public two guarantees. One is that the conclusions about behavior that it produces derive from scientific evidence. The second is that practical applications of psychology have been derived from and tested by scientific methods. Does psychology ever fall short of these goals? Yes, quite often (Lilienfeld, 2007; Lilienfeld, Ruscio, & Lynn, 2008; Lynn, Loftus, Lilienfeld, & Lock, 2003). This book is about how we might better attain them. I will return in Chapter 12 to the issue of psychologists themselves undermining their own legitimacy by not meeting appropriate scientific standards. But, in principle, these are the standards that justify psychology as an independent field. If psychology ever decides that these goals are not worth pursuing— that it does not wish to adhere to scientific standards—then it might as well fold its tent and let its various concerns devolve to other disciplines because it would be a totally redundant field of intellectual inquiry.

Clearly, then, the first and most important step that anyone must take in understanding psychology is to realize that its defining feature is that it is the data-based scientific study of behavior. Comprehending all of the implications of this fact will occupy us for the rest of this book, because it is the primary way that we develop the ability to think straight about psychology. Conversely, the primary way that people get confused in their thinking about psychology is that they fail to realize that it is a scientific discipline. For example, it is quite common to hear people outside the discipline voice the opinion that psychology is not a science. Why is this a common occurrence?

Attempts to convince the public that psychology cannot be a science stem from a variety of sources. As will be discussed in later chapters, much confusion about the actual discipline of psychology is deliberately fostered by purveyors of bogus psychology. There has grown up in our society a considerable industry of pseudoscientific belief systems that have a vested interest in convincing the public that anything goes in psychology and that there are no rational criteria for evaluating psychological claims. This is the perfect atmosphere in which to market such offers as "Lose weight through hypnosis," "Develop your hidden psychic powers," and "Learn French while you sleep," along with the many other parts of the multimillion-dollar self-help industry that either are not based on scientific evidence or, in many cases, are actually contradicted by much available evidence.

Another source of resistance to scientific psychology stems from the tendency to oppose the expansion of science into areas where unquestioned authorities and "common sense" have long reigned. History provides many examples of initial public resistance to the use of science rather than philosophical speculation, theological edict, or folk wisdom to explain the natural world. Each science has gone through a phase of resistance to its development. Learned contemporaries of Galileo refused to look into his new telescope because the existence of the moons of Jupiter would have violated their philosophical and theological beliefs. For centuries, the understanding of human anatomy progressed only haltingly because of lay and ecclesiastical prohibitions of the dissection of human cadavers (the Christian view was that the interior of the body was "God's province"; see Grice, 2001). Charles Darwin was repeatedly denounced. Paul Broca's Society of Anthropology was opposed in France in the nineteenth century because knowledge about human beings was thought to be subversive to the state.

Each scientific step to greater knowledge about human beings has evoked opposition. This opposition eventually dissipated, however, when people came to realize that science does not defile humanity by its investigations but contributes to human fulfillment by widening the sphere of knowledge. Who now believes that astronomy's mapping of the galaxies and its intricate theories about the composition of distant stars destroy our wonder at the universe? Who would substitute the health care available in their community for that available before human cadavers were routinely dissected? An empirical attitude toward the stars or the human body has not diminished humanity. More recently, Darwin's evolutionary synthesis laid the foundation for startling advances in genetics and biology. Nevertheless, as we get closer to the nature of human beings and their origins, vestiges of opposition remain. In the United States, religious advocates continue to press for the teaching of creationism in the public schools, and surveys show that the scientific fact that humans evolved by natural selection is not accepted by a large portion of the public (Laden, 2008; Lerner, 2005; Shtulman, 2006). If evolutionary biology, with its long and impressive record of scientific achievements, still engenders public opposition, is it any wonder that psychology, the most recent discipline to bring long-held beliefs about human beings under scientific scrutiny, currently provokes people to deny its validity?

What, Then, Is Science?

In order to understand what psychology is, we must understand what science is. We can begin by dealing with what science is not. In this way, we can rid ourselves of the vast majority of common misconceptions. First, science is not defined by subject matter. Any aspect of the universe is fair game for the development of a scientific discipline, including all aspects of human behavior. We cannot divide the universe into "scientific" and "nonscientific" topics. Although strong forces throughout history have tried to place human beings outside the sphere of scientific investigation, they have been unsuccessful, as we shall see. The reactions against psychology as a scientific discipline probably represent the modern remnants of this ancient struggle.

Science is also not defined by the use of particular experimental apparatus. It is not the test tube, the computer, the electronic equipment, or the investigator's white coat that defines science. (If this were the case, there would be no question at all about psychology's status, because psychology departments in all major universities are full of computers, chemicals, and electronic equipment of all types.) These are the trappings of science but are not its defining features. Science is, rather, a way of thinking about and observing the universe that leads to a deep understanding of its workings.

In the remainder of this chapter, we shall discuss three important and interrelated features that define science: (1) the use of systematic empiricism; (2) the production of public knowledge; and (3) the examination of solvable problems. Although we shall examine each feature separately, remember that the three connect to form a coherent general structure. (For a more detailed discussion of the general characteristics of a science, see the works of Bronowski, Haack, Medawar, Popper, Raymo, and Sagan listed in the references section of this book.)

Systematic Empiricism

If you look up the word *empiricism* in any dictionary, you will find that it means "the practice of relying on observation." Scientists find out about the world by examining it. The fact that this point may seem obvious to you is an indication of the spread of the scientific attitude in the past couple of centuries. In the past, it has not always seemed so obvious. Recall the example from history of the refusal to look into Galileo's telescope. It was long thought that knowledge was best obtained through pure thought or through appeal to authority. Galileo claimed to have seen moons around the planet Jupiter. Another scholar, Francesco Sizi, attempted to refute Galileo, not with observations, but with the following argument:

> There are seven windows in the head, two nostrils, two ears, two eyes and a mouth; so in the heavens there are two favorable stars, two unpropitious, two luminaries, and Mercury alone undecided and indifferent. From which and many other similar phenomena of nature such as the seven metals, etc., which it were tedious to enumerate, we gather that the number of planets is necessarily seven. . . . Besides, the Jews and other ancient nations, as well as modern Europeans, have adopted the division of the week into seven days, and have named them from the seven planets; now if we increase the number of planets, this whole system falls to the ground. . . . Moreover, the satellites are invisible to the naked eye and therefore can have no influence on the earth and therefore would be useless and therefore do not exist. (Holton & Roller, 1958, p. 160)

The point is not that the argument is laughably idiotic, but that it was seen as a suitable rebuttal to an actual observation! We laugh now because we have the benefit of hindsight. Three centuries of the demonstrated power of the empirical approach give us an edge on poor Sizi. Take away those years of empiricism, and many of us might have been there nodding our heads and urging him on. No, the empirical approach is not necessarily obvious, which is why we often have to teach it, even in a society that is dominated by science.

Empiricism pure and simple is not enough, however. Note that the heading for this section is "*Systematic* Empiricism." Observation is fine and necessary, but pure, unstructured observation of the natural world will not lead to scientific knowledge. Write down every observation you make from the time you get up in the morning to the time you go to bed on a given day. When you finish, you will have a great number of facts, but you will not have a greater understanding of the world. Scientific observation is termed *systematic* because it is structured so that the results of the observation reveal something about the underlying nature of the world. Scientific observations are usually theory driven; they test different explanations of the nature of the world. They are structured so that, depending on the outcome of the observation, some theories are supported and others rejected.

Publicly Verifiable Knowledge: Replication and Peer Review

Scientific knowledge is public in a special sense. By *public,* we, of course, do not mean that scientific observations are posted on community-center bulletin boards. Instead, we refer to the fact that scientific knowledge does not exist solely in the mind of a particular individual. In an important sense, scientific knowledge does not exist at all until it has been submitted to the scientific community for criticism and empirical testing by others. Knowledge that is considered "special"—the province of the thought processes of a particular individual, immune from scrutiny and criticism by others—can never have the status of scientific knowledge.

Science makes the idea of public verifiability concrete via the procedure of *replication.* In order to be considered in the realm of science, a finding must be presented to the scientific community in a way that enables other scientists to attempt the same experiment and obtain the same results. When this occurs, we say that the finding has been replicated. Scientists use replication to define the idea of public knowledge. Replication ensures that a particular finding is not due simply to the errors or biases of a particular investigator. In short, for a finding to be accepted by the scientific community, it must be possible for someone other than the original investigator to duplicate it. When a finding is presented in this way, it becomes public. It is no longer the sole possession of the original researcher; it is instead available for other investigators to extend, criticize, or apply in their own ways.

The poet John Donne told us that "no man is an island." In science, no researcher is an island. Each investigator is connected to the scientific community and its knowledge base. It is this interconnection that enables science to grow cumulatively. Researchers constantly build on previous knowledge in order to go beyond what is currently known. This process is possible only if previous knowledge is stated in such a way that any investigator can use it to build on.

By *publicly verifiable knowledge,* then, we mean findings presented to the scientific community in such a way that they can be replicated, criticized, or extended by anyone in the community. This is a most important criterion not only for scientists but also for the layperson, who, as a consumer, must evaluate scientific information presented in the media. As we shall see in Chapter 12, one important way to distinguish charlatans and practitioners of pseudoscience from legitimate scientists is that the former often bypass the normal channels of scientific publication and instead go straight to the media with their "findings." One ironclad criterion that will always work for the public when presented with scientific claims of uncertain validity is the question, Have the findings been published in a recognized scientific journal that uses some type of peer review procedure? The answer to this question will almost always separate pseudoscientific claims from the real thing.

Peer review is a procedure in which each paper submitted to a research journal is critiqued by several scientists, who then submit their criticisms to an editor. The editor is usually a scientist with an extensive history of work in the specialty area covered by the journal. The editor decides whether the weight of opinion warrants publication of the paper, publication after further experimentation and statistical analysis, or rejection because the research is flawed or trivial. Most journals carry a statement of editorial policy in each issue, so it is easy to check whether a journal is peer reviewed.

Not all information in peer-reviewed scientific journals is necessarily correct, but at least it has met a criterion of peer criticism and scrutiny. Peer review is a minimal criterion, not a stringent one, because most scientific disciplines publish dozens of different journals of varying quality. Most scientific ideas can get published somewhere in the legitimate literature if they meet some rudimentary standards. The idea that only a narrow range of data and theory can get published in science is false. This is an idea often suggested by purveyors of bogus remedies and therapies who try to convince the media and the public that they have been shut out of scientific outlets by a conspiracy of "orthodox science." But consider for a minute just how many legitimate outlets there are in a field like psychology. The publications *Psychological Abstracts* and *PsycINFO* summarize articles from over 2,000 different journals. Most of these journals are peer reviewed. Virtually all halfway legitimate theories and experiments can find their way into this vast array of publication outlets.

Again, I am not suggesting that all ideas published in the journals summarized in *Psychological Abstracts* and *PsycINFO* are necessarily valid. On the contrary, I emphasized earlier that this is only a minimal criterion. However, the point is that the failure of an idea, a theory, a claim, or a therapy to have adequate documentation in the peer-reviewed literature of a scientific discipline is a very sure sign. Particularly when the lack of evidence is accompanied by a media campaign to publicize the claim, *it is a sure sign that the idea, theory, or therapy is bogus.* For example, in a famous Pennsylvania court case in 2005 regarding attempts to teach creationism in school biology classes, one of the witnesses advocating for intelligent design (a form of creationism) admitted that "he was unable to name any peer-reviewed research generated by intelligent design, though the movement has been around for more than a decade" (Talbot, 2005, p. 68).

The mechanisms of peer review vary somewhat from discipline to discipline, but the underlying rationale is the same. Peer review is one way (replication is another) that science institutionalizes the attitudes of objectivity and public criticism. Ideas and experimentation undergo a honing process in which they are submitted to other critical minds for evaluation. Ideas that survive this critical process have begun to meet the criterion of public verifiability. The peer review process is far from perfect, but it is really the only consumer protection that we have. To ignore it (or not to be aware of it) is to leave ourselves at the mercy of the multimillion-dollar pseudoscience industries that are so good at manipulating the media to their own ends (see Chapter 12). In subsequent chapters, we shall discuss in much more detail the high price we pay for ignoring the checks and balances inherent in the true scientific practice of psychology.

Empirically Solvable Problems: Scientists' Search for Testable Theories

Science deals with solvable, or specifiable, problems. This means that the types of questions that scientists address are potentially answerable by means of currently available empirical techniques. If a problem is not solvable or a theory is not testable by the empirical techniques that scientists have at hand, then scientists will not attack it. For example, the question "Will three-year-old children given structured language stimulation during day care be ready for reading instruction at an earlier age than children not given such extra stimulation?" represents a scientific problem. It is answerable by currently available empirical methods. The question "Are human beings inherently good or inherently evil?" is not an empirical question and, thus, is simply not in the realm of science. Likewise, the question "What is the meaning of life?" is not an empirical question and so is outside the realm of science.

Science advances by positing theories to account for particular phenomena in the world, by deriving predictions from these theories, by testing the predictions empirically, and by modifying the theories based on the tests. The sequence might be portrayed as: theory → prediction → test → theory modification. So what a scientist often means by the term *solvable problem* is "*testable* theory." What makes a theory testable? The theory must have specific implications for observable events in the natural world; this is what is meant by *empirically testable*. This criterion of testability is often termed the *falsifiability criterion*, and it is the subject of Chapter 2.

By saying that scientists tackle empirically solvable problems, we do not mean to imply that different classes of problems are inherently solvable or unsolvable and that this division is fixed forever. Quite the contrary: Some problems that are currently unsolvable may become solvable as theory and empirical techniques become more sophisticated. For example, decades ago historians would not have believed that the controversial issue of whether Thomas Jefferson fathered a child by his slave Sally Hemings was an empirically solvable question. Yet by 1998 this problem had become solvable through advances in genetic technology, and a paper was published in the journal *Nature* (Foster et al., 1998) indicating that it was highly probable that Jefferson was the father of Eston Hemings Jefferson.

This is how science in general has developed and how new sciences have come into existence. There is always ample room for disagreement about what is currently solvable. Scientists themselves often disagree on this point as it relates to current problems of ambiguous status. Thus, although all scientists agree on the solvability criterion, they may disagree on its specific applications. Nobel laureate Peter Medawar titled one of his books *The Art of the Soluble* (1967) to illustrate that part of the creativity involved in science is finding the problem on the furthest edge of the frontier of human knowledge that will yield to empirical techniques.

Psychology itself provides many good examples of the development from the unsolvable to the solvable. There are many questions (such as "How does a child acquire the language of his or her parents?" "Why do we forget things we once knew?" "How does being in a group change a person's behavior and thinking?") that had been the subjects of speculation for centuries before anyone recognized that they could be addressed by empirical means. As this recognition slowly developed, psychology coalesced as a collection of problems concerning behavior in a variety of domains. Psychological issues gradually became separated from philosophy, and a separate empirical discipline evolved.

Cognitive psychologist Steven Pinker (1997) discusses how ignorance can be divided into *problems* and *mysteries.* In the case of problems, we know that an answer is possible and what that answer might look like even though we might not actually have the answer yet. In the case of mysteries, we can't even conceive of what an answer might look like. Using this terminology, we can see that science is a process that turns mysteries into problems. In fact, Pinker (1997) noted that he wrote his book *How the Mind Works* "because dozens of mysteries of the mind, from mental images to romantic love, have recently been upgraded to problems" (p. ix).

Psychology and Folk Wisdom: The Problem With "Common Sense"

We all have implicit models of behavior that govern our interactions and our thoughts about ourselves and other people. Indeed, some social, personality, and cognitive psychologists study the nature of these implicit psychological theories. Rarely do we state our theories clearly and logically. Instead, we usually become aware of them only when attention is drawn to them or when we find them challenged in some way. Actually, our personal models of behavior are not really coherent in the way that an actual theory would have to be. Instead, we carry around a ragbag of general principles, homilies, and clichés about human behavior that we draw on when we feel that we need an explanation. The problem with this commonsense knowledge about behavior is that much of it contradicts itself and is, therefore, unfalsifiable (the principle of falsifiability is the topic of the next chapter).

Often a person uses some folk proverb to explain a behavioral event even though, on an earlier occasion, this same person used a directly contradictory folk proverb to explain the same type of event. For example, most of us have heard or said, "look before you leap." Now there's a useful, straightforward bit of behavioral advice—except that I vaguely remember admonishing on occasion, "he who hesitates is lost." And "absence makes the heart grow fonder" is a pretty clear prediction of an emotional reaction to environmental events. But then what about "out of sight, out of mind"? And if "haste makes waste," why does "time wait for no man"? How could the saying "two heads are better than one" not be true? Except that "too many cooks spoil the broth." If I think "it's better to be safe than sorry," why do I also believe "nothing ventured, nothing gained"? And if "opposites attract," why do "birds of a feather flock together"? I have counseled many students to "never to put off until tomorrow what you can do today." But I hope my last advisee has never heard me say this, because I just told him, "cross that bridge when you come to it."

The enormous appeal of clichés like these is that, taken together as implicit "explanations" of behavior, they cannot be refuted. No matter what happens, one of these explanations will be cited to cover it. No wonder we all think we are such excellent judges of human behavior and personality. We have an explanation for anything and everything that happens. As British writer Matthew Parris (2007) has said, "folk wisdom is such a cowardly thing" (p. 28). By this he means that it takes no risk that it might be refuted.

So sometimes our implicit psychological theories can't be refuted. We will see in the next chapter why this inability to be refuted makes such theories not very useful. However, a further problem occurs even in cases in which our folk beliefs do have some specificity, that is, even when they are empirically testable. The problem is that psychological research has shown that, when many common cultural beliefs about behavior are subjected to empirical test, they turn out to be false.

It is not difficult to generate instances of folk beliefs (or "common sense") that are wrong. Take, for example, the idea that children who excel academically or who read a lot are not socially or physically adept. This idea still circulates in our society even though it is utterly false. There is voluminous evidence that, contrary to "commonsense" folk belief, readers and academically inclined individuals are more physically robust and are more socially involved than are people who do not read (Zill & Winglee, 1990). For example, children high in scholastic achievement are more likely to be accepted by their peers than children low in achievement. People who are avid readers are more likely to play sports, jog, camp, hike, and do car repair than are people who do not read very much.

Many of our folk beliefs about behavior arise and take on a life of their own. For example, throughout the 1990s the folk belief developed in our society and in schools that low self-esteem was a cause of aggression. But empirical investigations indicated that there was no connection between aggression and low self-esteem. If anything, the opposite appeared to be the case—aggression is more often associated with high self-esteem

(Baumeister, Bushman, & Campbell, 2000). Likewise, an extremely popular hypothesis in the 1990s was that school achievement problems were the result of low self-esteem. In fact, it turns out that the relationship between self-esteem and school achievement is more likely to be in the opposite direction from that assumed by educators and parents. It is superior accomplishment in school (and in other aspects of life) that leads to high self-esteem and not the reverse (Baumeister, Campbell, Krueger, & Vohs, 2003, 2005; Stout, 2000).

Consider another commonplace expression of folk wisdom: that "children bring happiness to their parents." This statement might have some degree of truth if used to refer to how we view the effects of our children from the vantage point of retirement. People do indeed *look back* on their children as having brought them great happiness. The problem is that people tend to confuse the perspective of looking back on an event with the actual experience of the event. Having children turns out to be a case where the two perspectives are very different. Looking back on having children from old age does indeed make people happy. However, in terms of ongoing, moment-to-moment happiness (as opposed to retrospectively looking back), children actually make people less happy. There is now a fairly sizable literature using so-called experience-sampling methods to look at how happy people are at various points in time (Ali, 2008; Brooks, 2008; Gilbert, 2006; Gorchoff, John, & Helson, 2008; Wargo, 2007), and this research shows a number of trends, for example, that getting married increases happiness. This literature also shows that parental happiness drops with the arrival of the first child. It rebounds a little until the first child reaches adolescence, and then it drops even further. Marital happiness returns to childless levels only when the last child leaves home.

In short, the folk wisdom "children bring happiness to their parents," when subjected to scientific examination, turns out to have a number of complications. It is true only from the retrospective standpoint—"children bring happiness" when they have finally left home and we can appreciate the accomplishment of raising them! This is not, though, what the phrase is often used to imply. It is often used to imply that having children will bring you happiness right now—in your short-term future. This is where this "folk wisdom" is most egregiously wrong.

Another example of folk wisdom run amok is the folk myth that we use only 10 percent of our brainpower. Despite having absolutely no basis in cognitive neuroscience (see Beyerstein, 1999; Boyd, 2008; Higbee & Clay, 1998; Radford, 1999), this one has been around for decades and has taken on the status of what has been termed a "psycho-fact." Radford quotes columnist Robert Samuelson's definition of a psycho-fact as "a belief that, though not supported by hard evidence, is taken as real because its constant repetition changes the way we experience life" (p. 53).

Folk beliefs are not always immune to evidence. Sometimes, when the contradictory evidence becomes too widely known, folk psychology ("common sense") does change. For example, years ago, one widely held cliché about children was "Early ripe, early rot" (Fancher, 1985, p. 141). The cliché reflected the belief that childhood precocity was associated with adult abnormality, a belief sustained by many anecdotes about childhood prodigies who came to ruin in later life. In this case, the psychological evidence documenting the inaccuracy of the cliché has been absorbed into the general culture, and you will almost never hear this bit of folk "wisdom" anymore.

This last example also carries a warning by reminding us to beware of today's "common sense"—because it is not difficult to show that yesterday's common sense has often turned into today's nonsense. After all, common sense is what "everybody knows," right? Right. Well, everybody knows that women shouldn't be able to vote, right? Everybody knows that African Americans shouldn't be taught to read, right? Everybody knows that individuals with disabilities should be institutionalized out of the sight of society, right? In fact, 150 years ago, all of these beliefs were what "everybody knew." Of course, we now recognize this common sense of the past as nonsense—as beliefs based on totally unverified assumptions. But in these examples we can see the critical role that psychology plays vis-à-vis common sense. Psychology tests the empirical basis of the assumptions of common sense. Sometimes the assumptions do not hold up when tested, as we saw in many of the previous examples. From the examples discussed—and many more could be cited—we can see that psychology's role as the empirical tester of much folk wisdom often brings it into conflict with many widely held cultural beliefs. Psychology is often the bearer of the "bad tidings" that comfortable folk beliefs do not stand up to the cold light of day. Perhaps it is not surprising that many people would like not only to ignore the message but also to do away with the messenger.

Psychology as a Young Science

There has always been opposition to an empirically based psychology. Just 100 years ago, Cambridge University refused to establish a psychophysics laboratory because the study of such a topic would "insult religion by putting the human soul on a pair of scales" (Hearst, 1979, p. 7). Psychology's battle to establish its problems as empirically solvable has only recently been won. But as the science progresses, psychologists will address more and more issues that are the subject of strongly held beliefs about human beings because many of these problems are empirically testable. Psychologists now study topics such as the development of moral reasoning, the psychology of romantic love, the nature of racial prejudice, and the psychological and social determinants of religious beliefs. Studies of childhood sexual activity have incited much controversy (Hagen, 2001; Rind, 2008; Rind,

Tromovitch, & Bauserman, 2001). Some people object to empirical investigation in these areas (Hunt, 1999); yet there has been scientific progress in each one of them.

Past-president of the APA Gerald Koocher (2006) boldly warned us about the nature of psychological research by titling one of his presidential columns "Psychological Science is not Politically Correct." In the article, he discussed research on topics such as the causes of obesity, what determines political attitudes, the relation between religion and sexual behavior, and domestic violence. He pointed out that the research findings on each of these topics have proved controversial, but that "psychological science cannot be held to a standard of political correctness by social liberals or conservatives" (p. 5).

Levin and O'Donnell (2000) discuss how opposition to some psychological research is based on what they claim is a "need *not* to know." They describe a school board where parents were given the option of having their child educated in K–2 multi-aged classrooms or in their usual age-graded classrooms. The school board disparaged their teachers' suggestion for a research study on the issue because they thought that if the research study showed one or the other method to be more effective, parents would force them to switch to this type of instruction completely. As Levin and O'Donnell (2000) note, "the school board simply did not want to know!" (p. 66). Thus, we should be aware that psychological research is often denigrated not because people think it is bad but because they desire to avoid the implications of the information that it might produce.

Psychology is often in a no-win situation as a discipline. On one hand, some people object to calling psychology a science and deny that psychologists can establish empirical facts about behavior. On the other hand, there are those who object to the investigation of certain areas of human behavior because they fear that facts uncovered by psychology might threaten their beliefs. Skinnerian psychologists regularly deal with these contradictory criticisms. For instance, critics have argued that the laws of reinforcement formulated by behaviorists do not apply to human behavior. At the same time, other critics are concerned that the laws will be used for the rigid and inhumane control of people. Thus, the behaviorists are faced with some critics who deny that their laws can be applied and others who charge that their laws can be applied too easily!

Examples such as this arise because the relatively new science of psychology has just begun to uncover facts about aspects of behavior that have previously escaped study. The relative youth of psychology as a science partially explains why many people are confused about the discipline. Nevertheless, during the past four decades, psychology has become firmly established in the interconnecting structure of knowledge that we call science. Failure to appreciate this fact is the source of almost all of the confused thinking about psychology that you will encounter.

Summary

Psychology is an immensely diverse discipline covering a range of subjects that are not always tied together by common concepts. Instead, what unifies the discipline is that it uses scientific methods to understand behavior. The scientific method is not a strict set of rules; instead it is defined by some very general principles. Three of the most important are that (1) science employs methods of systematic empiricism; (2) it aims for knowledge that is publicly verifiable; and (3) it seeks problems that are empirically solvable and that yield testable theories (the subject of the next chapter). The structured and controlled observations that define systematic empiricism are the subject of several later chapters of this book. Science renders knowledge public by procedures such as peer review and mechanisms such as replication.

Psychology is a young science and, thus, is often in conflict with so-called folk wisdom. This conflict is typical of all new sciences, but understanding it helps to explain some of the hostility directed toward psychology as a discipline. This characteristic of questioning common wisdom also makes psychology an exciting field. Many people are drawn to the discipline because it holds out the possibility of actually testing "common sense" that has been accepted without question for centuries.

CHAPTER 2

Falsifiability: How to Foil Little Green Men in the Head

In 1793, a severe epidemic of yellow fever struck Philadelphia. One of the leading doctors in the city at the time was Benjamin Rush, a signer of the Declaration of Independence. During the outbreak, Rush was one of the few physicians who were available to treat literally thousands of yellow fever cases. Rush adhered to a theory of medicine that dictated that illnesses accompanied by fever should be treated by vigorous bloodletting (the removal of blood from the body either by using an instrument such as a lancet or by the application of leeches). He administered this treatment to many patients, including himself when he came down with the illness. Critics charged that his treatments were more dangerous than the disease. However, following the epidemic, Rush became even more confident of the effectiveness of his treatment, even though many of his patients had died. Why?

One writer summarized Rush's attitude this way: "Convinced of the correctness of his theory of medicine and lacking a means for the systematic study of treatment outcome, he attributed each new instance of improvement to the efficacy of his treatment and each new death that occurred despite it to the severity of the disease" (Eisenberg, 1977, p. 1106). In other words, if the patient got better, this improvement was taken as proof that bloodletting worked. If instead the patient died, Rush interpreted this to mean that the patient had been too ill for *any* treatment to work. We now know that Rush's critics were right: His treatments were as dangerous as the disease. In this chapter, we will discuss how Rush went wrong. His error illustrates one of the most important principles of scientific thinking, one that is particularly useful in evaluating psychological claims.

In this chapter, we focus in more detail on the third general characteristic of science that we discussed in Chapter 1: Scientists deal with solvable problems. What scientists most often mean by a *solvable problem* is a "testable theory." The way scientists make sure they are dealing with testable theories is by ensuring that their theories are falsifiable, that is, that they have implications for actual events in the natural world. We will see why what is termed the *falsifiability criterion* is so important in psychology.

Theories and the Falsifiability Criterion

Benjamin Rush fell into a fatal trap when assessing the outcome of his treatment. His method of evaluating the evidence made it impossible to conclude that his treatment did not work. If the recovery of a patient meant confirmation of his treatment (and, hence, his theory of medicine), then it only seems fair that the death of a patient should have meant disconfirmation. Instead, he rationalized away these disconfirmations. By interpreting the evidence as he did, Rush violated one of the most important rules regarding the construction and testing of theories in science: He made it impossible to falsify his theory.

Scientific theories must always be stated in such a way that the predictions derived from them could potentially be shown to be false. Thus, the methods of evaluating new evidence relevant to a particular theory must always include the possibility that the data will falsify the theory. This principle is often termed the *falsifiability criterion*, and its importance in scientific progress has been most forcefully articulated by Karl Popper, a philosopher of science whose writings are read widely by working scientists.

The falsifiability criterion states that, for a theory to be useful, the predictions drawn from it must be specific. The theory must go out on a limb, so to speak, because in telling us what *should* happen, the theory must also imply that certain things will *not* happen. If these latter things *do* happen, then we have a clear signal that something is wrong with the theory: It may need to be modified, or we may need to look for an entirely new theory. Either way, we shall end up with a theory that is nearer to the truth. By contrast, if a theory does not rule out any possible observations, then the theory can never be changed, and we are frozen into our current way of thinking, with no possibility of progress. Thus, a successful theory is not one that accounts for every possible outcome because such a theory robs itself of any predictive power.

Because we shall often refer to the evaluation of theories in the remainder of this book, we must clear up one common misconception surrounding the term *theory*. The misconception is reflected in the commonly used phrase "Oh, it's only a theory." This phrase captures what *laypeople* often mean when they use the term *theory:* an unverified hypothesis, a mere guess, a hunch. It implies that one theory is as good as another. This is most definitely *not* the way the term *theory* is used in science. When scientists refer to theories, they do not mean unverified guesses.

A theory in science is an interrelated set of concepts that is used to explain a body of data and to make predictions about the results of future experiments. *Hypotheses* are specific predictions that are derived from theories (which are more general and comprehensive). Currently viable theories are those that have had many of their hypotheses confirmed. The theoretical structures of such theories are, thus, consistent with a large number of observations. However, when the database begins to contradict the hypotheses derived from a theory, scientists begin trying to construct a new theory (or, more often, simply make adjustments in the previous theory) that will provide a better interpretation of the data. Thus, the theories that are under scientific discussion are those that have been verified to some extent and that do not make many predictions that are contradicted by the available data. They are *not* mere guesses or hunches.

The difference between the layperson's and the scientist's use of the term *theory* has often been exploited by some religious fundamentalists who want creationism taught in the public schools (Forrest & Gross, 2004; Humes, 2007; Miller, 2008; Scott, 2005). Their argument often is "After all, evolution is only a theory." This statement is intended to suggest the *layperson's* usage of the term *theory* to mean "only a guess." However, the theory of evolution by natural selection is not a theory in the layperson's sense (to the contrary, in the layperson's sense, it would be called a fact; see Randall, 2005). Instead, it is a theory in the *scientific* sense. It is a conceptual structure that is supported by a large and varied set of data (Maynard Smith, 1998; Miller, 2008; Ridley, 2004; Shermer, 2006; Wilson, 2007). It is not a mere guess, equal to any other guess. Instead, it interlocks with knowledge in a host of other disciplines, including geology, physics, chemistry, and all aspects of biology. The distinguished biologist Theodosius Dobzhansky (1973) made this point by titling a well-known article, "Nothing in Biology Makes Sense Except in the Light of Evolution."

That scientific theories interconnect with other established knowledge and are not just conjectures is stressed by Michael Novacek (2006), curator of paleontology at the American Museum of Natural History. He notes that evolution "is the framework for all modern biology, from the study of fossils to the mapping of the genome, but it is also profoundly practical in application. Scientists are debating the likelihood and timing of a horrific pandemic caused by avian flu. Those who worry about that possibility and reject evolution live in a world of contradiction. If the H5N1 virus, the infective agent for avian flu, adopts a new lifestyle and moves directly from one human host to another, it would be because it evolved that capacity" (p. 60).

The Theory of Knocking Rhythms

A hypothetical example will show how the falsifiability criterion works. A student knocks at my door. A colleague in my office with me has a theory that makes predictions about the rhythms that different types of people use to knock. Before I open the door, my colleague predicts that the person behind it is a female. I open the door and, indeed, the student is a female. Later I tell my colleague that I am impressed, but only mildly so because he had a 50 percent chance of being correct even without his "theory of knocking rhythms"—actually even higher, because on most campuses females outnumber males. He says he can do better. Another knock comes. My colleague tells me it is a male under 22 years old. I open the door to find a male student whom I know to be just out of high school. I comment that I am somewhat impressed because our university has a considerable number of students over the age of 22. Yet I still maintain that, of course, young males are quite common on campus. Thinking me hard to please, my colleague proposes one last test. After the next knock, my colleague predicts, "Female, 30 years old, 5 feet 2 inches tall, carrying a book and a purse in the left hand and knocking with the right." After opening the door and confirming the prediction completely, I have quite a different response. I say that, assuming my colleague did not play a trick and arrange for these people to appear at my door, I am now in fact extremely impressed.

Why the difference in my reactions? Why do my friend's three predictions yield three different responses, ranging from "So what?" to "Wow!"? The answer has to do with the specificity and precision of the predictions. The more specific predictions made a greater impact when they were confirmed. Notice, however, that the specificity varied directly with the falsifiability. The more specific and precise the prediction was, the more potential observations there were that could have falsified it. For example, there are a lot of people who are *not* 30-year-old females and 5 feet 2 inches tall. Note that implicitly, by my varied reactions, I signaled that I would be more impressed by a theory that made predictions that maximized the number of events that should *not* occur.

Good theories, then, make predictions that expose themselves to falsification. Bad theories do not put themselves in jeopardy in this way. They make predictions that are so general that they are almost bound to be true (e.g., the next person to knock on my door will be less than 100 years old) or are phrased in such a way that they are completely protected from falsification (as in the Benjamin Rush example). In fact, a theory can be so protected from falsifiability that it is simply no longer considered scientific at all. Indeed, it was philosopher Karl Popper's attempt to define the criteria that separate science from nonscience that led him to emphasize the importance of the falsifiability principle. There is a direct link here to psychology and to our discussion of Freud in Chapter 1.

Freud and Falsifiability

In the early decades of the twentieth century, Popper was searching for the underlying reasons that some scientific theories seem to lead to advances in knowledge and others lead to intellectual stagnation (Hacohen, 2000). Einstein's general relativity theory, for example, led to startlingly new observations (for instance, that the light from a distant star bends when it passes near the sun) precisely because its predictions were structured so that many possible events could have contradicted them and, thus, falsified the theory.

Popper reasoned that this is not true of stagnant theories and pointed to Freudian psychoanalysis as an example. Freudian theory uses a complicated conceptual structure that explains human behavior after the fact—that is, after it has occurred—but does not predict things in advance. In short, Freudian theory can explain everything. However, as Popper argued, it is precisely this property that makes it scientifically useless. It makes no specific predictions. Adherents of psychoanalytic theory spend much time and effort in getting the theory to explain every known human event, from individual quirks of behavior to large-scale social phenomena. But their success in making the theory a rich source of after-the-fact explanation robs it of any scientific utility. Freudian psychoanalytic theory currently plays a much larger role as a spur to the literary imagination than as a theory in contemporary psychology. Its demise within psychology can be traced in part to its failure to satisfy the falsifiability criterion (Wade & Tavris, 2008).

But the existence of such unfalsifiable theories does real damage. As one critic has argued, "Incorrect but widely dispersed ideas about the mind inevitably end by causing social damage. Thanks to the once imposing prestige of psychoanalysis, people harboring diseases or genetic conditions have deferred effective treatment while scouring their infantile past for the sources of their trouble" (Crews, 1993, p. 65). For example, explanations for the cause of autism (in part a genetically determined disorder) were led down a blind alley by psychoanalytic explanations for the condition. Influenced by psychoanalytic ideas, psychologist Bruno Bettelheim popularized the now-discredited notion of "refrigerator mothers" as the cause and thought that "the precipitating factor in infantile autism is the parent's wish that his child should not exist" (Offit, 2008, p. 3). Ideas like this not only did damage, but they set back the study of autism.

As another example, consider the history of Gilles de la Tourette syndrome. This is a disorder characterized by physical tics and twitches that may involve any part of the body, as well as vocal symptoms such as grunts and barks, echolalia (involuntary repetition of the words of others), and coprolalia (compulsive repetition of obscene words). Tourette syndrome is an organically based disorder of the central nervous system and is now often successfully treated with drug therapies (Scahill et al., 2006; Smith, Polloway, Patton, & Dowdy, 2008). Throughout history, individuals with Tourette syndrome have been persecuted—earlier as witches by religious authorities, and in more modern times by being subjected to exorcisms (Hines, 2003). Importantly, understanding of the cause and treatment of the disorder was considerably hampered from 1921 to 1955, when explanations and treatments for Tourette syndrome were dominated by psychoanalytic conceptualizations (see Kushner, 1999). Author after author presented unfalsifiable psychoanalytic explanations for the syndrome. The resulting array of vague explanations created a conceptual sludge that obscured the true nature of the syndrome and probably impeded scientific progress toward an accurate understanding of it. For example, according to one author,

> [Tourette syndrome is] a classic example of the retrogressive effect of psychoanalysis on the investigation of brain disease. La Tourette had attributed the disease to a degenerative process of the brain. After Freud's theories became fashionable in the early decades of the present century, attention in such conditions was deflected from the brain. . . . The consequence of this retrograde movement was that patients tended to be referred to psychiatrists (usually of a psychoanalytic persuasion) rather than to neurologists, so that physical examinations and investigation were not performed. (Thornton, 1986, p. 210)

Shapiro et al. (1978) described one psychoanalyst who thought that his patient was "reluctant to give up the tic because it became a source of erotic pleasure to her and an expression of unconscious sexual strivings." Another considered the tics "stereotyped equivalents of onanism. . . . The libido connected with the genital sensation was displaced into other parts of the body." A third considered the tic a "conversion symptom at the anal-sadistic level." A fourth thought that a person with Tourette syndrome had a "compulsive character, as well as a narcissistic orientation" and that the patient's tics "represent[ed] an affective syndrome, a defense against the intended affect."

In fact, these examples were numerous and typical in their uninformed overconfidence. Developmental psychologist Jerome Kagan (2006) tells us how "Sandor Ferenczi, a disciple of Freud *who had never seen a patient with Tourette's syndrome* [italics added], made an equally serious error when he wrote that the frequent facial tics of people with Tourette's were the result of a repressed urge to masturbate" (p. 179).

The summary by Shapiro et al. (1978) of the resulting theoretical situation demonstrates quite well the harmful effects of ignoring the falsifiability criterion:

> Psychoanalytic theorizing of this kind in effect leaves no base untouched. Tics are a conversion symptom but not hysterical, anal but also erotic, volitional but also compulsive, organic but also dynamic in origin. . . . These psychological labels, diagnoses, and treatments were unfortunately imposed on patients and their families, usually with little humility, considerable dogmatism, and with much harm. . . . These papers, because of their subsequent widespread influence, had a calamitous effect on the understanding and treatment of this syndrome. (pp. 39–42, 50, 63)

Progress in the treatment and understanding of Tourette syndrome began to occur only when researchers recognized that the psychoanalytic "explanations" were useless. These explanations were enticing because they seemed to explain things. In fact, they explained everything—after the fact. However, the explanations they provided created only the illusion of understanding. By attempting to explain everything after the fact, they barred the door to any advance. Progress occurs only when a theory does not predict *everything* but instead makes specific predictions that tell us—in advance—something specific about the world. The predictions derived from such a theory may be wrong, of course, but this is a strength, not a weakness.

The Little Green Men

It is not difficult to recognize unfalsifiable conceptualizations when one is detached from the subject matter and particularly when one has the benefit of historical hindsight (as in the Benjamin Rush example). It is also easy to detect unfalsifiable conceptualizations when the instance is obviously concocted. For example, it is a little known fact that I have discovered the underlying brain mechanism that controls behavior. You will soon be reading about this discovery (in the *National Enquirer*, available at your local supermarket). In the left hemisphere of the brain, near the language areas, reside two tiny green men. They have the power to control the electrochemical processes taking place in many areas of the brain. And, well, to make a long story short, they basically control everything. There is one difficulty, however. The little green men have the ability to detect any intrusion into the brain (surgery, X-rays, etc.), and when they do sense such an intrusion, they tend to disappear. (I forgot to mention that they have the power to become invisible.)

I have no doubt insulted your intelligence by using an example more suitable for elementary school students. I have obviously concocted this example so that my hypothesis about the little green men could never be shown to be wrong. However, consider this. As a lecturer and public speaker on psychological topics, I am often confronted by people who ask me why I have not lectured on all the startling new discoveries in extrasensory perception (ESP) and parapsychology that have been made in the past few years. I have to inform these questioners that most of what they have heard about these subjects has undoubtedly come from the general media rather than from scientifically respectable sources. In fact, some scientists have looked at these claims and have not been able to replicate the findings. I remind the audience that replication of a finding is critical to its acceptance as an established scientific fact and that this is particularly true in the case of results that contradict either previous data or established theory.

I further admit that many scientists have lost patience with ESP research. Although one reason is undoubtedly that the area is tainted by fraud, charlatanism, and media exploitation, perhaps the most important reason for scientific disenchantment is the existence of what Martin Gardner (1972) years ago called the catch-22 of ESP research.

It works as follows: A "believer" (someone who believes in the existence of ESP phenomena before beginning an investigation) claims to have demonstrated ESP in the laboratory. A "skeptic" (someone who doubts the existence of ESP) is brought in to confirm the phenomena. Often, after observing the experimental situation, the skeptic calls for more controls (controls of the type we will discuss in Chapter 6), and though these are sometimes resisted, well-intentioned believers often agree to them. When the controls are instituted, the phenomena cannot be demonstrated (Farha, 2007; Hines, 2003; Hyman, 1992, 1996; Kelly, 2005; Marks, 2001; Milton & Wiseman, 1999; Park, 2008). The skeptic, who correctly interprets this failure as an indication that the original demonstration was due to inadequate experimental control and, thus, cannot be accepted, is often shocked to find that the believer does not regard the original demonstration as invalid. Instead, the believer invokes the catch-22 of ESP: Psychic powers, the believer maintains, are subtle, delicate, and easily disturbed. The "negative vibes" of the skeptic were probably responsible for the disruption of the "psi powers." The believer thinks that the powers will undoubtedly return when the negative aura of the skeptic is removed.

This way of interpreting failures to demonstrate ESP in experiments is logically analogous to my story about the little green men. ESP operates just as the little green men do. It's there as long as you don't intrude to look at it carefully. When you do, it disappears. If we accept this explanation, it will be impossible to demonstrate the phenomenon to any skeptical observers. It appears only to believers. Of course, this position is unacceptable in science. We do not have the magnetism physicists and the nonmagnetism physicists (those for whom magnetism does and does not "work"). Interpreting ESP experiments in this way makes the hypothesis of ESP unfalsifiable just as the hypothesis of the little green men is. Interpreting the outcomes in this way puts it outside the realm of science.

Not All Confirmations Are Equal

The principle of falsifiability has important implications for the way we view the confirmation of a theory. Many people think that a good scientific theory is one that has been confirmed repeatedly. They assume that the amount of confirming evidence is critical in the evaluation of a theory. But falsifiability implies that the number of times a theory has been confirmed is not the critical element. The reason is that, as our example of the "theory of knocking rhythms" illustrated, not all confirmations are equal. Confirmations are more or less impressive depending on the extent to which the prediction exposes itself to potential disconfirmation. One confirmation of a highly specific, potentially falsifiable prediction (for instance, a female, 30 years old, 5 feet 2 inches tall, carrying a book and a purse in the left hand and knocking with the right) has a greater impact than the confirmation of 20 different predictions that are all virtually unfalsifiable (for instance, a person less than 100 years old).

Thus, we must look not only at the *quantity* of the confirming evidence, but also at the *quality* of the confirming instances. Using the falsifiability criterion as a tool to evaluate evidence will help the research consumer resist the allure of the nonscientific, all-explaining theory that inevitably hinders the search for deeper understanding. Indeed, such theoretical dead ends are often tempting precisely because they can never be falsified. They are islands of stability in the chaotic modern world.

Popper often made the point that "the secret of the enormous psychological appeal of these [unfalsifiable] theories lay in their ability to explain everything. To know in advance that whatever happens you will be able to understand it gives you not only a sense of intellectual mastery but, even more important, an emotional sense of secure orientation in the world" (Magee, 1985, p. 43). However, the attainment of such security is not the goal of science, because such security would be purchased at the cost of intellectual stagnation. Science is a mechanism for continually challenging previously held beliefs by subjecting them to empirical tests in such a way that they can be shown to be wrong. This characteristic often puts science—particularly psychology—in conflict with so-called folk wisdom or common sense (as we discussed in Chapter 1).

Falsifiability and Folk Wisdom

Psychology is a threat to the comfort that folk wisdom provides because, as a science, it cannot be content with explanations that cannot be refuted. The goal of psychology is the empirical testing of alternative behavioral theories in order to rule out some of them. Aspects of folk wisdom that are explicitly stated and that do stand up to empirical testing are, of course, welcomed, and many have been incorporated into psychological theory. However, psychology does not seek the comfort of explanatory systems that account for everything after the fact but predict nothing in advance. It does not accept systems of folk wisdom that are designed never to be changed and that end up being passed on from generation to generation. It is self-defeating to try to hide this fact from students or the public. Unfortunately, some psychology instructors and popularizers are aware that psychology's threat to folk wisdom disturbs some people, and they sometimes seek to soothe such feelings by sending a false underlying message that implies, "You'll learn some interesting things, but don't worry—psychology won't challenge things you believe in strongly." This is a mistake, and it contributes to confusion both about what science is and about what psychology is. Recall from the discussion in the last chapter (see Koocher, 2006) that psychology establishes facts about sexual behavior, intelligence, crime, financial behavior, and many other topics that people feel strongly about. It would be amazing if the investigation of subjects such as these failed to uncover something that did not upset *somebody*!

Science *seeks* conceptual change. Scientists try to describe the world as it really is, as opposed to what our prior beliefs dictate it should be. The dangerous trend in modern thought is the idea that people must be shielded from the nature of the world—that a veil of ignorance is necessary to protect a public unequipped to deal with the truth. Psychology is like other sciences in rejecting the idea that people need to be shielded from the truth.

Furthermore, we all lose when we are surrounded by others who hold incorrect views of human behavior. Our world is shaped by public attitudes toward education, crime, health, industrial productivity, child care, and many other critical issues. If these attitudes are the products of incorrect theories of behavior, then we are all harmed.

The Freedom to Admit a Mistake

Scientists have found that one of the most liberating and useful implications of the falsifiability principle is that, in science, making a mistake is not a sin. Falsified hypotheses provide information that scientists use to adjust their theories so that these theories accord more closely with the data. Philosopher Daniel Dennett (1995) has said that the essence of science is "making mistakes in public—making mistakes for all to see, in the hopes of getting the others to help with the corrections" (p. 380). By the process of continually adjusting theory when data do not accord with it, scientists collectively arrive at theories that better reflect the nature of the world.

In fact, our way of operating in everyday life might be greatly improved if we could use the falsifiability principle on a personal level. This is why the word *liberating* was used in the opening sentence of this section. It has a personal connotation that was specifically intended—because the ideas developed here have implications beyond science. We would have many fewer social and personal problems if we could only understand that, when our beliefs are contradicted by evidence in the world, it is better to adjust our beliefs than to deny the evidence and cling tenaciously to dysfunctional ideas. Physicist J. Robert Oppenheimer argued,

> There's a point in anybody's train of reasoning when he looks back and says, "I didn't see this straight." People in other walks of life need the ability to say without shame, "I was wrong about that." Science is a method of having this happen all the time. You notice a conflict or some oddity about a number of things you've been thinking about for a long time. It's the shock that may cause you to think another thought. That is the opposite of the worldly person's endless web of rationalization to vindicate an initial error. (Dos Passos, 1964, pp. 150–151)

How many times have you been in an intense argument with someone when right in the middle—perhaps just as you were giving a heated reply and defending your point of view—you realized that you were wrong about some critical fact or piece of evidence? What did you do? Did you back down and admit to the other person that you had assumed something that wasn't true and that the other person's interpretation now seemed more correct to you? Probably not. If you are like most of us, you engaged in an "endless web of rationalization to vindicate an initial error." You tried to extricate yourself from the argument without admitting defeat. The last thing you would have done was admit that you were wrong. Thus, both you and your partner in the argument became a little more confused about which beliefs more closely tracked the truth. If refutations never become public (as they do in science), if both true and false beliefs are defended with equal vehemence, and if the correct feedback about the effects of argument is not given (as in this example), there is no mechanism for getting beliefs more reliably in sync with reality. This is why so much of our private and public discourse is confused and why the science of psychology is a more reliable guide to the causes of behavior than is so-called common sense.

Many scientists have attested to the importance of understanding that making errors in the course of science is normal and that the real danger to scientific progress is our natural human tendency to avoid exposing our beliefs to situations in which they might be shown to be wrong. Nobel Prize winner Peter Medawar (1979) wrote,

> Though faulty hypotheses are excusable on the grounds that they will be super-seded in due course by acceptable ones, they can do grave harm to those who hold them because scientists who fall deeply in love with their hypotheses are proportionately unwilling to take no as an experimental answer. Sometimes instead of exposing a hypothesis to a cruelly critical test, they caper around it, testing only subsidiary implications, or follow up sidelines that have an indirect bearing on the hypothesis without exposing it to the risk of refutation. . . . I can-not give any scientist of any age better advice than this: *the intensity of the conviction that a hypothesis is true has no bearing on whether it is true or not.* (p. 39; italics in original)

Here is a way of thinking about what Medawar is saying. On his show on October 17, 2005, comedian Stephen Colbert coined the term "truthiness." Truthiness is the "quality of a thing *feeling* true without any evidence sug-gesting it actually was" (Manjoo, 2008, p. 189). What Medawar is saying is that science rejects truthiness. This often puts science at odds with modern society, where truthiness is more prevalent than ever.

Many of the most renowned scientists in psychology have followed Medawar's advice—"the intensity of the conviction that a hypothesis is true has no bearing on whether it is true or not." In an article on the career of noted experimental psychologist Robert Crowder, one of his colleagues, Mahzarin Banaji, is quoted as saying that "he is the least defensive scientist I know. If you found a way to show that his theory was wobbly or that his experimental finding was limited or flawed, Bob would beam with pleasure and plan the demise of his theory with you" (Azar, 1999, p. 18). Azar (1999) describes how Crowder developed a theory of one component of memory called precategorical acoustic storage and then carefully designed the studies that falsified his own model. Finally, in an eloquent statement about the attitudes that led to Darwin's monumental contributions to science, evolutionary psychologist John Tooby (2002) said that "Darwin went farther than his contemporaries because he was less bound by the compulsion to make the universe conform to his predilections" (p. 12).

But the falsifying attitude doesn't always have to characterize each and every scientist for *science* to work. Jacob Bronowski (1973, 1977) often argued in his many writings that the unique power of science to reveal knowledge about the world does *not* arise because scientists are uniquely virtuous (that they are completely objective; that they are never biased in interpreting findings, etc.) but instead it arises because fallible scientists are immersed in a process of checks and balances—in a process in which other scientists are always there to criticize and to root out the errors of their peers. Philosopher Daniel Dennett (2000) has made the same point by arguing that it is not necessary for every scientist to display the objectivity of Robert Crowder. Like Bronowski, Dennett stresses that "scientists take themselves to be just as weak and fallible as anybody else, but recognizing these very sources of error in themselves and in the groups to which they belong, they have devised elaborate systems to tie their own hands, forcibly preventing their frailties and prejudices from infecting their results" (p. 42). More humorously, psychologist Ray Nickerson (1998) makes the related point that the vanities of scientists are actually put to use by the scientific process, by noting that it is "not so much the critical attitude that individual scientists have taken with respect to their own ideas that has given science its success . . . but more the fact that individual scientists have been highly motivated to demonstrate that hypotheses that are held by some other scientists are false" (p. 32). These authors suggest that the strength of scientific knowledge comes not because scientists are virtuous, but from the social process where scientists constantly cross-check each others' knowledge and conclusions.

Thoughts Are Cheap

Our earlier discussion of the idea of testing folk wisdom leads us to another interesting corollary of the falsifiability principle: Thoughts are cheap. To be specific, what we mean here is that certain *kinds* of thoughts are cheap. Biologist and science writer Stephen J. Gould (1987) illustrated this point:

> Fifteen years of monthly columns have brought me an enormous correspondence from nonprofessionals about all aspects of science. . . . I have found that one common misconception surpasses all others. People will write, telling me that they have developed a revolutionary theory, one that will expand the boundaries of science. These theories, usually described in several pages of

single-spaced typescript, are speculations about the deepest ultimate questions we can ask—what is the nature of life? the origin of the universe? the beginning of time? But thoughts are cheap. Any person of intelligence can devise his half dozen before breakfast. Scientists can also spin out ideas about ultimates. We don't (or, rather, we confine them to our private thoughts) because we cannot devise ways to test them, to decide whether they are right or wrong. What good to science is a lovely idea that cannot, as a matter of principle, ever be affirmed or denied? (p. 18)

The answer to Gould's last question is "No good at all." The type of thoughts that Gould is saying are cheap are those that we referred to in our discussion of Karl Popper's views: grand theories that are so global, complicated, and "fuzzy" that they can be used to explain anything—theories constructed more for emotional support because they are not meant to be changed or discarded. Gould was telling us that such theories are useless for scientific purposes, however comforting they may be. Science is a creative endeavor, but the creativity involves getting conceptual structures to fit the confines of empirical data. This is tough. These types of thoughts—those that explain the world as it *actually is*—are not cheap. Probably this is why good scientific theories are so hard to come by and why unfalsifiable pseudoscientific belief systems proliferate everywhere—the latter are vastly easier to construct.

Theories in science make contact with the world. They are falsifiable. They make specific predictions. Actually coming up with the theories that are truly scientific explanations is a difficult task. However, understanding the general logic by which science works is *not* so difficult. Indeed, there are materials about the logic of scientific thinking that have been written for children (Epstein, 2008; Kramer, 1987; Swanson, 2001, 2004).

Errors in Science: Getting Closer to the Truth

In the context of explaining the principle of falsifiability, we have outlined a simple model of scientific progress. Theories are put forth and hypotheses are derived from them. The hypotheses are tested by a variety of techniques that we shall discuss in the remainder of this book. If the hypotheses are confirmed by the experiments, then the theory receives some degree of corroboration. If the hypotheses are falsified by the experiments, then the theory must be altered in some way, or it must be discarded for a better theory.

Of course, saying that knowledge in science is tentative and that hypotheses derived from theories are potentially false does not mean that everything is up for grabs. There are many relationships in science that have been confirmed so many times that they are termed *laws* because it is extremely doubtful that they will be overturned by future experimentation. It is highly unlikely that we shall find one day that blood does not circulate in the veins and arteries or that the earth does not orbit the sun. These mundane facts are not the type of hypotheses that we have been talking about. They are of no interest to scientists precisely because they are so well established. Scientists are interested only in those aspects of nature that are on the fringes of what is known. They are not interested in things that are so well confirmed that there is no doubt about them.

This aspect of scientific practice—that scientists gravitate to those problems on the fringes of what is known and ignore things that are well confirmed (so-called laws)—is very confusing to the general public. It seems that scientists are always emphasizing what they don't know rather than what is known. This is true, and there is a very good reason for it. To advance knowledge, scientists must be at the outer limits of what is known. Of course, this is precisely where things are uncertain. But science advances by a process of trying to reduce the uncertainty at the limits of knowledge. This can often make scientists look "uncertain" to the public. But this perception is deceiving. Scientists are only uncertain at the fringes of knowledge—where our understanding is currently being advanced. Scientists are *not* uncertain about the many facts that have been well established by replicable research.

It should also be emphasized that, when scientists talk about falsifying a theory based on observation and about replacing an old, falsified theory with a new one, they do not mean that all the previous facts that established the old theory are thrown out (we shall talk about this at length in Chapter 8). Quite the contrary, the new theory must explain all of the facts that the old theory could explain plus the new facts that the old theory could not explain. So the falsification of a theory does not mean that scientists have to go back to square one. Science writer Isaac Asimov illustrated the process of theory revision very well in an essay titled "The Relativity of Wrong" (1989), in which he wrote about how we have refined our notions of the earth's shape. First, he warned us not to think that the ancient belief in a flat earth was stupid. On a plain (where the first civilizations with writing developed), the earth looks pretty flat, and Asimov urged us to consider what a quantitative comparison of different theories would reveal. First, we could express the different theories in terms of how much curvature per mile they hypothesized. The flat-earth theory would say that the curvature is 0 degrees per mile. This theory is wrong, as we know. But in one sense, it is close. As Asimov (1989) wrote,

> About a century after Aristotle, the Greek philosopher Eratosthenes noted that the sun cast a shadow of different lengths at different latitudes (all the shadows would be the same length if the earth's surface were flat). From the difference in shadow length, he calculated the size of the earthly sphere and it turned out to be 25,000 miles circumference. The curvature of such a sphere is about 0.000126 degrees per mile, a quantity very close to 0 per mile, as you can see. . . . The tiny difference between 0 and 0.000126 accounts for the fact that it took so long to pass from the flat earth to the spherical earth. Mind you, even a tiny difference, such as that between 0 and 0.000126, can be extremely

important. The difference mounts up. The earth cannot be mapped over large areas with any accuracy at all if the difference isn't taken into account and if the earth isn't considered a sphere rather than a flat surface. (pp. 39–40)

But science, of course, did not stop with the theory that the earth was spherical. As we discussed earlier, scientists are always trying to refine their theories as much as possible and to test the limits of current knowledge. For example, Newton's theories of gravitation predicted that the earth should not be perfectly spherical, and indeed this prediction has been confirmed. It turns out that the earth bulges a little at the equator and that it is a little flat at the poles. It is something called an *oblate spheroid*. The diameter of the earth from North Pole to South Pole is 7,900 miles, and the equatorial diameter is 7,927 miles. The curvature of the earth is not constant (as in a perfect sphere); instead, it varies slightly from 7.973 inches to 8.027 inches to the mile. As Asimov (1989) noted, "The correction in going from spherical to oblate spheroidal is much smaller than going from flat to spherical. Therefore, although the notion of the earth as a sphere is wrong, strictly speaking, it is not as wrong as the notion of the earth as flat" (p. 41). Asimov's example of the shape of the earth illustrates for us the context in which scientists use such terms as *mistake, error,* or *falsified.* Such terms do not mean that the theory being tested is wrong in every respect, only that it is incomplete. So when scientists emphasize that knowledge is tentative and may be altered by future findings, they are referring to a situation such as this example. When scientists believed that the earth was a sphere, they realized that, in detail, this theory might someday need to be altered. However, the alteration from spherical to oblate spheroidal preserves the "roughly correct" notion that the earth is a sphere. We do not expect to wake up one day and find that it is a cube.

Clinical psychologist Scott Lilienfeld (2005) contextualizes Asimov's point for the psychology student:

> When explaining to students that scientific knowledge is inherently tentative and open to revision, some students may mistakenly conclude that genuine knowledge is impossible. This view, which is popular in certain postmodernist circles, neglects to distinguish knowledge claims that are more certain from those that are less certain. Although absolute certainty is probably unattainable in science, some scientific claims, such as Darwin's theory of natural selection, have been extremely well corroborated, whereas others, such as the theory underpinning astrological horoscopes, have been convincingly refuted. Still others, such as cognitive dissonance theory, are scientifically controversial. Hence, there is a continuum of confidence in scientific claims; some have acquired virtual factual status whereas others have been resoundingly falsified. The fact that methodological skepticism does not yield completely certain answers to scientific questions—and that such answers could in principle be overturned by new evidence—does not imply that knowledge is impossible, only that this knowledge is provisional. (p. 49)

The mistaken notion the science must yield certain knowledge is often used to undermine science itself. Paleontologist Neil Shubin has described how creationists use this tactic. In an interview with science writer Natalie Angier (2007), Shubin notes how "creationists first try to paint science as a body of facts and certainties, and then they attack this or that 'certainty' for not being so certain after all. They cry 'Aha! You can't make up your mind. You can't be trusted. Why should we believe you about anything?' Yet they are the ones who constructed the straw man of scientific infallibility in the first place" (p. 20).

Summary

What scientists most often mean by a *solvable problem* is a *testable theory*. The definition of a testable theory is a very specific one in science: It means that the theory is potentially falsifiable. If a theory is not falsifiable, then it has no implications for actual events in the natural world and, hence, is useless. Psychology has been plagued by unfalsifiable theories, and that is one reason why progress in the discipline has been slow.

Good theories are those that make specific predictions, and such theories are highly falsifiable. The confirmation of a specific prediction provides more support for the theory from which it was derived than the confirmation of a prediction that was not precise. In short, one implication of the falsifiability criterion is that all confirmations of theories are not equal. Theories that receive confirmation from highly falsifiable, highly specific predictions are to be preferred. Even when predictions are not confirmed (i.e., when they are falsified), this falsification is useful to theory development. A falsified prediction indicates that a theory must either be discarded or altered so that it can account for the discrepant data pattern. Thus, it is by theory adjustment caused by falsified predictions that sciences such as psychology get closer to the truth.

CHAPTER 3

Operationism and Essentialism: "But, Doctor, What Does It Really Mean?"

Do physicists really know what gravity is? I mean *really*. What is the real *meaning* of the term *gravity*? What is the underlying essence of it? What does it ultimately mean even to speak of gravity? When you get down to rock bottom, what is it all about?

Questions such as these reflect a view of science that philosopher Karl Popper called *essentialism*. This is the idea that the only good scientific theories are those that give ultimate explanations of phenomena in terms of their underlying essences or their essential properties. People who hold this view usually also believe that any theory that gives less than an ultimate explanation of a phenomenon is useless. It does not reflect the true underlying situation, the essence of the way the world is. In this chapter, we shall discuss why science does not answer essentialist questions and why, instead, science advances by developing *operational definitions* of concepts.

Why Scientists Are Not Essentialists

Scientists, in fact, do not claim to acquire the type of knowledge that the essentialist seeks. The proper answer to the preceding questions is that physicists do *not* know what gravity is in this sense. Science does not attempt to answer "ultimate" questions about the universe. Peter Medawar (1984) wrote,

> [There exist] questions that science cannot answer and that no conceivable advance of science would empower it to answer. These are the questions that children ask—the "ultimate questions." . . . I have in mind such questions

35

as: How did everything begin? What are we all here for? What is the point of living? (p. 66)

[However,] the failure of science to answer questions about first and last things does not in any way entail the acceptance of answers of other kinds; nor can it be taken for granted that because these questions can be put they can be answered. So far as our understanding goes, they cannot. (p. 60)

[Finally, however,] there is no limit upon the ability of science to answer the kind of questions that science can answer. . . . Nothing can impede or halt the advancement of scientific learning except a moral ailment such as the failure of nerve. (p. 86)

One reason that scientists are suspicious of claims that some person, theory, or belief system provides absolute knowledge about ultimate questions is that scientists consider questions about "ultimates" to be unanswerable. Scientists do not claim to produce perfect knowledge; the unique strength of science is not that it is an error-free process, but that it provides a way of eliminating the errors that are part of our knowledge base. Furthermore, claims of perfect or absolute knowledge tend to choke off inquiry. Because a free and open pursuit of knowledge is a prerequisite for scientific activity, scientists are always skeptical of claims that the ultimate answer has been found.

Essentialists Like to Argue About the Meaning of Words

A common indication of the essentialist attitude is an obsessive concern about defining the meaning of terms and concepts before the search for knowledge about them begins. "But we must first define our terms" is a frequent essentialist slogan. "What does that theoretical concept really *mean?*" The idea seems to be that, before a word can be used as a concept in a theory, we must have a complete and unambiguous understanding of all the underlying language problems involved in its usage. In fact, this is exactly the opposite of the way scientists work. Before they begin to investigate the physical world, physicists do not engage in debates about how to use the word *energy* or whether the word *particle* really captures the essence of what we mean when we talk about the fundamental constituents of matter.

The meaning of a concept in science is determined *after* extensive investigation of the phenomena the term relates to, not before such an investigation. The refinement of conceptual terms comes from the interplay of data and theory that is inherent in the scientific process, not from debates on language usage. Essentialism leads us into endless argument about words, and many scientists believe that such language games distract us from matters of substance. For example, concerning the question "What is the true meaning of the word *life?*" two biologists answer "There is no true meaning. There is a usage that serves the purposes of working biologists well enough, and it is not the subject of altercation or dispute" (Medawar & Medawar, 1983, pp. 66–67). In short, the explanation of phenomena, not the analysis of language, is the goal of the scientist. The key to progress in all the sciences has been to abandon essentialism and to adopt operationism, our topic of inquiry in this chapter. Nowhere is this more evident than in psychology.

Operationists Link Concepts to Observable Events

Where, then, does the meaning of concepts in science come from if not from discussions about language? What are the criteria for the appropriate use of a scientific concept? To answer these questions, we must discuss operationism, an idea that is crucial to the construction of theory in science and one that is especially important for evaluating theoretical claims in psychology.

Although there are different forms of operationism, it is most useful for the consumer of scientific information to think of it in the most general way. *Operationism* is simply the idea that concepts in scientific theories must in some way be grounded in, or linked to, observable events that can be measured. Linking the concept to an observable event makes the concept public. The operational definition removes the concept from the feelings and intuitions of a particular individual and allows it to be tested by anyone who can carry out the measurable operations.

For example, defining the concept *hunger* as "that gnawing feeling I get in my stomach" is not an operational definition because it is related to the personal experience of a "gnawing feeling" and, thus, is not accessible to other observers. By contrast, definitions that involve some measurable period of food deprivation or some physiological index such as blood sugar levels are operational because they involve observable measurements that anyone can carry out. Similarly, psychologists cannot be content with a definition of *anxiety,* for example, as "that uncomfortable, tense feeling I get at times" but must define the concept by a number of operations such as questionnaires and physiological measurements. The former definition is tied to a personal interpretation of bodily states and is not replicable by others. The latter puts the concept in the public realm of science.

It is important to realize that a concept in science is defined by a *set* of operations, not by just a single behavioral event or task. Instead, several slightly different tasks and behavioral events are used to converge on a concept (we will talk more about the idea of converging operations in Chapter 8). For example, educational psychologists define a concept such as *reading ability* in terms of performance on a standardized instrument such as the Woodcock Reading Mastery Tests (Woodcock, 1998) that contains a whole *set* of tasks. The total reading ability score on the Woodcock Reading Mastery instrument comprises indicators of performance on a number of different subtests that test slightly different skills but are all related to reading, for example, reading a passage and thinking of an appropriate word to fill in a blank in the passage, coming up with a synonym for a word, pronouncing a difficult word correctly in isolation, and several others. Collectively, performance on all of these tasks defines the concept *reading ability.*

Operational definitions force us to think carefully and empirically—in terms of observations in the real world—about how we want to define a concept. Imagine trying to define operationally something as seemingly conceptually simple as typing ability. Imagine you need to do this because you want to compare two different methods of teaching typing. Think of all the decisions you would have to make. You would want to measure typing speed, of course. But over how long a passage? A passage of only 100 words would seem too short, and a passage of 10,000 words would seem to long. But exactly how long then? How long does speed have to be sustained to match how we best conceive of the theoretical construct *typing ability?* And what kind of material has to be typed? Should it include numbers and formulas and odd spacing? And how are we going to deal with errors? It seems that both time and errors should come into play when measuring typing ability, but exactly what should the formula be that brings the two together? Do we want time and errors to be equally weighted, or is one somewhat more important than the other? The need for an operational definition would force you to think carefully about all of these things; it would make you think very thoroughly about how to conceptualize typing ability.

Reliability and Validity

For an operational definition of a concept to be useful, it must display both reliability and validity. *Reliability* refers to the consistency of a measuring instrument—whether you would arrive at the same measurement if you assessed the same concept multiple times. The scientific concept of reliability is easy to understand because it is very similar to its layperson's definition and very like one of its dictionary definitions: "an attribute of any system that consistently produces the same results."

Consider how a layperson might talk about whether something was reliable or not. Imagine a New Jersey commuter catching the bus to work in Manhattan each morning. The bus is scheduled to arrive at the commuter's stop at 7:20 A.M. One week the bus arrives at 7:20, 7:21, 7:20, 7:19, and 7:20, respectively. We would say that the bus was pretty reliable that week. If the next week the bus arrived at 7:35, 7:10, 7:45, 7:55, and 7:05, respectively, we would say that the bus was very unreliable that week.

The reliability of an operational definition in science is assessed in much the same way. If the measure of a concept yields similar numbers for multiple measurements of the same concept, we say that the measuring device displays high reliability. If we measured the same person's intelligence with different forms of an IQ test on Monday, Wednesday, and Friday of the same week and got scores of 110, 109, and, 110, we would say that that particular IQ test seems to be very reliable. By contrast, if the three scores were 89, 130, and 105, we would say that that particular IQ test does not seem to display high reliability. There are specific statistical techniques for assessing the reliability of different types of measuring instruments, and these are discussed in all standard introductory methodology textbooks.

But remember that reliability is only about consistency and nothing else. Reliability alone is not enough for an operational definition to be adequate. Reliability is necessary but not sufficient. To be a good operational definition of a concept, the operations assessed must also be a *valid* measure of that concept. The term *construct validity* refers to whether a measuring instrument (operational definition) is measuring what it is supposed to be measuring. In his methodology textbook, Professor Paul Cozby (2008) gives us a humorous example of reliability without validity. Imagine you are about to get your intelligence assessed. The examiner tells you to stick out your foot and clamps on a measuring device like those at the shoe store and reads out a number. You would, of course, think that this was a joke. But note that this measuring instrument would display many of the types of reliability that are discussed in methodology textbooks. It would give virtually the same readings on Monday, Wednesday, and Friday (what is termed *test–retest reliability*) and it would give the same reading no matter who used it (what is termed *interrater reliability*).

The problem with the shoe device as a measure of intelligence is not reliability (which it has) but validity. It is not a good measure of the concept it purports to measure (intelligence). One way we would know that it is not a valid measure of intelligence is that we would find that it does not relate to many other variables that we would expect a measure of intelligence to relate to. Measures from the shoe instrument would not relate to academic success; they would not relate to neurophysiological measures of brain functioning; they would not relate to job success; and they would not relate to measures of the efficiency of information processing developed by cognitive psychologists. By contrast, actual measures of intelligence relate to all of these things (Deary, 2001; Deary et al., 2008; Duncan et al., 2008; Flynn, 2007; Geary, 2005; Hunt & Carlson, 2007; Lubinski, 2004). Actual measures of intelligence in psychology have validity as well as reliability, whereas the shoe-size measure of intelligence has reliability without validity.

You might be wondering about another combination of affairs at this point, so let me recapitulate where we are. In operational definitions, we are looking for both reliability and validity, so high reliability and high validity are sought. We have just discussed the shoe-size IQ test in order to demonstrate that high reliability and low validity get us nowhere. A third case, low reliability and low validity, is so obviously useless that it is not worth discussing. But you might be wondering about the fourth and last possible combination: What if something has high validity and low reliability? The answer is that, like its converse case of low validity and high reliability (the shoe-size example), this state of affairs gets you nowhere. And, actually, it is more accurate to say that this state of affairs is impossible—because you cannot claim to be measuring validly if you cannot measure reliably.

Direct and Indirect Operational Definitions

The link between concepts and observable operations varies greatly in its degree of directness or indirectness. Few scientific concepts are defined almost entirely by observable operations in the real world. Most concepts are defined more indirectly. For example, the use of some concepts is determined by both a set of operations and the particular concept's relationship to other theoretical constructs. Finally, there are concepts that are not directly defined by observable operations but linked to other concepts that are. These are sometimes called latent constructs, and they are common in psychology.

For example, much research has been done on the so-called type A behavior pattern because it has been linked to the incidence of coronary heart disease (Chida & Hamer, 2008; Curtis & O'Keefe, 2002; Matthews, 2005; Smith, 2003; Suls & Bunde, 2005). We will discuss the type A behavior pattern in more detail in Chapter 8. The important point to illustrate here, however, is that the type A behavior pattern is actually defined by a set of subordinate concepts: a strong desire to compete, a potential for hostility, time-urgent behavior, an intense drive to accomplish goals, and several others. However, each one of these defining features of the type A behavior pattern (a strong desire to compete, etc.) is *itself* a concept in need of operational definition. Indeed, considerable effort has been expended in operationally defining each one. The important point for our present discussion is that the concept of the type A behavior pattern is a complex concept that is not directly defined by operations. Instead, it is linked with other concepts, which, in turn, have operational definitions. The type A behavior pattern provides an example of a concept with an indirect operational definition. Although theoretical concepts differ in how closely they are linked to observations, all concepts acquire their meaning partially through their link to such observations.

Scientific Concepts Evolve

It is important to realize that the definition of a scientific concept is not fixed but constantly changing as the observations that apply to the concept are enriched. If the original operational definition of a concept turns out to be theoretically unfruitful, it will be abandoned in favor of an alternative set of defining operations. Thus, concepts in science are continually evolving and can increase in abstractness as the knowledge concerning them increases. For example, at one time the electron was thought of as a tiny ball of negative charge circling the nucleus of an atom. Now it is viewed as a probability density function having wavelike properties in certain experimental situations.

In psychology, the development of the concept of intelligence provides a similar example. At first, the concept had only a strict operational definition: Intelligence is what is measured by tests of mental functioning. As empirical evidence accumulated relating intelligence to scholastic achievement, learning, brain injury, neurophysiology, and other behavioral and biological variables, the concept was both enriched and refined (Duncan et al., 2008; Flynn, 2007; Geary, 2005; Lubinski, 2004; Sternberg & Grigorenko, 2002; Unsworth & Engle, 2005; Zimmer, 2008). It now appears that intelligence is best conceptualized as a higher order construct defined by several more specific information-processing operations. These hypothesized processes, in turn, have more direct operational definitions stated in terms of measurable performance.

The concepts in theories of human memory have likewise evolved. Psychologists now rarely use global concepts like *remembering* or *forgetting;* instead, they test the properties of more specifically defined memory subprocesses, such as short-term acoustic memory, iconic storage, semantic memory, and episodic memory. The older concepts of remembering and forgetting have been elaborated with more specifically operationalized concepts.

Thus, the usage of theoretical terms evolves from scientific activity rather than from debates about the meaning of words. This is one of the most salient differences between the operational attitude of science and the essentialist quest for absolute definition. Philosopher Paul Churchland (1988) emphasized the idea that concepts in science derive meaning not from language definitions but from observations and other concepts to which they are related:

> To fully understand the expression "electric field" is to be familiar with the network of theoretical principles in which that expression appears. Collectively, they tell us what an electric field is and what it does. This case is typical. Theoretical terms do not, in general, get their meanings from single, explicit definitions stating conditions necessary and sufficient for their application. They are implicitly defined by the network of principles that embed them. (p. 56)

As scientific concepts evolve, they often become enmeshed in several different theoretical systems and acquire alternative operational definitions. There is not necessarily anything wrong with the concept when this happens. For example, many believe that psychology is discredited by the fact that many of its important theoretical constructs, such as intelligence, are operationalized and conceptualized in more than one way. But such a situation is not unique to psychology, and it is not a matter for despair or hand-wringing. In fact, it is a relatively common occurrence in science. Heat, for example, is conceptualized in terms of thermodynamic theory and in terms of kinetic theory. Physics is not scandalized by this state of affairs. Consider the electron. Many of its properties are explained by its being conceptualized as a wave. Other properties, however, are better handled if it is viewed as a particle. The existence of these alternative conceptualizations has tempted no one to suggest that physics be abandoned.

People got a lesson in this point in 2006 when the media reported that the International Astronomical Union had recently reoperationalized the term *planet* in a way that excluded Pluto (Adler, 2006). That something as seemingly basic as the concept "planet" could be the subject of alternative views was a surprise to many in the public. But in fact it is a common occurrence in science. In this case, one group of astronomers prefers to stress the composition and geologic composition of astronomical bodies. Another group likes to emphasize their dynamical properties, for example, their orbits and gravitational effects. The operational definitions of the former group include Pluto as a planet, but the operational definitions of the latter group exclude Pluto. The differing operational definitions do not reflect badly on the field of astronomy. They merely reflect differing ways of triangulating concepts in the discipline. The same is true in psychology, where there are sometimes alternative operational definitions of concepts. Just because something is hard to define does not mean that there is not something real there to study.

It is likewise with other well-established scientific concepts such as the gene in biology. We first learn the concept in its simplest form—as a unit of DNA that codes for a protein. However, science writer Natalie Angier (2008) tells us that in recent years the concept of the gene has been complexified beyond that simple definition. But Harvard Medical School scientist Jonathan Beckwith advises us not to worry because "It's the normal process of doing science. You start off simple and you develop complexity" (p. D2). Researchers are not confused by these shifting and complexifying definitions. Instead, they welcome them as a sign of scientific progress. A scientist interviewed by Angier warns us that "Geneticists happily abuse 'gene' to mean many things in many settings. This can be a source of enormous consternation to onlookers who want to understand the conversation, but geneticists aren't bothered" (p. D2). It is likewise in psychology when concepts complexify and their operational definitions shift.

Operational Definitions in Psychology

Many people understand the necessity of operationism when they think about physics or chemistry. They understand that if scientists are going to talk about a particular type of chemical reaction, or about energy, or about magnetism, they must have a way of measuring these things. Unfortunately, when people think and talk about psychology, they often fail to recognize the need for operationism. Why is it not equally obvious that psychological terms must be operationally defined, either directly or indirectly, in order to be useful explanatory constructs in scientific theories?

One reason is what has been termed the *preexisting-bias problem* in psychology. We alluded to this problem in Chapter 1. People do not come to the study of geology with emotionally held beliefs about the nature of rocks. The situation in psychology is very different. We all have intuitive theories of personality and human behavior because we have been "explaining" behavior to ourselves all our lives. All our personal psychological theories contain theoretical concepts (e.g., *smart, aggressive, anxiety*). Thus, it is only natural to ask why we have to accept some other definition. Although this attitude seems reasonable on the surface, it is a complete bar to any scientific progress in understanding human behavior and is the cause of much public confusion about psychology.

One of the greatest sources of misunderstanding and one of the biggest impediments to the accurate presentation of psychological findings in the media is the fact that many technical concepts in psychology are designated by words used in everyday language. This everyday usage opens the door to a wide range of misconceptions. The layperson seldom realizes that when psychologists use words such as *intelligence, anxiety, aggression,* and *attachment* as theoretical constructs, they do not necessarily mean the same thing that the general public does when using these words.

The nature of this difference should be apparent from the previous discussion of operationism. When terms such as *intelligence* and *anxiety* are used in psychological theories, their direct or indirect operational definitions determine their correct usage. These definitions are often highly technical, usually fairly specific, and often different from popular usage in many ways. For example, when hearing the phrase "the first principal component of the factor analysis of a large sampling of cognitive tasks," many people would not recognize it as part of the operational definition of the term *intelligence*.

Similarly, in lay usage, the term *depression* has come to mean something like "feeling down in the dumps." By contrast, the technical definition of major depressive disorder takes up over a dozen pages in the *Diagnostic and Statistical Manual of Mental Disorders* (American Psychiatric Association, 2000) and means something quite different from being "down in the dumps." A clinical psychologist's depression is not the same as the layperson's depression (Hollon, Thase, & Markowitz, 2002). Other sciences also have this problem, although perhaps in a less severe form than psychology. Recall the previous discussion of the concept *life*. As Medawar and Medawar (1983) pointed out, "The trouble is that 'life,' like many other technical terms in science, has been pirated from the vernacular and is used in scientific contexts far removed from those that might arise in common speech" (p. 66).

Physicist Lisa Randall (2005) discusses how this problem obscures the understanding of physics by the public. She points out that the term *relativity* in Einstein's theory has been taken by the public to imply that "there are no absolutes because everything is relative" when in fact the theory says just the opposite! Randall points out that actually Einstein's theory implies that "although the measurements any observer makes depend on his coordinates and reference frame, the physical phenomena he measures have an invariant description that transcends that observer's particular coordinates. Einstein's theory of relativity is really about finding an invariant description of physical phenomena. Indeed, Einstein agreed with the suggestion that his theory would have been better named 'invariantentheorie.' But the term 'relativity' was already too entrenched at the time for him to change" (p. 13).

Randall goes on to point out that even in physics "ambiguous word choices are the source of some misunderstandings. Scientists often employ colloquial terminology, which they then assign a specific meaning that is impossible to fathom without proper training" (p. 13). And the same is true in psychology. When the psychologist and the layperson use the same word to mean different things, they often misinterpret each other. Such confusion would be less prevalent if new words had been coined to represent psychological constructs. On occasion such words have been coined. Just as physicists have their *erg* and *joule*, psychology has its *dissonance* and *encoding*, words that are not actually coined but are uncommon enough to prevent confusion.

"But," the layperson may object, "why do psychologists inflict this on us? New jargon, highly technical definitions, uncommon uses of words. Why do we need them? Why is my idea of 'intelligence' not an acceptable idea to talk about?"

Here we see exemplified a critical misunderstanding of psychological research—a misunderstanding that is often reflected in media reports of psychological research. A national newspaper report on the 1996 meeting of the American Psychological Association (Immen, 1996) is headlined "Could You Repeat That in Klingon?" and refers to "psychologists speaking a language all their own." The article ridicules the following title of a paper delivered at the conference: "Interpreting WJ-R and KAIT Joint Factor Analyses from Gf-Gc Theory." Although the reporter states that he would "not even dare to speculate about the true meaning" of the title, almost all properly trained psychologists would recognize the title as referring to developments in intelligence test theory. And this is as it should be. Gf-Gc theory is a technical development in intelligence theory. There is no reason for the reporter to have heard of this concept—just as one would not expect the reporter to know the details of the latest elementary particle to be identified by physicists. Somehow, however, the reporter's (quite understandable) ignorance of the technical terminology is seen as reflecting negatively on modern psychology.

We come here to the crux of the problem. The first step in resolving it is to emphasize a point from our earlier discussion: Operationism is not unique to psychology. It is characteristic of all sciences. Most of the time, we accept it readily, recognizing its obvious nature. If a scientist is investigating radioactivity, we take it for granted that he or she must have some observable way of measuring the phenomenon—a method that another investigator could use to obtain the same results. This method is what makes possible the public nature of science, one of its defining features. Two different scientists agree on the same operational definition so that it is possible for one to replicate the other's results. However, what seems obvious in other contexts is sometimes not so clear when we think about psychology. The necessity for operational definitions of concepts like *intelligence* and *anxiety* is often not recognized because we use these terms all the time, and, after all, don't we all just "know" what these things mean?

The answer is "No, we don't"—not in the sense that a scientist has to know, that is, in a public sense. A scientist must "know" what intelligence means by being able to define, precisely, how another laboratory could measure it in exactly the same way and be led to the same conclusions about the concept. This is vastly different—in terms of explicitness and precision—than the vague verbal connotations that are needed in order to achieve casual understanding in general conversation.

Operationism as a Humanizing Force

The problem with relying on what we all just "know" is the same problem that plagues all intuitive (i.e., nonempirical) systems of belief. What you "know" about something may not be quite the same as what Jim "knows" or what Jane "knows." How do we decide who is right? You may say, "Well, I feel strongly about this, so strongly that I *know* I'm right." But what if Jim, who thinks somewhat differently, feels even more strongly than you do? And then there's Jane, who thinks differently from you or Jim, claiming that she must be right because she feels *even more* strongly than Jim does.

This simple parody is meant only to illustrate a fundamental aspect of scientific knowledge, one that has been a major humanizing force in human history: In science, the truth of a knowledge claim is not determined by the strength of belief of the individual putting forth the claim. The problem with all intuitively based systems of belief is that they have no mechanism for deciding among conflicting claims. When everyone knows intuitively, but the intuitive claims conflict, how do we decide who is right? Sadly, history shows that the result of such conflicts is usually a power struggle.

Some people mistakenly claim that an operational approach to psychology dehumanizes people and that instead we should base our views of human beings on intuition. Psychologist Donald Broadbent (1973) argued that the truly humane position is one that bases theoretical views of human beings on observable behavior rather than on the intuition of the theorizer:

> We can tell nothing of other people except by seeing what they do or say in particular circumstances. . . . The empirical method is a way of reconciling differences. If one rejects it, the only way of dealing with a disagreement is by emotional polemic. (p. 206)

Thus, the humanizing force in science is that of making knowledge claims public so that conflicting ideas can be tested in a way that is acceptable to all disputants. Recall the concept of replication from Chapter 1. This allows a selection among theories to take place by peaceful mechanisms that we all agree on in advance. The public nature of science rests critically on the idea of operationism. By operationally defining concepts, we put them in the public realm, where they can be criticized, tested, improved, or perhaps rejected.

Psychological concepts cannot rest on someone's personal definition, which may be uncommon, idiosyncratic, or vague. For this reason, psychology must reject all personal definitions of concepts—just as physics, for example, rejects personal definitions of energy and meteorology rejects personal definitions of what a cloud is. Psychologists instead must rely on publicly accessible concepts defined by operations that anyone with proper training and facilities can perform. In rejecting personal definitions, psychology is not shutting out the layperson but is opening up the field—as all sciences do—to the quest for a common, publicly accessible knowledge that all can share.

Such publicly accessible knowledge is available to solve human problems only when concepts have become grounded in operational definitions and are not the focus of essentialist arguments about the meaning of words. For example, Monk (1990) describes how during World War II the concept of *wound shock* had become problematic in medicine. Some physicians identified the condition based on an abnormally high concentration of red blood cells thought to be due to a leakage of plasma from the blood into tissue. Others identified wound shock on the basis of low blood pressure, skin pallor, and rapid pulse. In other words, operational definitions of the concept were inconsistent (and even idiosyncratic) and, thus, one physician by the name of Grant working for the British Medical Research Council recommended "that the very concept of 'wound shock' should be abandoned and that detailed observations of casualties should be made without using the term. . . . The lack of a common basis of diagnosis renders it impossible to assess the efficacy of the various methods of treatment adopted" (Monk, 1990, pp. 445–446). In other words, the concept was doing more harm than good because it did not have a definition that was common enough so that it could be considered public knowledge (i.e., generally shared and agreed upon).

Sometimes the changes in the meaning of concepts in science will put scientific understanding of a concept in conflict with the nonspecialist's understanding. Farber and Churchland (1995) discuss such a situation surrounding the concept of fire. The classical concept was used "to classify not only burning carbon-stuffs, but also activity on the sun and various stars (actually nuclear fusion), lightning (actually electrically induced incandescence), the northern lights (actually spectral emission), and the flash of fireflies (actually phosphorescence). In our modern conceptual scheme, since none of these things involves oxidation, none belongs to the same class as wood fires. Moreover, some processes that turned out to belong to the oxidation class—rusting, tarnishing, and metabolism—were not originally considered to share anything with burning, since felt heat was taken to be an essential feature of this class" (p. 1296). In short, the principle of oxidation uniting the phenomena of a campfire and rusting—and separating them from the phenomenon of lightning—may be a sign of progress to a scientist, but it can be confusing and disorienting to the layperson.

Essentialist Questions and the Misunderstanding of Psychology

Another reason many people seem to abandon the idea of operationism when they approach psychology is that they seek essentialist answers to certain human problems. Whether the cause is psychology's relatively recent separation from philosophy or the public's more limited understanding of psychology than of other sciences is unclear. In a sense, however, it does not matter. The net result is the same. Psychology is expected to provide absolute answers to complex questions in a way that other sciences are not.

Recall the questions at the beginning of this chapter: What is the real meaning of the word *gravity?* What is the underlying essence of it? What does it ultimately mean even to speak of gravity? Most people would recognize that these questions require knowledge of the ultimate, underlying nature of a phenomenon and that current theories in physics cannot provide answers to questions of this type. Anyone familiar with popular writing about the progress of physical science in the last few centuries will recognize that gravity is a theoretical construct of great complexity and that its conceptual and operational relationships have been in constant flux.

However, substitute the word *intelligence* for the word *gravity* in each of the preceding questions and, suddenly, a miracle occurs. Now the questions are imbued with great meaning. They seem natural and meaningful. They literally beg for an ultimate answer. When the psychologist gives the same answer as the physicist—that intelligence is a complex concept that derives meaning from the operations used to measure it and from its theoretical relationships to other constructs—he or she is belittled and accused of avoiding the real issues.

One problem facing psychology, then, is that the public demands answers to essentialist questions that it does not routinely demand of other sciences. These demands often underlie many of the attempts to disparage the progress that has been made in the field. Although these demands do not hinder the field itself—because psychologists, like other scientists, ignore demands for essentialist answers and simply go about their work— they are an obstacle to the public's understanding of psychology. The public becomes confused when an uninformed critic claims that there has been no progress in psychology. The fact that this claim so frequently goes unchallenged reflects the unfortunate truth of the major premise of this book: Public knowledge of what scientific achievement within psychology would actually mean is distressingly meager. When examined closely, such criticisms usually boil down to the contention that psychology has not yet provided the ultimate answer to any of its questions. To this charge, psychology readily pleads guilty—as do all the other sciences.

Some may find it discomforting to learn that no science, including psychology, can give answers to essentialist questions. Holton and Roller (1958) discussed the uneasiness that the layperson may feel when told that physicists cannot answer essentialist questions. They discuss the phenomenon of radioactive decay in which the number of atoms of a radioactive element that have decayed can be related to time via an exponential mathematical function. That function, however, does not explain *why* radioactive decay occurs. It does not answer the layperson's question of *why* it follows this function. It does not answer the question of what radioactive decay *really is*. Holton and Roller tell us that "we must try to make our peace with the limitations of modern science; it does not claim to find out 'what things really are' " (pp. 219–220). As science writer Robert Wright (1988) explained,

> There was something bothersome about Isaac Newton's theory of gravitation. . . . How, after all, could "action at a distance" be realized? . . . Newton sidestepped such questions. . . . Ever since Newton, physics has followed his example. . . . Physicists make no attempt to explain why things obey laws of electromagnetism or of gravitation. (p. 61)

Likewise, those who seek essentialist answers to questions concerning human nature are destined to be disappointed if they are looking to psychology. Psychology is not a religion. It is a broad field that seeks a scientific understanding of all aspects of behavior. Therefore, psychology's current explanations are temporary theoretical constructs that account for behavior better than alternative explanations. These constructs will certainly be superseded in the future by superior theoretical conceptualizations that are closer to the truth.

Operationism and the Phrasing of Psychological Questions

The idea of an operational definition can be a very useful tool in evaluating the falsifiability of a psychological theory. The presence of concepts that are not directly or indirectly grounded in observable operations is an important clue to recognizing a nonfalsifiable theory. These concepts are usually intended to rescue such a theory from disconfirmation after the data have been collected. Thus, the presence of loose concepts—those for which the theorist cannot provide direct or indirect operational links—should be viewed with suspicion.

A principle that scientists term *parsimony* is relevant here. The principle of parsimony dictates that when two theories have the same explanatory power, the simpler theory (the one involving fewer concepts and conceptual relationships) is preferred. The reason is that the theory with fewer conceptual relationships will likely be the more falsifiable of the two in future tests.

A strong grasp of the principle of operationism will also aid in the recognition of problems or questions that are scientifically meaningless. For example, I have in my files a wire service article, from United Press International, entitled "Do Animals Think?" The article describes recent experimentation in animal behavior. There is nothing wrong with the research described in the article, but it is clear that the title is merely a teaser. The question in the title is scientifically meaningless unless some operational criteria are specified for the term *think*, and none is given in the article. A similar problem concerns the many newspaper articles that have asked, "Can computers think?" Without some operational criteria, this question is also scientifically meaningless, even though it is infinitely useful as grist for cocktail party conversation.

Actually it is instructive to observe people debating this last question because such a debate provides an opportunity to witness concretely the preexisting-bias problem in psychology that we discussed earlier. Most people are strongly biased toward not wanting a computer to be able to think. Why? For a variety of reasons, the layperson's concept *think* has become so intertwined with the concept *human* that many people have an emotional reaction against the idea of nonhuman things thinking (e.g., computers or extraterrestrial life forms that look nothing like the humans on our planet).

However, despite their strong feelings against the idea of thinking computers, most people have not thought about the issue very carefully and are at a loss to come up with a definition of thinking that would include most humans (babies, for example) and exclude all computers. It is sometimes humorous to hear the criteria that people who are unfamiliar with current work in artificial intelligence come up with, for they invariably choose something that computers can actually do. For example, many people propose the criterion "ability to learn from experience," only to be told that some robots and artificial intelligence systems have fulfilled this criterion (Clark, 2001; McCorduck, 2004). The strength of preexisting bias can be observed in this situation. Is the person's response "Oh, I didn't know. Well, since the criterion for thinking that I put forth is met by some computers, I will have to conclude that at least those computers think"? Usually this intellectually honest response is not the one that is given. More commonly, the person begins groping around for another criterion in the hope that computers cannot meet it.

Usually the second choice is something like "creativity" ("coming up with something that people judge as useful that no person has thought of before"—we will ignore the question of whether most *humans* would meet this criterion). When told that most experts agree that computers have fulfilled this criterion (Boden, 2003), the person still does not admit the possibility of thinking machines. Often the person abandons the attempt to derive an operational definition at this point and instead attempts to argue that computers could not possibly think because "humans built them and programmed them; they only follow their programs."

Although this argument is one of the oldest objections to thinking machines (McCorduck, 2004; Woolley, 2000), it is actually fallacious. Preexisting bias prevents many people from recognizing that it is totally irrelevant to the question at issue. Almost everyone would agree that thinking is a process taking place in the natural world. Now notice that we do not invoke the "origins" argument for other processes. Consider the process of heating food. Consider the question "Do ovens heat?" Do we say, "Ovens don't really heat, because ovens are built by *people*. Therefore, it only makes sense to say that *people* heat. Ovens don't really heat?" Or what about lifting? Do cranes lift? Is our answer "Cranes don't really lift because cranes are built by *people*. Therefore, it only makes sense to say that *people* lift. Cranes don't really lift?" Of course not. The origin of something is totally irrelevant to its ability to carry out a particular process. The process of thinking is just the same. Whether or not an entity thinks is independent of the origins of the entity.

The failure to think rationally about the possibility of thinking machines was one reason that the noted computer scientist Alan Turing developed his famous test of whether computers think. What is important for our discussion is that the test Turing devised is an *operational* test. Turing (1950) began his famous article "Computing Machinery and Intelligence" by writing, "I propose to consider the question 'Can machines think?' " Not wanting discussion of the issue to descend to the usual circular cocktail-party chatter or endless essentialist arguments about what we mean by *think*, Turing proposed a strict operational test of whether a computer could think. His proposal was that it would be reasonable to grant a computer thinking powers if it could carry on an intelligent conversation.

The creativity in the Turing proposal was that he put forth a way to operationalize the question while at the same time guarding against the preexisting-bias problem. Turing strictly specified the logistics of the test of whether the computer could carry on an intelligent conversation. It was not to be done by having a tester interact with the computer via keyboard and screen and then having the tester judge whether the computer had, in fact, carried on an intelligent conversation. Turing did not propose this type of test because he was concerned about the preexisting-bias problem. Turing was sure that once the person sat down before a computer, keyboard, and screen—something obviously a *machine*—the person would deny it thinking capabilities no matter what it did. Therefore, Turing proposed a test that controlled for the irrelevant external characteristics of the thinking device. His well-known proposal was to have the tester engage in conversation via two keyboards—one connected to a computer and the other to a human, both out of sight—and then to decide which was which. If the tester could not identify the human with greater-than-chance accuracy, then one reasonable inference was that the conversational abilities—the operational definition of thinking—of the computer were equal to those of a human.

Turing's key insight was the "same insight that inspires the practice among symphony orchestras of conducting auditions with an opaque screen between the jury and the musician. What matters in a musician, obviously, is musical ability and only musical ability: such features as sex, hair length, skin color, and weight are strictly irrelevant. . . . Turing recognized that people might be similarly biased in their judgments of intelligence by whether the contestant had soft skin, warm blood, facial features, hands and eyes— which are obviously not themselves essential components of intelligence" (Dennett, 1998, p. 5). Turing's test teaches us the necessity of operational definitions if we are to discuss psychological concepts rationally; that is, in a principled way rather than merely as a reflection of our own biases about the question at issue.

The intellectual style revealed when we observe people discussing the issue of artificial intelligence illustrates well the difference between scientific and nonscientific styles of thinking. The scientific approach is to develop an operational definition that seems reasonable and then to see what conclusions about thinking, computers, and humans it leads to. By contrast, preexisting bias dominates the thinking of most people. They have already arrived at certain conclusions and are not interested in what is actually known about the relative contrasts between computer and human performance. Instead, with minds made up, they spend their intellectual energies in a desperate juggling of words designed to protect their prior beliefs from change. What we see, then, is a combination of preexisting bias and nonoperational essentialist attitudes that fuel the assumption that people "just know" what thinking "really" is without any necessity of operational criteria. Such attitudes are what make most people's intuitive psychological theories unfalsifiable and, hence, useless. These very attitudes illustrate precisely why we need the *science* of psychology!

Summary

Operational definitions are definitions of concepts stated in terms of observable operations that can be measured. One of the main ways that we ensure that theories are falsifiable is by making certain that the key concepts in theories have operational definitions stated in terms of well-replicated behavioral observations. Operational definitions are one major mechanism that makes scientific knowledge publicly verifiable. Such definitions are in the public domain so that the theoretical concepts that they define are testable by all— unlike "intuitive," nonempirical definitions that are the special possession of particular individuals and not open to testing by everyone.

Because psychology employs terms from common discourse, such as *intelligence* and *anxiety,* and because many people have preexisting notions about what these terms mean, the necessity of operationally defining these terms is often not recognized. Psychology is like all other sciences in requiring operational definitions of its terms. However, people often demand answers to essentialist questions (questions about the absolute, underlying nature of a concept) of psychology that they do not demand of other sciences. No science provides such answers to ultimate questions. Instead, psychology, like other sciences, seeks continually to refine its operational definitions so that the concepts in theories more accurately reflect the way the world actually is.

CHAPTER 4

Testimonials and Case Study Evidence: Placebo Effects and the Amazing Randi

Cut to the *Oprah Winfrey Show,* one of the most popular television talk shows of the last decade. Today's guest is Dr. Alfred Pontificate, director of the Oedipus Institute of Human Potential. Oprah attempts to elicit questions about the doctor's provocative new Theory of Birth Order, which is based on the idea that the course of one's life is irrevocably set by family interactions that are determined by birth order. The discussion inevitably turns from theoretical concerns to requests for explanations of personal events of importance to members of the audience. The doctor complies without much prodding.

For example, "Doctor, my brother is a self-destructive workaholic. He ignores his wife and family and places work-related problems above everything else. He has an ulcer and a drinking problem that he refuses to acknowledge. His family hasn't been on a real vacation in two years. He's headed for divorce and doesn't seem to care. Why has he chosen such a self-destructive course?"

To which the doctor replies, "What is his birth order, my dear?"

"Oh, he is the oldest of the children."

"Yes," the doctor says, "this is quite common. We see it often in the clinic. The underlying dynamics of a situation like this arise because parents transfer their life hopes and frustrations to their firstborn child. Through a process of unconscious wish transference, the child absorbs these hopes and frustrations, even if the parents never articulate them. Then, through the unconscious process that I call the dynamic expectation spiral, the aspirations of the parents become manifest as a pathological need for achievement in the child."

Although the audience members on the *Oprah* show sometimes asks hostile questions when the guest challenges their beliefs, this rarely happens when a behavioral "expert" seems to confirm conventional wisdom. Once in a while, however, the show is enlivened by an audience member who questions the evidence behind the guest's declarations. In this case, an eager, forthright questioner is in the studio. "But wait a minute, Doctor," the questioner begins. "My brother is a firstborn, too. My parents sent the bum to Harvard and told me to go to a two-year school to be a dental hygienist. So, this 'great brain' of theirs drops out after one year, goes to some mountaintop in Colorado, and the last time we saw him he was weaving baskets! I don't understand what you're saying about firstborns."

The audience tenses for the confrontation, but alas, the doctor always wins in the end: "Oh, yes, I have seen many cases like your brother. Yes, I often meet them in my practice. They are people for whom the dynamic expectation spiral has short-circuited, creating an unconscious desire to thwart wish transference. Thus, the individual's life develops in such a way as to reject conventional achievement aspirations." A hushed pause follows; then on we go to the next "case."

Of course, we are dealing with something quite familiar here. This is another example of the Benjamin Rush problem discussed in Chapter 2. This "theory" of birth order is structured so that no observation can disconfirm it. Because it is an unfalsifiable theory, the confirmations put forth to prove it are meaningless because nothing is ruled out by the theory.

However, our concern in this chapter is not with the theory itself, but with the nature of the evidence that is presented to support it. When pressed for evidence, Dr. Pontificate presents his own "clinical experience" or "case studies" as proof. This is an extremely common occurrence in the realm of media psychology. Talk shows and paperback book racks are full of psychological theories based on the clinical experience of the author. Many of the therapies presented to the public through these outlets are backed by nothing more than the testimonials of individuals who have undergone them and consider themselves improved or cured. In this chapter, we shall develop a principle of great use to consumers of psychological information: Case studies and testimonials are virtually worthless as evidence for the evaluation of psychological theories and treatments.

In this chapter, we will demonstrate why this is true, and we will also discuss the proper role of the case study in psychology.

The Place of the Case Study

A case study is an investigation that looks intensely and in detail at a single individual or very small number of individuals. The usefulness of case study information is strongly determined by how far scientific investigation has advanced in a particular area. The insights gained from case studies or clinical experience may be quite useful in the early stages of the investigation of certain problems as indicators of which variables deserve more intense study. Case studies have played a prominent role in opening up new areas of study in psychology (Martin & Hull, 2006). Well-known examples occur in the work of Jean Piaget. Piaget's investigations raised the possibility that children's thinking is not just a watered-down or degraded version of adults' thinking but has a structure of its own. Some of Piaget's conjectures about children's thinking have been confirmed, but many have not (Bjorklund, 2004; Goswami, 2008). However, what is important for our discussion here is not how many of Piaget's conjectures have been confirmed. Instead, what is important is to understand the fact that Piaget's case studies did not *prove* anything but, rather, suggested incredibly fruitful areas for developmental psychologists to investigate. It was subsequent correlational and experimental studies of the type to be described in Chapters 5 and 6 that provided the confirmatory and disconfirmatory evidence for the hypotheses that were generated by Piaget's case studies.

However, when we move from the early stages of scientific investigation, where case studies may be very useful, to the more mature stages of theory testing, the situation changes drastically. Case studies are not useful at the later stages of scientific investigation because they cannot be used as confirming or disconfirming evidence in the test of a particular theory. The reason is that case studies and testimonials are isolated events that lack the comparative information necessary to rule out alternative explanations.

One of the limitations of Freud's work was that he never took the second step of moving from interesting hypotheses based on case studies to actually *testing* those hypotheses (Dufresne, 2007). One of the leading writers about Freud's work, Frank Sulloway, has said that "science is a two-step process. The first step is the development of hypotheses. Freud had developed a set of extremely compelling, extremely plausible hypotheses for his day, but he never took that key, second procedural step in the rigorous manner that is required for true science" (Dufresne, 2007, p. 53).

Testimonials are like case studies in that they are isolated events. The problem of relying on testimonial evidence is that there are testimonials to support virtually every therapy tried. Thus, it is wrong to use them to support any *specific* remedy, because all of the competing remedies *also* have supporting testimonials. What we want to know, of course, is which remedy is *best*, and we cannot determine this by using testimonial evidence. As psychologist Ray Nickerson (1998) has said in his review of the cognitive processes we use to deceive ourselves, "Every practitioner of a form of pseudomedicine can point to a cadre of patients who will testify, in all sincerity, to having benefited from the treatment" (p. 192). For example, subliminal self-help audiotapes (tapes that use messages below hearing threshold) that are purported to raise memory performance or self-esteem generate plenty of testimonials despite the fact that controlled studies indicate that they have absolutely no effect on memory or self-esteem (Moore, 1995).

The idea of alternative explanations is critical to an understanding of theory testing. The goal of experimental design is to structure events so that support of one particular explanation simultaneously disconfirms other explanations. Scientific progress can occur only if the data that are collected rule out some explanations, as discussed in Chapter 2. Science sets up conditions for the natural selection of ideas. Some survive empirical testing and others do not. Those that remain are closer to the truth. This is the honing process by which ideas are sifted so that those that contain the most truth are found. But there must be selection and elimination in this process: Data collected as support for a particular theory must not leave many other alternative explanations as equally viable candidates. For this reason, scientists construct control or comparison groups in their experimentation. Control groups are formed so that, when their results are compared with those from an experimental group, some alternative explanations are ruled out. How this is done will be a main topic in several later chapters.

Case studies and testimonials stand as isolated phenomena. They lack the comparative information necessary to prove that a particular theory or therapy is superior. It is thus wrong to cite a testimonial or a case study as support for a *particular* theory or therapy. Those who do so mislead the public if they do not point out that such evidence is open to a wide range of alternative explanations. In short, the isolated demonstration of a phenomenon may be highly misleading. This point can be illustrated more specifically by the example of placebo effects.

Why Testimonials Are Worthless: Placebo Effects

Virtually every therapy that has ever been devised in medicine and psychology has garnered supporters and has been able to produce individuals who will testify sincerely to its efficacy. Medical science has documented testimonials to the curative powers of swine teeth, crocodile dung, powdered Egyptian mummy, and many other even more imaginative remedies (Begley, 2008a; Harrington, 2008). In fact, it has long been known that the mere suggestion that treatment is being administered is enough to make many people feel better.

The tendency of people to report that any treatment has helped them, regardless of whether it has a real therapeutic element, is known as the *placebo effect* (Bausell, 2007; Begley, 2008a; Goldacre, 2008; Harrington, 2008; Moerman & Harrington, 2005; Stewart-Williams & Podd, 2004). The concept of the placebo effect was well illustrated in the movie *The Wizard of Oz*. The wizard did not *actually* give the tin man a heart, the scarecrow a brain, and the lion courage, but they all felt better nevertheless. In fact, because it is only in the last hundred years or so that medical science has developed a substantial number of treatments that actually have therapeutic efficacy, it has been said that "prior to the twentieth century, the whole history of medicine was simply the history of the placebo effect" (Postman, 1988, p. 96).

We can illustrate the concept of a placebo effect by considering biomedical research, where all studies of new medical procedures must include controls for placebo effects. Typically, if a new drug is being tested on a group of patients, an equivalent group will also be formed and given a pill that does not contain the drug (a placebo). Neither group will know what it is receiving. Thus, when the two groups are compared, the placebo effect—that is, the tendency to feel better when any new treatment is introduced—is controlled for. It would not be sufficient merely to show that a percentage of patients receiving the new drug report relief from their symptoms, because in the absence of a control group it would be impossible to know what percentage is reporting relief due to a placebo effect rather than to the efficacy of the drug itself.

The placebo effect has been found to be 29 percent (of patients reporting satisfactory relief after receiving a placebo) for major depression, 36 percent for duodenal ulcer, 29 percent for migraine headache, and 27 percent for reflux esophagitis (Cho, Hotopf, & Wessely, 2005). One study (Bower, 1996) suggested that the placebo effect associated with taking the popular antidepressant drug Prozac is as large as the effect of the drug itself (Kirsch et al., 2008). Placebo effects can be very powerful—so powerful that there have even been reports of people who have become addicted to placebo pills (Ernst & Abbot, 1999), needing more and more to maintain their state of health! One bizarre study (see Begley, 2008a) found that a group of subjects who received sham surgery (incision, but no actual procedure) reported almost as much pain relief from osteoarthritis as those actually receiving a real arthroscopy. It is no doubt examples like this that account for the fact that almost 50 percent of physicians report that they deliberately prescribe placebos (Tilburt, Emanuel, Kaptchuk, Curlin, & Miller, 2008). Finally, placebo effects can be modulated by the context of expectation. Research has demonstrated (Waber, Shiv, Carmon, & Ariely, 2008) that a costly placebo provides more pain relief than a cheap placebo!

Of course, in actual research on drug therapies, the placebo control is not a pill containing nothing but instead is one containing the best currently known agent for the condition. The issue isolated by the experimental comparison is whether the new drug is superior to the best one currently available.

You are given information about placebo effects every time that you take a prescription medication. The next time you receive a prescription medication (or, if you are too healthy, take a look at your grandmother's!), examine carefully the sheet of information that comes with the drug (or look on the drug manufacturer's website) and you will find information about its placebo effects on the medical problem in question. For example, I take a medication called Imitrex (sumatriptan succinate) for relief from migraine headaches. The information sheet accompanying this drug tells me that controlled studies have demonstrated that, at a particular dosage level, 57 percent of patients taking this medication receive relief in two hours (I am one of the lucky 57 percent!). But the sheet also tells me that the same studies have shown a placebo effect of 21 percent for this type of headache—21 percent of people receive relief in two hours when their pill is filled with a neutral substance rather than sumatriptan succinate.

Placebo effects are implicated in all types of psychological therapy (Lilienfeld, 2007). Many people with psychological problems of mild to moderate severity report improvement after receiving psychotherapy. However, controlled studies have demonstrated that some proportion of this recovery rate is due to a combination of placebo effects and the mere passage of time, often termed *spontaneous remission*. As Dodes (1997) notes, "Even serious diseases have periods of exacerbation and remission; arthritis and multiple sclerosis are prime examples. There are even cases of cancer inexplicably disappearing" (p. 45).

Most therapeutic treatments are some unknown combination of an active therapeutic component and a placebo effect. Dodes (1997) cautions us to realize that a positive response to a placebo does not mean that a patient's problem was imaginary and warns that, contrary to popular belief, placebos can be harmful: "Placebo responses can 'teach' chronic illness by confirming and/or reinforcing the delusion of imagined disease. Patients can become dependent on nonscientific practitioners who employ placebo therapies" (Dodes, 1997, p. 45).

In studies of psychotherapy effectiveness, it is often difficult to determine exactly how to treat the placebo control group, but these complications should not concern us here. Instead, it is important to understand why researchers are concerned about separating true therapeutic effects from placebo effects and spontaneous remission. A study of therapeutic effectiveness by Gordon Paul (1966, 1967) provides an example of what the outcomes of such investigations reveal. Paul studied groups of students who suffered from maladaptive anxiety in public-speaking situations. Of an experimental group that received desensitization therapy specific to their speech anxiety problem, 85 percent showed significant improvement. A placebo group received a pill that they were told was a potent tranquilizer but that was actually a bicarbonate capsule. Of this group, 50 displayed significant improvement. Of a third group that did not receive any therapy at all, 22 percent also displayed significant improvement. Thus, it appears that the spontaneous remission rate was 22 percent for this particular problem, that an additional 28 percent of the subjects displayed improvement due to generalized placebo effects (50 percent minus 22 percent), and that the desensitization therapy did have a specific effect over and above that of the placebo plus spontaneous remission (85 percent compared with 50 percent).

Like the Paul study, other research has shown that psychotherapies do have a positive effect over and above what would be expected purely as the result of a placebo (Hollon et al., 2002; Lipsey & Wilson, 1993; Nathan & Gorman, 1998; Shadish & Baldwin, 2005). But experiments using placebo controls have demonstrated that merely citing the overall percentage of people who report improvement vastly overestimates the degree of improvement that is uniquely due to the particular treatment. The problem here is that testimonials are just too easy to generate. Cornell University psychologist Thomas Gilovich (1991) noted that "with the body so effective in healing itself, many who seek medical assistance will experience a positive outcome even if the doctor does nothing beneficial. Thus, even a worthless treatment can appear effective when the base-rate of success is so high" (p. 128). In short, placebo effects are potentially occurring whenever a therapeutic intervention is undertaken, *regardless of the efficacy of the intervention.* The problem is that placebo effects are so potent that, no matter how ludicrous the therapy one uses, if it is administered to a large group of people a few will be willing to give a testimonial to its efficacy (the early-morning whack-on-the-head therapy—use it every day and you'll feel better! Send $10.95 for your special, medically tested rubber hammer).

But we really should not joke about such a serious matter. Unwarranted reliance on testimonials and case study evidence may have disastrous consequences. Members of a research team that contributed to the modern conceptualization of Tourette syndrome as an organically based disorder (Shapiro et al., 1978; see Chapter 2) pointed out that inappropriate reliance on case study evidence helped to perpetuate the unfalsifiable psychoanalytic explanations of the syndrome that impeded true scientific progress in investigating the nature of the disorder.

An editorial in the *New England Journal of Medicine* illustrates what practitioners in the medical sciences believe to be the place of the case study and the testimonial in medicine. "If, for example, the *Journal* were to receive a paper describing a patient's recovery from cancer of the pancreas after he had ingested a rhubarb diet . . . we might publish a case report—not to announce a remedy, but only to suggest a hypothesis that should be tested in a proper clinical trial. In contrast, anecdotes about alternative remedies (usually published in books and magazines for the public) have no such documentation and are considered insufficient in themselves as support for therapeutic claims" (Angell & Kassirer, 1998, pp. 839–840).

The "Vividness" Problem

It is fine to point out how the existence of placebo effects renders testimonials useless as evidence, but we must recognize another obstacle that prevents people from understanding that testimonials cannot be accepted as proof of a claim. Social and cognitive psychologists have studied what is termed the *vividness effect* in human memory and decision making (Ruscio, 2000; Slovic, 2007; Stanovich, 2009; Trout, 2008). When faced with a problem-solving or decision-making situation, people retrieve from memory the information that seems relevant to the situation at hand. Thus, they are more likely to use the facts that are more accessible to solve a problem or make a decision. One factor that strongly affects accessibility is the vividness of information.

The problem is that there is nothing more vivid or compelling than sincere personal testimony that something has occurred or that something is true. The vividness of personal testimony often overshadows other information of much higher reliability. How often have we carefully collected information on different product brands before making a purchase, only to be dissuaded from our choice at the last minute by a chance recommendation of another product by a friend or an advertisement? Car purchases are a typical example. We may have read surveys of thousands of customers in *Consumer Reports* and decided on car X. After consulting the major automotive magazines and confirming that the experts also recommend car X, we feel secure in our decision—until, that is, we meet a friend at a party who knows a friend who knows a friend who bought an X and got a real lemon, spent hundreds on repairs, and would never buy another. Obviously, this single instance should not substantially affect our opinion, which is based on a survey of thousands of owners and the judgment of several experts. Yet how many of us could resist the temptation to overweight this evidence?

The auto purchase situation illustrates that the problems created by vivid testimonial evidence are not unique to psychology. Instances of how vividness affects people's opinions are not hard to find in any domain. Writer Michael Lewis (1997) describes how political commentator George Will—a notorious opponent of government regulation—published a column calling for mandatory air bags after seeing a death in a car crash outside of his home.

Imagine that you saw the following headline one Friday morning in your newspaper: "Jumbo Jet Crash Kills 413 People." Goodness, you might think, what a horrible accident. What a terrible thing to happen. Imagine, though, that the following Thursday you got up and your newspaper said, "Another Jumbo Jet Disaster: 442 Die." Oh, no, you might think. Not another disaster! How horrible. What in the world is wrong with our air traffic system? And then imagine—please imagine as best you can—getting up the following Friday and seeing in the paper: "Third Tragic Airline Crash: 431 Dead." Not only you but also the nation would be beside itself. A federal investigation would be demanded. Flights would be grounded. Commissions would be appointed. Massive lawsuits would be filed. *Newsweek* and *Time* would run cover stories. It would be the lead item on television news programs for several days. Television documentaries would explore the issue. The uproar would be tremendous.

But this is not an imaginary problem. It is real. A jumbo jet *does* crash every week. Well, not one jet, but a lot of little jets. Well, not little jets really, but little transportation devices. These devices are called automobiles. And over 350 people die in them *each week* in the United States (over 19,000 people each year; National Highway Traffic Safety Administration, 2004), enough to fill a jumbo jet.

A jumbo jet's worth of people die in passenger cars on our nation's highways every week, *yet we pay no attention*. This is because the "Jumbo Jet's Worth of People Who Die" are not presented to us in a vivid way by the media. Hence, the 350 people who die *each week* in passenger cars (plus the additional 330 who die *each week* in trucks and on motorcycles) have no vividness for us. We don't talk about them at the dinner table as we do when a jet goes down and kills a lot of people. We do not debate the safety and necessity of car travel as we would the safety of the air traffic system if a jumbo jet crashed every week killing 350 people each time. The 350 are not on the news because they are distributed all over the country and, thus, are a statistical abstraction to most of us. The media do not vividly present to us these 350 deaths because they do not happen in the same place. Instead, the media present to us (occasionally) a number (e.g., 350 per week). This *should* be enough to get us thinking, but it is not. Driving automobiles is an extremely dangerous activity, compared to almost any other activity in our lives (Galovski, Malta, & Blanchard, 2006; National Safety Council, 2001; Sunstein, 2002), yet there has never been a national debate about its risk relative to the benefits involved. Is this an acceptable toll for a suburban lifestyle that demands a lot of driving? We never ask the question because no problem is recognized. No problem is recognized because the cost is not presented to us in a vivid way, as is the cost of airline crashes.

Think of the absurdity of the following example. A friend drives you 20 miles to the airport where you are getting on a plane for a trip of about 750 miles. Your friend is likely to say, "Have a safe trip," as you part. This parting comment turns out to be sadly ironic, because your friend is *three times more likely to die in a car accident on the 20-mile trip back home than you are on your flight of 750 miles*. It is the vividness problem that accounts for the apparent irrationality of person A's wishing person B safety, when it is person A who is in more danger (Sivak & Flannagan, 2003).

These examples are not just hypothetical. Subsequent to the terrorist attacks of September 11, 2001, travel by airlines decreased because people were afraid of flying. Of course, people continued to travel. They did not just stay home. They simply took their trips by other means—in most cases by automobile. Since automobile travel is so much more dangerous than flying, it is a statistical certainty that more people died because they switched to driving. In fact, researchers have estimated that at least 300 more people died in the final months of 2001 because they took trips by car rather than flew (Gigerenzer, 2004, 2006). One group of researchers was able to come up with a vivid statistic to convey just how dangerous driving is. Sivak and Flannagan (2003) have calculated that for driving to be as dangerous as flying, an incident on the scale of September 11 would have to occur once a month!

Misleading personal judgments based on the vividness of media-presented images are widespread in other areas as well. Studies have surveyed parents to see which risks to their children worried them the most

(Cole, 1998; Radford, 2005). Parents turned out to be most worried about their children being abducted, an event with a probability of 1 in 700,000. By contrast, the probability of their child being killed in a car crash, which the parents worried about much less, is well over *100 times more likely* than their child being abducted. Of course, the fears of abduction are mostly a media-created worry. Cognitive psychologist Paul Slovic lamented our inability to worry about the right things: "We don't have the same sense of dread around cars that we do around carcinogens" (Fountain, 2006, p. 15).

Likewise, risks that we face such as the possibility of developing diabetes cause less worry than risks such as developing staph infections in hospitals, even though the former will affect 45 million Americans and the latter only 1,500 in a year (Fountain, 2006). This is despite the fact that, personally, we can do something about the former (by changing our diet and exercising) but not the latter. Because of the dominance of vivid stimuli, argues Paul Offit (2008), "people are more frightened by things that are less likely to hurt them. They are scared of pandemic flu but not epidemic flu (which kills more than 30,000 people a year in the United States); of botulism tsunamis, and plagues but not strokes and heart attacks; of radon and dioxin but not French Fries; of flying but not driving" (p. 217).

Just how easy it is to exploit vividness to skew our perception of risk was shown in a study (Sinaceur, Heath, & Cole, 2005), in which subjects were presented with the following hypothetical situation: "Imagine that you have just finished eating your dinner. You have eaten a packaged food product made with beef that was bought at the supermarket. While listening to the evening news on the television, you find out that eating this packaged food may have exposed you to the human variant of bovine spongiform encephalopathy (BSE)." After reading this, the subjects were asked to respond on a seven-point scale to the following questions: "After hearing this, to what extent would you decrease your consumption of this type of packaged beef?" and "To what extent would you alter your dietary habits to de-emphasize red meats and increase the consumption of other foods?" Not surprisingly, after hearing this hypothetical situation, subjects felt that they would decrease their consumption of beef. However, another group of subjects was even *more* likely to say they would decrease their consumption of beef when they heard the same story identically except for the very last words. Instead of "human variant of bovine spongiform encephalopathy (BSE)," the second group read "human variant of Mad Cow Disease." It is clear what is going on here. Our old friend vividness is rearing its head again. Mad Cow Disease conjures creepy imagines of an animal-born disease in a way that bovine spongiform encephalopathy does not.

The vividness of presentations can even affect the way we interpret scientific evidence itself. In one study, subjects were given descriptions of psychological phenomena and explanations for those phenomena (Weisberg, Keil, Goodstein, Rawson, & Gray, 2008). Some of the explanations were good ones (involving actual psychological concepts) and others were poor ones (simply redescribing the phenomenon in a circular fashion rather than explaining it). Ratings of the quality of both types of explanations (especially the poor ones) were substantially higher when the explanations were preceded by the words "brain scans indicate." Likewise, McCabe and Castel (2008) found that the conclusions of scientific experiments in cognitive neuroscience were rated as more credible if they contained a brain image summarizing the results instead of a graph depicting the identical outcome. In short, the vividness of the presentation of scientific results influences how the research is evaluated.

The Overwhelming Impact of the Single Case

Psychologists have extensively studied the tendency for people's judgments to be dominated by a single, salient example when more accurate information is available. Wilson and Brekke (1994) demonstrated how insidious the vividness problem is and also how it influences actual consumer behavior. They investigated how people were influenced by two different types of information about two different brands (brand A and brand B) of condom. One type of information was a survey and analysis in *Consumer Reports* magazine, and the other was the opinions of two university students about their preferences for condom brands. First, Wilson and Brekke surveyed a group of subjects on which type of information they would want to be influenced by. Over 85 percent of the subjects said that they would *want* to be more influenced by the *Consumer Reports* article than by the opinions of the two students. A similar group of subjects were then recruited for a study in which they were told that they would be given, free of charge, some condoms of their own choosing. The subjects were told that they could consult either or both of two types of information: a survey and analysis in *Consumer Reports* magazine and the opinions of two university students about their preferences. Even though less than 15 percent of a similar group of subjects wanted to be influenced by the opinions of the two students, 77 percent of the subjects requested *both* types of information. Apparently the subjects could not resist seeing the testimonials even though they did not believe that they should be affected by them. And they were indeed affected by them. When the subjects chose to see both types of information and the recommendations of the two sources of information differed, 31 percent of the subjects chose the brand of condom recommended in the student testimonials over the brand recommended by *Consumer Reports.*

Another example of how people respond differently to vivid anecdotal information comes from the media coverage of the Vietnam War in the mid to late 1960s. As the war dragged on and the death toll of Americans killed continued without an end in sight, the media took to reporting the weekly number of American service personnel who had been killed that week. Week after week, the figure varied between 200 and 300, and the public, seemingly, became quite accustomed to this report. However, one week a major magazine published a spread, running on for several pages, of the individual pictures of those persons who had died in the previous week. The public was now looking, concretely, at the approximately 250 individual lives that had been lost in a typical week. The result was a major outcry against the toll that the war was taking. The 250 pictures had an effect that the weekly numbers had not had. But we, as a society, must overcome this tendency not to believe numbers—to have to see everything. Most of the complex influences on our society are accurately captured only by numbers. Until the public learns to treat these numerical abstractions of reality as seriously as images, public opinion will be as fickle as the latest image to flicker across the screen.

History repeated itself in 2004 when the *Nightline* television program ran the names and photographs of the over 700 soldiers who had died at the time of the first anniversary of the start of the Iraq war. This was exactly the same format that the *Nightline* program had used when it ran the names and photographs of the victims of the September 11 attack on its first anniversary. Both sets of photographs were run with the permission of the families of those pictured. However, the photos of the dead soldiers drew howls of protest from supporters of the war. There were charges that the show's host, Ted Koppel, was hostile to the war, but these charges were misplaced because Koppel had not been opposed to the war. Instead, Koppel said that "Some of you are convinced that I am opposed to the war. I am not, but that's beside the point. I am opposed to sustaining the illusion that war can be waged by the sacrifice of the few without burdening the rest of us in any way" (CNN.com, 2004). It is not that the number who had died had not been reported. That over 700 had died to that point was reported day after day in every newspaper in the country. But both sides in this controversy knew that the public had, in some sense, not yet "processed" that number—had not yet calculated the cost because the number was an abstraction. Both sides knew that many people would really become conscious of the costs—would really only process the information for the first time—when they had seen the pictures.

But it is not only the public that is plagued by the vividness problem. Experienced clinical practitioners in both psychology and medicine struggle all the time with the tendency to have their judgment clouded by the overwhelming impact of the single case. Writer Francine Russo (1999) describes the dilemma of Willie Anderson, an oncologist at the University of Virginia. Anderson is an advocate of controlled experimentation and routinely enrolls his patients in controlled clinical trials, but he still struggles with his own reactions to single, salient cases that have an emotional impact on his decisions. Despite his scientific orientation, he admits that "when it's real people looking you in the eye, you get wrapped up in their hopes and your hopes for their hopes, and it's *hard*" (p. 36). But Anderson knows that sometimes the best thing for his patients is to ignore the "real person looking you in the eye" and go with what the best evidence says. And the best evidence comes from a controlled clinical trial (described in Chapter 6), not from the emotional reaction to that person looking you in the eye.

In summary, the problems created by reliance on testimonial evidence are ever present. The vividness of such evidence often eclipses more reliable information and obscures understanding. Psychology instructors worry that merely pointing out the logical fallacies of reliance on testimonial evidence is not enough to provide a deep understanding of the pitfalls of these types of data. What else can be done? Is there any other way to get this concept across to people? Fortunately, there is an alternative—an alternative somewhat different from the academic approach. The essence of this approach is to fight vividness with vividness. To hoist testimonials by their own petard! To let testimonials devour themselves with their own absurdity. A practitioner of this approach is the one, the only, the indubitable Amazing Randi!

The Amazing Randi: Fighting Fire with Fire

James Randi is a magician and jack-of-all-trades who has received a MacArthur Foundation "genius" grant. For many years, he has been trying to teach the public some basic skills of critical thinking. The Amazing Randi (his stage name) has done this by exposing the fraud and charlatanism surrounding claims of "psychic" abilities. Although he has uncovered many magicians and conjurors masquerading as psychics, he is best known for exposing the trickery of Uri Geller, the psychic superstar of the 1970s. Bursting on the scene with his grand claims of psychic powers, Geller captivated the media to an extraordinary degree. He was featured in newspapers, on television shows, and in major news magazines on several continents (Geller is still around, writing books; Radford, 2006). Randi detected and exposed the common and sometimes embarrassingly simple magic tricks that Geller used to perform his psychic "feats," which included bending keys and spoons, and starting watches—mundane fare for a good magician. Since the Geller exposé, Randi has continued to use his considerable talents in the service of the public's right to know the truth in spite of itself by exposing the fallacies behind ESP, biorhythms, psychic surgery, levitation, and other pseudosciences (Randi, 1983, 1995, 2005; Sagan, 1996).

One of Randi's minor diversions consists of demonstrating how easy it is to garner testimonial evidence for any preposterous event or vacuous claim. His technique is to let people be swallowed up in a trap set by their own testimonials. Randi makes much use of that fascinating American cultural institution, the talk show, often appearing as a guest in the guise of someone other than himself. On a New York show a few years ago, he informed the audience that, while driving through New Jersey earlier in the day, he had seen a formation of orange V-shaped objects flying overhead in a northerly direction. Within seconds, as Randi put it, "the station switchboard lit up like an electronic Christmas tree." Witness after witness called in to confirm this remarkable sighting. Unfortunately for them, the "sighting" was only a product of Randi's imagination. Callers provided many details that Randi had "omitted," including the fact that there had been more than one pass of the "saucers." This little scam illustrates how completely unreliable are individual reports that "something happened."

On a different radio show, Randi demonstrated the basis for the popularity of another pseudoscience: biorhythms (Hines, 1998, 2003). One listener agreed to keep a day-by-day diary and compare it with a two-month biorhythm chart that had been prepared especially for her. Two months later, the woman called back to inform the audience that biorhythms should be taken very seriously because her chart was more than 90 percent accurate. Randi had to inform her of the silly mistake made by his secretary, who had sent someone else's chart to her, rather than her own. However, the woman did agree to evaluate the correct chart, which would be mailed to her right away, and to call back. A couple of days later, the woman called back, relieved. Her own chart was just as accurate—in fact, even more accurate. On the next show, however, it was discovered that, whoops, another error had been made. The woman had been sent Randi's secretary's chart rather than her own!

Randi's biorhythm scams are actually an example of a phenomenon that has been termed the *P. T. Barnum effect* (Barnum, the famous carnival and circus operator, coined the statement "There's a sucker born every minute"). This effect has been extensively studied by psychologists (e.g., Dickson & Kelly, 1985), who have found that the vast majority of individuals will endorse generalized personality summaries as accurate and specific descriptions of themselves. Here is an example taken from Shermer (2005, p. 6):

> You can be a very considerate person, very quick to provide for others, but there are times, if you are honest, when you recognize a selfish streak in yourself. . . . Sometimes you are too honest about your feelings and you reveal too much of yourself. You are good at thinking things through and you like to see proof before you change your mind about anything. When you find yourself in a new situation you are very cautious until you find out what's going on, and then you begin to act with confidence. . . . You know how to be a good friend. You are able to discipline yourself so that you seem in control to others, but actually you sometimes feel somewhat insecure. You wish you could be a little more popular and at ease in your interpersonal relationships than you are now. You are wise in the ways of the world, a wisdom gained through hard experience rather than book learning.

Large numbers of people find this summary to be a very accurate description of their personality. But very few people spontaneously realize that most other people would also find it indicative of *themselves!* There are well-known sets of statements and phrases (like this example) that most people see as applicable to themselves. Anyone can feed them to a "client" as individualized psychological "analysis" and the client will usually be very impressed by the individualized accuracy of the "personality reading," not knowing that the same reading is being given to everyone. The Barnum effect is, of course, the basis of belief in the accuracy of palm readers and astrologists (Kelly, 1997, 1998). The Barnum effect also provides an example of how easy it is to generate testimonials and, of course, shows why they are worthless.

This is exactly what James Randi was trying to do in his little scams described previously—to teach people a lesson about the worthlessness of testimonial evidence. He consistently demonstrates how easy it is to generate testimonials in favor of just about any bogus claim. For this reason, presenting a testimonial in support of a particular claim is meaningless. Only evidence from controlled observations (to be described in Chapter 6) is sufficient to actually *test* a claim.

Testimonials Open the Door to Pseudoscience

It is sometimes claimed that pseudosciences like parapsychology, astrology, biorhythms, and fortune-telling are simply a way to have a little fun, that they really do no harm. After all, why should we care? Isn't it just a case of a few people engaging in wishful thinking and a few others making a couple of bucks out of them?

First, people tend not to think about what economists call *opportunity costs*. When you take time to do one thing, you have lost the time to do something else. You have lost the opportunity to spend your time otherwise. When you spend money on one thing you no longer have the money to do something else—you have lost the opportunity to spend otherwise. Pseudosciences have massive opportunity costs. When people spend time (and money) on pseudosciences they gain nothing and they waste time that might have been spent on more productive endeavors.

A complete examination of the problem reveals that the harm done to society by the prevalence of pseudosciences is more widespread than is generally believed. And the costs extend beyond opportunity costs. In a complex, technological society, the influence of pseudoscience can be propagated by decisions that affect thousands of other people. That is, you may be affected by pseudoscientific beliefs even if you do not share those beliefs. For example, one third of Americans are drinking unfluoridated water despite voluminous scientific evidence that fluoridation can significantly reduce tooth decay (Beck, 2008; Griffin, Regnier, Griffin, & Huntley, 2007; Singh, Spencer, & Brennan, 2007). Millions of Americans in areas without fluoridation are suffering needless cavities because their neighbors are in the grip of pseudoscientific conspiracy theories about the harmful effects of fluoridation. Small groups of people with these pseudoscientific beliefs have pressured various communities to keep fluoridation out and have thus denied its benefits to everyone who lives near them. In short, the pseudoscientific beliefs of the few have negatively affected the many.

Consider another example of how you might be affected by pseudoscience even though you do not believe in it yourself. Major banks and several *Fortune* 500 companies employ graphologists for personnel decisions (Sutherland, 1992) even though voluminous evidence indicates that graphology is useless for this purpose (Hines, 2003). To the extent that pseudodiagnostic graphological cues lead employers to ignore more valid criteria, both economic inefficiency and personal injustice are the result. How would you like to lose your chance for a job that you really want because you have a particular little "loop" in your handwriting? Or, alternatively, how would you feel if you were denied a job because a "psychic" saw a disturbance in your "aura"? In fact, this is actually happening to some people. Some corporations are paying for "psychic readings" of individuals who are candidates for hiring. For example, Susan King is a so-called clairvoyant whom companies pay to give them "readings" to aid in personnel decisions. She claims that she doesn't even need to meet the applicant—that she can work from photos and first names—although "some clients call her in to observe shortlisted candidates during final interviews and even at cocktail parties afterwards" (Kershaw, 1991). In competitive economic times, is this how you want your employment opportunities to be determined?

Unfortunately, these examples are not rare (Shermer, 2005; Stanovich, 2009; Sternberg, 2002). We are all affected in numerous ways when pseudoscientific beliefs permeate society—even if we do not subscribe to the beliefs. For example, police departments hire psychics to help with investigations (Marshall, 1980) even though research has shown that this practice has no effectiveness (Hines, 2003; Rowe, 1993). Programmers at the ABC television network hired a Hollywood psychic to help make decisions about the content of the most influential communications technology in our society (Auletta, 1992, p. 114). And, most astonishingly, an astrologer was employed in the Reagan White House to advise on the "timing of presidential speeches, appearances, meetings with heads of state, airplane travel schedules, and even discussion topics" (Johnson, 1991, p. 454).

Pseudosciences such as astrology are now large industries, involving newspaper columns, radio shows, book publishing, the Internet, magazine articles, and other means of dissemination. The leading horoscope magazines have circulations larger than that of many legitimate science magazines. The House of Representatives Select Committee on Aging has estimated that the amount wasted on medical quackery nationally reaches into the billions. In short, pseudosciences are lucrative businesses, and the incomes of thousands of individuals depend on their public acceptance.

Some associations and organizations have been more aggressive than psychology in rooting out pseudoscience. In 2007 the Federal Trade Commission (FTC) levied multi-million dollar fines against four diet-drug marketers who sold by using infomercials and celebrity endorsements. In announcing the fines, the FTC Chairwoman Deborah Platt Majoras tried to educate the public by stating that "Testimonials from individuals are not a substitute for science, and that's what Americans need to understand" (de la Cruz, 2007, p. A10). Likewise, medical associations have been more aggressive than psychology in attacking pseudoscience and dissociating legitimate medical practice from the illegitimate. Consider the guidelines published by the Arthritis Foundation and cited by the House Committee on Aging for spotting the unscrupulous promoter:

1. He may offer a "special" or "secret" formula or device for "curing" arthritis.
2. He advertises. He uses "case histories" and testimonials from satisfied "patients."
3. He may promise (or imply) a quick or easy cure.
4. He may claim to know the cause of arthritis and talk about "cleansing" your body of "poisons" and "pepping up" your health. He may say surgery, X- rays and drugs prescribed by a physician are unnecessary.
5. He may accuse the "medical establishment" of deliberately thwarting progress, or of persecuting him . . . but he doesn't allow his method to be tested in tried and proven ways. (U. S. Congress, 1984, p. 12)

This list could also serve as a guide for spotting fraudulent psychological treatments and claims. Note, of course, point 2, which is the focus of this chapter. But also note that points 1 and 5 illustrate the importance of something discussed earlier: Science is public. In addition to putting forth testimonials as "proof," the practitioners of pseudoscience often try to circumvent the public verifiability criterion of science by charging that there is a conspiracy to suppress their "knowledge." They use this as justification for going straight to the media with their "findings" rather than submitting their work to the normal scientific publication processes. The ploy is usually more successful in the area of psychology than anywhere else because the media often show less respect for the normal scientific mechanisms of psychology than they do for those of other sciences. It is important to keep this bias in mind (it will receive an extended discussion in Chapter 12). Unverified claims that the media would never think of reporting if they occurred in the physical sciences are seen as legitimate topics of psychological reporting because journalists have been convinced by the purveyors of pseudoscience that "anything goes" in psychology. Thus, the consumer must be aware that television and the print media will publicize virtually any outlandish claim in the area of psychology if they think there is an audience for it, no matter how much the claim is contradicted by the available evidence.

Claims of miracle cures raise false hopes that can cause psychological damage when they are dashed. One of the most despicable examples in my files on this subject is an article from a grocery store tabloid entitled "Psychic Shows the Blind How to See Using ESP." People can fail to take advantage of the real knowledge available to them because they become involved in pseudosciences. Proponents of psychic surgery implicitly encourage people to spend money on bogus cures and to ignore traditional "nonpsychic" medical procedures that may help them (Angell & Kassirer, 1998).

A clear example of how we are all hurt when pseudoscientific beliefs spread is provided by the theory (first put forth in the early 1990s and continuing to this day) that autism is connected to the early vaccination of children. This theory is false (Honda, Shimizu, & Rutter, 2005; Judelsohn, 2007; Novella, 2007; Offit, 2008; Taylor, 2006), but no reader of this chapter should be surprised at how the belief arose. Many children are diagnosed with autism around the time of their first vaccinations and many begin to show clearly discernible signs of the condition (delayed language acquisition, difficulties in reciprocal social interaction, and a restricted repertoire of activities) around this time. Not surprisingly given that there are thousands of children with this condition, some parents become fully aware of their child's difficulties (either through diagnosis or increased awareness based on their own observations) shortly after the child receives a vaccination. These parents then provide the vivid and heartfelt testimonials that there must be a connection between their child's condition and the vaccination. However, many different experimental and epidemiological studies have converged (see Chapter 8) on the conclusion that no such connection exists. This pseudoscientific belief, though, had more costs than just the opportunity costs to the parents and children involved. The false belief in a connection spawned an anti-vaccination movement. As a result, immunization rates have decreased, many more children have been hospitalized with measles than would have been the case otherwise, and some have died (Goldacre, 2008; Judelsohn, 2007; Novella, 2007; Offit, 2008). Again, the lesson is that in an interconnected society, your neighbor's pseudoscientific belief might affect you even if you reject the belief yourself.

Physicians are increasingly concerned about the spread of medical quackery on the Internet (Offit, 2008) and its real health costs. Dr. Max Coppes was prompted to write a letter to the *New England Journal of Medicine* warning of the real human costs of pseudoscience in medicine (Scott, 1999). He described the case of a nine-year-old girl who, after cancer surgery, had a 50 percent chance of three more years of life if she had undergone chemotherapy. Instead, her parents found an unproven treatment that utilized shark cartilage and opted for that instead. The young girl was dead in four months.

When I am speaking on this topic, at about this point in my lecture someone always asks a very relevant question: "Haven't you just employed vivid cases to illustrate a point—what you said shouldn't be done?" This is a good question and it allows me to elaborate on some of the subtleties involved in the argument of this chapter. The answer to the question is that yes, I *have* employed vivid cases to illustrate a point. To *illustrate* the point—but not to *prove* it. The key issue here is to distinguish two things: (1) the claim being made and (2) the communication of the claim.

For each one we could ask, is its basis a vivid testimonial, yes or no? This yields four possible situations:

a. a claim based on vivid testimonials communicated by vivid testimonials
b. a claim based on vivid testimonials communicated without testimonials
c. a claim based on evidence other than testimonials communicated by vivid testimonials
d. a claim based on evidence other than testimonials communicated without testimonials

Some of the discussion in this chapter falls into category c: claims based on evidence other than testimonials communicated by vivid testimonials. For example, I cite much nontestimonial evidence throughout the chapter to establish claims such as the following: Case study evidence cannot be used to establish a causal influence, vivid examples are overweighted in people's judgments, pseudoscience is costly, and so on. I present in the citations and the reference list the public evidence for each of these claims. Nonetheless, for communicative purposes I have used some vivid cases to draw attention to these claims and to make them memorable. The key point, though, is that the claims themselves are supported by more than vivid testimonial evidence. So, for example, I have used some vivid examples to demonstrate the fact that vivid examples are overweighted in people's judgments. But the real evidence for the claim that vivid examples are overweighted in people's judgments is in the peer-reviewed scientific evidence I have cited (e.g., Lassiter et al., 2002; Sinaceur et al., 2005: Slovic, 2007; Stanovich, 2009).

So, to return to the main point of this section, and to summarize it, the spread of pseudoscience is quite costly. And nothing fosters the spread of pseudosciences more than confusion about what type of evidence does and does not justify belief in a claim about a phenomenon. By providing readily available support for virtually any claim and by the impact that they have when used, testimonials open the door to the development of and the belief in pseudosciences. There is no more important rule for the consumer of psychological information than to beware of them. In the next several chapters, we shall see what type of evidence *is* required to justify claims.

Summary

Case study and testimonial evidence is useful in psychology (and other sciences) in the very earliest stages of an investigation, when it is important to find interesting phenomena and important variables to examine further. As useful as case study evidence is in the early, pretheoretical, stages of scientific investigation, it is virtually useless in the later stages, when theories are being put to specific tests. This is because, as an isolated phenomenon, the outcome of a case study leaves many alternative explanations. One way to understand why case studies and testimonial evidence are useless for theory testing is to consider the placebo effect. The placebo effect is the tendency of people to report that any treatment has helped them, regardless of whether the treatment had a real therapeutic element. The existence of placebo effects makes it impossible to prove the effectiveness of a psychological (or medical) treatment by producing testimonials to its effectiveness. The reason is that the placebo effect guarantees that no matter what the treatment, it will be possible to produce testimonial evidence to its effectiveness.

Despite the uselessness of testimonial evidence in theory testing, psychological research has indicated that such evidence is often weighted quite heavily by people because of the vividness effect: People overweight evidence that is more vivid and, hence, more retrievable from memory. One thing that is particularly vivid for most people is testimonial evidence. The result is an overreliance on such evidence in the justification of specific psychological claims. In fact, testimonial and case study evidence cannot be used to justify general theoretical claims.

CHAPTER 5

Correlation and Causation: Birth Control by the Toaster Method

Many years ago, a large-scale study of the factors related to the use of contraceptive devices was conducted in Taiwan. A large research team of social scientists and physicians collected data on a wide range of behavioral and environmental variables. The researchers were interested in seeing what variables best predicted the adoption of birth control methods. After collecting the data, they found that the one variable most strongly related to contraceptive use was the number of electrical appliances (toaster, fans, etc.) in the home (Li, 1975).

This result probably does not tempt you to propose that the teenage pregnancy problem should be dealt with by passing out free toasters in high schools. But why *aren't* you tempted to think so? The correlation between appliances and contraceptive use was indeed strong, and this variable was the single best predictor among the many variables that were measured. Your reply, I hope, will be that it is not the strength but the *nature* of the relationship that is relevant. Starting a free toaster program would imply the belief that toasters *cause* people to use contraceptives. The fact that we view this suggestion as absurd means that, at least in clear-cut cases such as this, we recognize that two variables may be associated without having a causal relationship.

In this example, we can guess that the relationship exists because contraceptive use and the number of electrical appliances in the home are linked through some other variable that relates to both. Socioeconomic status (SES) would be one likely candidate for a mediating variable. We know that SES is related to contraceptive use. All we need now is the fact that families at higher socioeconomic levels tend to have more electrical appliances in their

73

homes, and we have the linkage. Of course, other variables may mediate this correlation. However, the point is that, no matter how strong the correlation is between the number of toasters and contraceptive use, the relationship does not indicate a causal connection.

The contraceptive example makes it very easy to understand the fundamental principle of this chapter: The presence of a correlation does not necessarily imply causation. In this chapter, we will discuss the two problems that prevent the drawing of a causal inference: the third-variable problem and the directionality problem. We will also discuss how the third-variable problem often results from selection bias.

The limitations of correlational evidence are not always so easy to recognize as the toaster example. When the causal link seems obvious to us, when we have a strong preexisting bias, or when our interpretations become dominated by our theoretical orientation, it is tempting to treat correlations as evidence of causation.

The Third-Variable Problem: Goldberger and Pellagra

In the early 1900s, thousands of Americans in the South suffered and died of a disease called *pellagra.* Characterized by dizziness, lethargy, running sores, vomiting, and severe diarrhea, the disease was thought to be infectious and to be caused by a living microorganism of "unknown origin." It is not surprising, then, that many physicians of the National Association for the Study of Pellagra were impressed by evidence that the disease was linked to sanitary conditions. It seemed that homes in Spartanburg, South Carolina, that were free of pellagra invariably had inside plumbing and good sewerage. By contrast, the homes of pellagra victims often had inferior sewerage. This correlation coincided quite well with the idea of an infectious disease transmitted, because of poor sanitary conditions, via the excrement of pellagra victims.

One physician who doubted this interpretation was Joseph Goldberger, who, at the direction of the surgeon general of the United States, had conducted several investigations of pellagra. Goldberger thought that pellagra was caused by inadequate diet—in short, by the poverty common throughout the South. Many victims had lived on high-carbohydrate, extremely low-protein diets, characterized by small amounts of meat, eggs, and milk and large amounts of corn, grits, and mush. Goldberger thought that the correlation between sewage conditions and pellagra did not reflect a causal relationship in either direction (much as in the toaster–birth control example). Goldberger thought that the correlation arose because families with sanitary plumbing were likely to be economically advantaged. This economic discrepancy would also be reflected in their diets, which would contain more animal protein.

But wait a minute! Why should Goldberger get away with his causal inference? After all, both sides were just sitting there with their correlations, Goldberger with pellagra and diet and the other physicians with pellagra and sanitation. Why shouldn't the association's physicians be able to say that Goldberger's correlation was equally misleading? Why was he justified in rejecting the hypothesis that an infectious organism was transmitted through the excrement of pellagra victims because of inadequate sewage disposal? Well, the reason Goldberger was justified has to do with one small detail that I neglected to mention: Goldberger had eaten the excrement of pellagra victims.

Why Goldberger's Evidence Was Better

Goldberger had a type of evidence (a controlled manipulation, discussed further in the next chapter) that is derived when the investigator, instead of simply observing correlations, actually manipulates the critical variable. This approach often involves setting up special conditions that rarely occur naturally—and to call Goldberger's special conditions unnatural is an understatement!

Confident that pellagra was not contagious and not transmitted by the bodily fluids of the victims, Goldberger had himself injected with the blood of a victim. He inserted throat and nose secretions from a victim into his own mouth. In addition,

> he selected two patients—one with scaling sores and the other with diarrhea. He scraped the scales from the sores, mixed the scales with four cubic centimeters of urine from the same patients, added an equal amount of liquid feces, and rolled the mixture into little dough balls by the addition of four pinches of flour. The pills were taken voluntarily by him, by his assistants and by his wife. (Bronfenbrenner & Mahoney, 1975, p. 11)

Neither Goldberger nor the other volunteers came down with pellagra. In short, Goldberger had created the conditions necessary for the infectious transmission of the disease, and nothing had happened.

Goldberger had now manipulated the causal mechanism suggested by others and had shown that it was ineffective, but it was still necessary to test his own causal mechanism. Goldberger got two groups of prisoners from a Mississippi state prison farm who were free of pellagra to volunteer for his experiment. One group was given the high-carbohydrate, low-protein diet that he suspected was the cause of pellagra, while the other group received a more balanced diet. Within five months, the low-protein group was ravaged by pellagra, while the other group showed no signs of the disease. After a long struggle, during which Goldberger's ideas were opposed by those with political motives for denying the existence of poverty, his hypothesis was eventually accepted because it matched the empirical evidence better than any other.

The history of pellagra illustrates the human cost of basing social and economic policy on mistaken inferences from correlational studies. This is not to say that we should never use correlational evidence. Quite the contrary. In many instances, it is all we have to work with (see Chapter 8), and in some cases, it is all we need (for instance, when prediction, rather than determination of cause, is the goal). Scientists often have to use incomplete knowledge to solve problems. The important thing is that we approach correlational evidence with a certain skepticism. Examples such as the pellagra–sewage case occur with considerable frequency in all areas of psychology. The example illustrates what is sometimes termed the *third-variable problem:* the fact that the correlation between the two variables—in this case, pellagra incidence and sewage conditions—may not indicate a direct causal path between them but may arise because both variables are related to a third variable that has not even been measured. Pellegra incidence is related to SES (and to diet—the real causal variable) and SES is also related to sewerage quality. Correlations like that between sewage and pellagra are often termed *spurious correlations:* correlations that arise not because a causal link exists between the two variables that are measured, but because both variables are related to a third variable.

Let's consider a more contemporary example. For decades, debates have raged over the relative efficacy of public and private schools. Some of the conclusions drawn in this debate vividly demonstrate the perils of inferring causation from correlational evidence. The question of the efficacy of private versus public schools is an empirical problem that can be attacked with the investigative methods of the social sciences. This is not to imply that it is an easy problem, only that it is a scientific problem, potentially solvable. All advocates of the superiority of private schools implicitly recognize this, because at the crux of their arguments is an empirical fact: Student achievement in private schools exceeds that in public schools. This fact is not in dispute—educational statistics are plentiful and largely consistent across various studies. The problem is the use of these achievement data to conclude that the education received in private schools *causes* the superior test scores.

The outcome of educational testing is a function of many different variables, all of which are correlated. In order to evaluate the relative efficacy of public schools and private schools, we need more complex statistics than merely the relationship between the type of school attended and school achievement. For example, educational achievement is related to many different indicators of family background, such as parental education, parental occupation, SES, the number of books in the home, and other factors. These characteristics are also related to the probability of sending a child to a private school. Thus, family background is a potential third variable that may affect the relationship between academic achievement and the type of school. In short, the relationship may have nothing to do with the effectiveness of private schools but may be the result of the fact that economically advantaged children do better academically and are more likely to attend private schools.

Fortunately, there exist complex correlational statistics such as *multiple regression, partial correlation,* and *path analysis* (statistics developed in part by psychologists) that were designed to deal with problems such as this one. These statistics allow the correlation between two variables to be recalculated after the influence of other variables is removed, or "factored out" or "partialed out." Using these more complex correlational techniques, Ellis Page and Timothy Keith (1981), two researchers at Duke University, analyzed a large set of educational statistics on high-school students that were collected under the auspices of the National Center for Educational Statistics. They found that, after variables reflecting the students' home backgrounds and general mental ability were factored out, there was virtually no relationship between school achievement and the type of school attended. Their results have been confirmed by other researchers (Berliner & Biddle, 1995; Carnoy, Jacobsen, Mishel, & Rothstein, 2005; Hendrie, 2005).

Thus, it appears that advocating private schools as a means of improving educational achievement is the same as arguing for birth control by the toaster method. Academic achievement is linked to private school attendance not because of any direct causal mechanism, but because the family background and the general cognitive level of students in private schools are different from those of children in public schools.

The complex correlational statistics that allow us to partial out the effects of a third variable do not always reduce the magnitude of the original correlation. Sometimes the original correlation between two variables remains even after the partialing out of the third variable, and this result itself can be informative. Such an outcome indicates that the original correlation was not due to a spurious relationship with that particular third variable. Of course, it does not remove the possibility of a spurious relationship due to some other variable.

A good example is provided in the data analyzed by Thomas, Alexander, and Eckland (1979). These investigators found that the probability that a high-school student will attend university is related to the SES of the student's family. This is an important finding that strikes at the heart of the merit-based goals of our society. It suggests that opportunities for success in life are determined by a person's economic class. However, before jumping to this conclusion, we must consider several other alternative hypotheses. That is, the correlation between university attendance and SES should be examined closely for spuriousness. One obvious candidate for a third variable is academic ability. Perhaps this is related to both university attendance and SES, and if it is partialed out, the correlation between the first two variables may disappear. The investigators calculated the appropriate statistics and found that the correlation between university attendance and SES remained significant even after academic aptitude was partialed out. Thus, the fact that children of higher economic classes are more likely to attend university is not entirely due to differences in academic aptitude. This finding, of course, does not rule out the possibility that some other variable leads to the relationship between the first two, but it is clearly important, both practically and theoretically, to be able to rule out a major alternative explanation such as academic aptitude.

Consider another example in which the technique of partial correlation was used. It turns out that the violent crime in the United States is higher in the southern states than in the northern states. Anderson and Anderson (1996) tested what has been called the *heat hypothesis*—that "uncomfortably warm temperatures produce increases in aggressive motives and (sometimes) aggressive behavior" (p. 740). Not surprisingly, they did find a correlation between the average temperature in a city and its violent crime rate. What gives the heat hypothesis more credence, however, is that they found that the correlation between temperature and violent crime remained significant even after variables such as unemployment rate, per capita income, poverty rate, education, population size, median age of population, and several other variables were statistically controlled.

The Directionality Problem

There is no excuse for making causal inferences on the basis of correlational evidence when it is possible to manipulate variables in a way that would legitimately justify a causal inference. Yet this is a distressingly common occurrence when psychological issues are involved, and the growing importance of psychological knowledge in the solution of social problems is making this tendency increasingly costly. A well-known example in the area of educational psychology illustrates this point quite well.

Since the beginning of the scientific study of reading about a hundred years ago, researchers have known that there is a correlation between eye movement patterns and reading ability. Poorer readers make more erratic movements, display more regressions (movements from right to left), and make more fixations (stops) per line of text. On the basis of this correlation, some educators hypothesized that deficient oculomotor skills were the cause of reading problems, and many eye movement–training programs were developed and administered to elementary-school children. These programs were instituted long before it was ascertained whether the correlation really indicated that erratic eye movements caused poor reading.

It is now known that the eye movement–reading-ability correlation reflects a causal relationship that runs in exactly the opposite direction. Erratic eye movements do not cause reading problems. Instead, slow recognition of words and difficulties with comprehension lead to erratic eye movements. When children are taught to recognize words efficiently and to comprehend better, their eye movements become smoother. Training children's eye movements does nothing to improve their reading comprehension.

For more than a decade now, research has clearly pointed to word decoding and a language problem in phonological processing as the sources of reading problems (Snowling & Hulme, 2005; Stanovich, 2000; Vellutino, Fletcher, Snowling, & Scanlon, 2004). Very few cases of reading disability are due to difficulties in the area of eye movement patterns. Yet, if most school districts of at least medium size were to search diligently in their storage basements, they would find dusty eye movement trainers that represent thousands of dollars of equipment money wasted because of the temptation to see a correlation as proof of a causal hypothesis.

Consider another somewhat similar example. An extremely popular hypothesis in the fields of education and counseling psychology has been that school achievement problems, drug abuse, teenage pregnancy, and many other problem behaviors were the result of low self-esteem. It was assumed that the causal direction of the linkage was obvious: Low self-esteem led to problem behaviors, and high self-esteem led to high educational achievement and accomplishments in other domains. This assumption of causal direction provided the motivation for many educational programs for improving self-esteem. The problem here was the same as that in the eye movement example: An assumption of causal direction was made from the mere existence of a correlation. It turns out that the relationship between self-esteem and school achievement, if it exists at all, is more likely to be in the opposite direction: Superior accomplishment in school (and in other aspects of life) leads to high self-esteem (Baumeister, Campbell, Krueger, & Vohs, 2003, 2005; Krueger, Vohs, & Baumeister, 2008).

Problems of determining the direction of causation are common in psychological research. For example, cognitive psychologist Jonathan Haidt (2006) has discussed research showing that there is a correlation between altruism and happiness. There is research showing, for instance, that people who do volunteer work are happier than those who do not. Of course, it was necessary to make sure that a third variable wasn't accounting for the link between altruism and happiness. Once third variables were eliminated, it was necessary to determine the *direction* of the linkage: Was it that happiness caused people to be altruistic or was it that acts of altruism made people happy ("it is more blessed to give than to receive")? When the proper controlled studies were done, using the logic of the true experiment to be described in Chapter 6, it was found that there was a causal relationship running in *both* directions: Being happy makes people more altruistic, and performing altruistic acts makes people happier.

Our discussion thus far has identified the two major classes of ambiguity present in a simple correlation between two variables. One is called the *directionality problem* and is illustrated by the eye movement and self-esteem examples. Before immediately concluding that a correlation between variable A and variable B is due to changes in A causing changes in B, we must first recognize that the direction of causation may be the opposite, that is, from B to A. The second problem is the third-variable problem, and it is illustrated by the pellagra example (and the toaster–birth control and private-school–achievement examples). The correlation between the two variables may not indicate a causal path in either direction but may arise because both variables are related to a third variable.

Selection Bias

There are certain situations in which the possibility of a spurious correlation is very likely. These are situations in which there is a high probability that selection bias has occurred. The term *selection bias* refers to the relationships between certain subject and environmental variables that may arise when people with different biological, behavioral, and psychological characteristics select different types of environments. Selection bias creates a spurious correlation between environmental characteristics and behavioral-biological characteristics.

Let's look at a straightforward example that illustrates the importance of selection factors in creating spurious correlations: Quickly, name a state with an above average incidence of deaths due to respiratory illness. One answer to this question would be, of course, Arizona. What? Wait a minute! Arizona has clean air, doesn't it? Does the smog of Los Angeles spread that far? Has the suburban sprawl of Phoenix become that bad? No, it can't be. Let's slow down a minute. Maybe Arizona *does* have good air. And maybe people with respiratory illnesses tend to move there. And then they die. There you have it. A situation has arisen in which, if we're not careful, we may be led to think that Arizona's air is killing people.

However, selection factors are not always so easy to discern. They are often overlooked, particularly when there is a preexisting desire to see a certain type of causal link. Tempting correlational evidence combined with a preexisting bias may deceive even the best of minds. Let's consider some specific cases.

The importance of considering selection factors was illustrated quite well in the national debate over the quality of American education that has taken place throughout most of the last two decades. During this debate, the public was inundated with educational statistics but was not provided with corresponding guidance for avoiding the danger of inferring causal relationships from correlational data that are filled with misleading selection factors.

Throughout the continuing debate, many commentators with a political agenda repeatedly attempted to provide evidence that educational quality is not linked to teacher salary levels or class size, despite evidence that both are important (Ehrenberg, Brewer, Gamoran, & Williams, 2001; Nye, Hedges, & Konstantopoulos, 2000). One set of findings put forth was the SAT test results for each of the 50 states. The average scores on this test, taken by high-school students who intend to go to certain universities, did indeed show little relation to teacher salaries and general expenditure on education. If anything, the trends seemed to run opposite to the expected direction. Several states that had very high average teacher salaries had very low average SAT scores, and many states at the bottom of the teacher salary rankings had very high average SAT scores. A close look at the data patterns provides an excellent lesson in how easily selection factors can produce spurious correlations.

On further examination, we see that Mississippi students, for example, score higher than California students on the SAT (Powell & Steelman, 1996; Taube & Linden, 1989). In fact, the difference is considerable. The average Mississippi scores are over 100 points higher. Because Mississippi teachers' salaries are the lowest in the nation, this was cause for celebration among commentators arguing for cuts in teachers' salaries. But wait. Is it really true that schools are better in Mississippi than in California—that the general state of education is superior in the former? Of course not. Virtually any other objective index would show that California schools are superior. But if this is true, what about the SAT?

The answer lies in selection factors. The SAT is not taken by all high-school students. Unlike much standardized testing that schools conduct, in which all children are uniformly tested, the SAT involves selection bias (Hauser, 1998; Powell & Steelman, 1996; Taube & Linden, 1989). Only students hoping to go to a university take the test. This factor accounts for some of the state-by-state variance in average scores on the test and also explains why some of the states with the very best educational systems have very low average SAT scores.

Selection factors operate on the SAT scores of states in two different ways. First, some state university systems require the American College Testing (ACT) program test scores rather than the SAT scores. Thus, the only students who take the SAT in these states are students planning to go to a university out of state. It is more likely that these students will be from advantaged backgrounds and/or will have higher academic aptitude than the average student. This is what happened in the Mississippi–California example. Only 4 percent of Mississippi high-school students took the SAT, whereas the figure in California was 47 percent (Powell & Steelman, 1996).

The second selection factor is a bit more subtle. In states with good educational systems, many students intend to continue their education after high school. In such states, a high proportion of students take the SAT, including a greater number with lesser abilities. States with high dropout rates and lower overall quality have a much smaller proportion of students who aspire to a university education. The group of students who eventually take the SAT in such states represents only those best qualified to go to a university. The resulting average SAT scores in these states naturally tend to be higher than those from states where larger proportions of students pursue further education.

The misuse of SAT scores also provides us with an unfortunate example of how hard it is to correct the misleading use of statistics as long as the general public lacks the simple methodological and statistical thinking skills taught in this book. Brian Powell (1993), an Indiana University professor, analyzed a column written by political columnist George Will in which Will argued against public expenditures on education because states with high SATs do not have high expenditures on education. Powell pointed out that the states that Will singled out as having particularly high scores—Iowa, North Dakota, South Dakota, Utah, and Minnesota—have SAT participation rates of only 5 percent, 6 percent, 7 percent, 4 percent, and 10 percent, respectively, whereas more than 40 percent of all high-school seniors in the United States take the SAT. The reason is that in these states, the test required for admission to public institutions is the ACT test. Only students planning on studying out of state, "often at prestigious private schools" (Powell, 1993, p. 352), take the SAT. By contrast, in New Jersey, which Will used as an example of a state with low SAT scores and high expenditures, 76 percent of high-school seniors take the test. Obviously the students in North and South Dakota who take the SAT are a more select group than those in New Jersey, where three-quarters of all students take the test.

In the journal *Educational Researcher*, psychometrician Howard Wainer (1993) analyzed an article in the June 22, 1993, *Wall Street Journal* that featured a study by the Heritage Foundation, an ideologically biased think tank. The foundation argued against spending money on education because—you guessed it—SAT scores were lower in states where more money was spent on education. Wainer's article goes beyond merely showing how selection bias causes this result, however. Wainer demonstrated that when a test that uses a representative sample rather than a self-selected sample is analyzed (the National Assessment for Educational Progress, or NAEP), the relationship reverses: States that spend more on education have higher scores.

Using the partial correlation techniques mentioned earlier, Powell and Steelman (1996) confirmed this relationship. They found that once the states were statistically equated for the proportion of students who took the test, each additional $1,000 of per pupil expenditure was associated with a 15-point *increase* in the average SAT scores for the state. Nevertheless, despite the overwhelming evidence that selection effects make the state-by-state comparison of SAT scores meaningless unless statistical adjustments are made, the media and politicians continue to use the unadjusted scores to advance political agendas.

An example from clinical psychology demonstrates how tricky and "perverse" the selection bias problem can be. It has sometimes been demonstrated that the cure rate for various addictive-appetite problems such as obesity, heroin use, and cigarette smoking is lower for those who have had psychotherapy than for those who have not (Rzewnicki & Forgays, 1987;

Schachter, 1982). The reason, you will be glad to know, is not that psychotherapy makes addictive behavior more resistant to change. It is that, among those who seek psychotherapy, the disorder is more intractable, and self-cures have been ineffective. In short, "hard cases" seek psychotherapy more than "easy cases."

Wainer (1999) tells a story from World War II that reminds us of the sometimes perverse aspects of selection bias. He describes an aircraft analyst who was trying to determine where to place extra armor on an aircraft based on the pattern of bullet holes in the returning planes. His decision was to put the extra armor in the places that were free of bullet holes on the returning aircraft that he analyzed. He did *not* put the extra armor in the places where there were a lot of bullet holes. His reasoning was that the planes had probably been pretty uniformly hit with bullets. Where he found the bullet holes on the returning aircraft told him that, in those places, the plane could be hit and still return. Those areas that were free of bullet holes on returning planes had probably been hit—but planes hit there did not return. Hence, it was the places on the returning planes *without* bullet holes that needed more armor!

In short, the consumer's rule for this chapter is simple: Be on the lookout for instances of selection bias, and avoid inferring causation when data are only correlational. It is true that complex correlational designs do exist that allow limited causal inferences. It is also true that correlational evidence is helpful in demonstrating convergence on a hypothesis (see Chapter 8). Nevertheless, it is probably better for the consumer to err on the side of skepticism than to be deceived by correlational relationships that falsely imply causation.

Summary

The central point of this chapter was to convey that the mere existence of a relationship between two variables does not guarantee that changes in one are causing changes in the other—that correlation does not imply causation. Two problems in interpreting correlational relationships were discussed. In the third-variable problem, the correlation between the two variables may not indicate a direct causal path between them but may arise because both variables are related to a third variable that has not even been measured. If, in fact, the potential third variable has been measured, correlational statistics such as partial correlation (to be discussed again in Chapter 8) can be used to assess whether that third variable is determining the relationship. The other thing that makes the interpretation of correlations difficult is the existence of the directionality problem: the fact that even if two variables have a direct causal relationship, the direction of that relationship is not indicated by the mere presence of the correlation.

Selection bias is the reason for many spurious relationships in the behavioral sciences: the fact that people choose their own environments to some extent and thus create correlations between behavioral characteristics and environmental variables. As the example of Goldberger illustrated, and as will be illustrated extensively in the next two chapters, the only way to ensure that selection bias is not operating is to conduct a true experiment in which the variables are manipulated.

CHAPTER 6

Getting Things Under Control: The Case of Clever Hans

This chapter starts with a quiz. Don't worry; it's not about what you read in the last chapter. In fact, it should be easy because it's about the observable motion of objects in the world, something with which we have all had much experience. There are just three questions in the quiz.

For the first, you will need a piece of paper. Imagine that a person is whirling a ball attached to a string around his or her head. Draw a circle that represents the path of the ball as viewed from above the person's head. Draw a dot somewhere on the circle and connect the dot to the center of the circle with a line. The line represents the string, and the dot represents the ball at a particular instant in time. Imagine that at exactly this instant, the string is cut. Your first task is to indicate with your pencil the subsequent flight of the ball.

For your next problem, imagine that you are a bomber pilot flying toward a target at 500 miles per hour at a height of 20,000 feet. To simplify the problem, assume that there is no air resistance. The question here is, at which location would you drop your bomb: before reaching the target, directly over the target, or when you have passed the target? Indicate a specific distance in front of the target, directly over the target, or a specific distance past the target.

Finally, imagine that you are firing a rifle from shoulder height. Assume that there is no air resistance and that the rifle is fired exactly parallel to the ground. If a bullet that is dropped from the same height as the rifle takes one-half second to hit the ground, how long will it take the bullet that is fired from the rifle to hit the ground if its initial velocity is 2,000 feet per second?

And the answers—oh, yes, the answers. They appear later on in this chapter. But, first, in order to understand what the accuracy of our knowledge about moving objects has to do with psychology, we need to explore more fully the nature of the experimental logic that scientists use. In this chapter, we will discuss principles of experimental control and manipulation.

Snow and Cholera

In his studies of pellagra, Joseph Goldberger was partially guided by his hunch that the disease was not contagious. But 70 years earlier, John Snow, in his search for the causes of cholera, bet the opposite way and also won (Johnson, 2007; Shapin, 2006; Tufte, 1997). Many competing theories had been put forth to explain the repeated outbreaks of cholera in London in the 1850s. Many doctors believed that the exhalations of victims were inhaled by others who then contracted the disease. This was called the miasmal theory. By contrast, Snow hypothesized that the disease was spread by the water supply, which had become contaminated with the excrement of victims.

Snow set out to test his theory. Fortunately, there were many different sources of water supply in London, each serving different districts, so the incidence of cholera could be matched with the different water supplies, which varied in degree of contamination. Snow realized, however, that such a comparison would be subject to severe selection biases (recall the discussion in Chapter 5). The districts of London varied greatly in wealth, so any correlation between water supply and geography could just as easily be due to any of the many other economically related variables that affect health, such as diet, stress, job hazards, and quality of clothing and housing. In short, the possibility of obtaining a spurious correlation was nearly as high as in the case of the pellagra–sewage example discussed in Chapter 5. However, Snow was astute enough to notice and to exploit one particular situation that had occurred.

In one part of London, there happened to be two water companies that supplied a single neighborhood unsystematically. That is, on a particular street, a few houses were supplied by one company, then a few by the other, because in earlier days the two companies had been in competition. There were even cases in which a house had water from a company different from the one supplying the houses on either side of it. Thus, Snow had uncovered a case in which the SES of the people supplied by two water companies was virtually identical, or at least as close as it could be in a naturally occurring situation like this. Such a circumstance would still not have been of any benefit if the water from the two companies had been equally contaminated because Snow would have had no difference to associate with cholera incidence. Fortunately, this was not the case.

After the previous London cholera epidemic, one company, the Lambeth Company, had moved upstream on the Thames to escape the London sewage. The Southwark and Vauxhall Company, however, had stayed downstream. Thus, the probability was that the water of the Lambeth Company was much less contaminated than the water of the Southwark and Vauxhall Company. Snow confirmed this by chemical testing. All that remained was to calculate the cholera death rates for the houses supplied by the two water companies. The rate for the Lambeth Company was 37 deaths per 10,000 houses, compared with a rate of 315 per 10,000 houses for the Southwark and Vauxhall Company.

In this chapter, we will discuss how the Snow and Goldberger stories both illustrate the logic of scientific thinking. Without an understanding of this logic, the things scientists do may seem mysterious, odd, or downright ridiculous.

Comparison, Control, and Manipulation

Although many large volumes have been written on the subject of scientific methodology, it is simply not necessary for the layperson, who may never actually carry out an experiment, to become familiar with all the details and intricacies of experimental design. The most important characteristics of scientific thinking are actually quite easy to grasp. Scientific thinking is based on the ideas of *comparison, control,* and *manipulation.* To achieve a more fundamental understanding of a phenomenon, a scientist compares conditions in the world. Without this comparison, we are left with isolated instances of observations, and the interpretation of these isolated observations is highly ambiguous, as we saw in Chapter 4 in our discussion of testimonials and case studies.

By comparing results obtained in different—but controlled—conditions, scientists rule out certain explanations and confirm others. The essential goal of experimental design is to *isolate a variable.* When a variable is successfully isolated, the outcome of the experiment will eliminate a number of alternative theories that may have been advanced as explanations. Scientists weed out the maximum number of incorrect explanations either by directly controlling the experimental situation or by observing the kinds of naturally occurring situations that allow them to test alternative explanations.

The latter situation was illustrated quite well in the cholera example. Snow did not simply pick any two water companies. He was aware that water companies might supply different geographic localities that had vastly different health-related socioeconomic characteristics. Merely observing the frequency of cholera in the various localities would leave many alternative explanations of any observed differences in cholera incidence. Highly cognizant that science advances by eliminating possible explanations (recall our discussion of falsifiability in Chapter 2), Snow looked for and found a comparison that would eliminate a large class of explanations based on health-related correlates of SES.

Snow was fortunate to find a naturally occurring situation that allowed him to eliminate alternative explanations. But it would be absurd for scientists to sit around waiting for circumstances like Snow's to occur. Instead, most scientists try to restructure the world in ways that will differentiate alternative hypotheses. To do this, they must manipulate the variable believed to be the cause (contamination of the water supply, in Snow's case) and observe whether a differential effect (cholera incidence) occurs while they keep all other relevant variables constant. The variable manipulated is called the *independent variable* and the variable upon which the independent variable is posited to have an effect is called the *dependent variable.*

Thus, the best experimental design is achieved when the scientist can manipulate the variable of interest and control all the other extraneous variables affecting the situation. Note that Snow did not do this. He was not able to manipulate the degree of water contamination himself but instead found a situation in which the contamination varied and in which other variables, mainly those having to do with SES, were—by lucky chance—controlled. However, this type of naturally occurring situation is not only less common but also less powerful than direct experimental manipulation.

Joseph Goldberger did directly manipulate the variables he hypothesized to be the causes of the particular phenomenon he was studying (pellagra). Although Goldberger observed and recorded variables that were correlated with pellagra, he also directly manipulated two other variables in his series of studies. Recall that he induced pellagra in a group of prisoners given a low-protein diet and also failed to induce it in a group of volunteers, including himself and his wife, who ingested the excrement of pellagra victims. Thus, Goldberger went beyond observing naturally occurring correlations and created a special set of circumstances designed to yield data that would allow a stronger inference by ruling out a wider set of alternative explanations than Snow's did. This is precisely the reason why scientists attempt to manipulate a variable and to hold all other variables constant: in order to eliminate alternative explanations.

Random Assignment in Conjunction with Manipulation Defines the True Experiment

We are not saying here that Snow's approach was without merit. But scientists do prefer to manipulate the experimental variables more directly because direct manipulation generates stronger inferences. Consider Snow's two groups of subjects: those whose water was supplied by the Lambeth Company and those whose water was supplied by the Southwark and Vauxhall Company. The mixed nature of the water supply system in that neighborhood probably ensured that the two groups would be of roughly equal social status. However, the drawback of the type of research design used by Snow is that the subjects themselves determined which group they would be in. They did this by signing up with one or the other of the two water companies years before. We must consider why some people signed up with one company and some with another. Did one company offer better rates? Did one advertise the medicinal properties of its water? We do not know. The critical question is, might people who respond to one or another of the advertised properties of the product differ in other, health-related ways? The answer to this question has to be, it is a possibility.

A design such as Snow's cannot rule out the possibility of spurious correlates more subtle than those that are obviously associated with SES. This is precisely the reason that scientists prefer direct manipulation of the variables they are interested in. When manipulation is combined with a procedure known as *random assignment* (in which the subjects themselves do not determine which experimental condition they will be in but, instead, are randomly assigned to one of the experimental groups), scientists can rule out alternative explanations of data patterns that depend on the particular characteristics of the subjects. Random assignment ensures that the people in the conditions compared are roughly equal on all variables because, as the sample size increases, random assignment tends to balance out chance factors. This is because the assignment of the participants is left up to an unbiased randomization device rather than the explicit choices of a human. Please note here that random *assignment* is *not* the same thing as random *sampling*. The difference will be discussed in Chapter 7.

Random assignment is a method of assigning subjects to the experimental and control groups so that each subject in the experiment has the same chance of being assigned to either of the groups. Flipping a coin is one way to decide to which group each subject will be assigned to. In actual experimentation, a computer-generated table of random numbers is most often used. By using random assignment, the investigator is attempting to equate the two groups on all behavioral and biological variables prior to the investigation—even ones that the investigator has not explicitly measured or thought about.

How well random assignment works depends on the number of subjects in the experiment. As you might expect, the more the better. That is, the more subjects there are to assign to the experimental and control groups, the closer the groups will be matched on all variables prior to the manipulation of the independent variable. Fortunately for researchers, random assignment works pretty well even with relatively small numbers (e.g., 20–25) in each of the groups.

The use of random assignment ensures that there will be no systematic bias in how the subjects are assigned to the two groups. The groups will always be matched fairly closely on any variable, but to the extent that they are not matched, random assignment removes any bias toward either the experimental or the control group. Perhaps it will be easier to understand how random assignment eliminates the problem of systematic bias if we focus on the concept of replication: the repeating of an experiment in all of its essential features to see if the same results are obtained.

Imagine an experiment conducted by a developmental psychologist who is interested in the effect of early enrichment experiences for preschool children. Children randomly assigned to the experimental group receive the enrichment activities designed by the psychologist during their preschool day-care period. Children randomly assigned to the control group participate in more traditional playgroup activities for the same period. The dependent variable is the children's school achievement, which is measured at the end of the children's first year in school to see whether children in the experimental group have outperformed those in the control group.

An experiment like this would use random assignment to ensure that the groups start out relatively closely matched on all extraneous variables that could affect the dependent variable of school achievement. These extraneous variables are sometimes called *confounding variables.* Some possible confounding variables are intelligence test scores and home environment. Random assignment will roughly equate the two groups on these variables. However, particularly when the number of subjects is small, there may still be some differences between the groups. For example, if after random assignment the intelligence test scores of children in the experimental group were 105.6 and those of children in the control group were 101.9 (this type of difference could occur even if random assignment has been properly used), we might worry that any difference in academic achievement in favor of the experimental group was due to the higher intelligence test scores of children in that group rather than to the enrichment program. Here is where the importance of replication comes in. Subsequent studies may again show IQ differences between the groups after random assignment, but the lack of systematic bias in the random assignment procedure ensures that the difference will not always be in favor of the experimental group. In fact, what the property of no systematic bias ensures is that, across a number of similar studies, any IQ differences will occur approximately half of the time in favor of the experimental group and half of the time in favor of the control group. In Chapter 8 we will discuss how multiple experiments such as this are used to converge on a conclusion.

Thus, there are really two strengths in the procedure of random assignment. One is that in any given experiment, as the sample size gets larger, random assignment ensures that the two groups are relatively matched on all extraneous variables. However, even in experiments where the matching is not perfect, the lack of systematic bias in random assignment allows us to be confident in any conclusions about cause—as long as the study can be replicated. This is because, across a *series* of such experiments, differences between the two groups on confounding variables will balance out.

The Importance of Control Groups

All sciences contain examples of mistaken conclusions drawn from studies that fell short of the full controls of the true experiment. Ross and Nisbett (1991) discuss the state of the evidence in the mid-1960s on the portacaval shunt, a once-popular treatment for cirrhosis of the liver. The studies on the treatment were assembled in 1966, and an interesting pattern was revealed. In 96.9 percent of the studies that did not contain a control group, the physicians judged the treatment to be at least moderately effective. In the studies in which there was a control group but in which random assignment to conditions was not used (thus falling short of true experimental design), 86.7 percent of the studies were judged to have shown at least moderate effectiveness. However, in the studies in which there was a control group formed by true random assignment, only 25 percent of the studies were judged to have shown at least moderate effectiveness. Thus, the effectiveness of this particular treatment—now known to be ineffective—was vastly overestimated by studies that did not employ complete experimental controls. Ross and Nisbett (1991) note that "the positive results found using less formal procedures were the product either of 'placebo effects' or of biases resulting from nonrandom assignment" (p. 207). Ross and Nisbett discuss how selection effects (see Chapter 5) may operate to cause spurious positive effects when random assignment is not used. For example, if the patients chosen for a treatment tend to be "good candidates" or tend to be those with vocal and supportive families, there may be differences between them and the control group irrespective of the effectiveness of the treatment.

The tendency to see the necessity of acquiring comparative information before coming to a conclusion is apparently not a natural one—which is why training in all the sciences includes methodology courses that stress the importance of constructing control groups. The "nonvividness" of the control group—the group treated just like the experimental group except for the absence of a critical factor—makes it difficult to see how essential such a group is. Psychologists have done extensive research on the tendency for people to ignore essential comparative (control group) information. For example, in a much researched paradigm (Fiedler & Freytag, 2004; Novick & Cheng, 2004), subjects are shown a 2 × 2 matrix such as the one shown here that summarizes the data from an experiment.

	Improvement	*No Improvement*
Treatment	200	75
No Treatment	50	15

The numbers in the table represent the number of people in each cell. Specifically, 200 people received the treatment and showed improvement in the condition being treated, 75 received the treatment and showed no improvement, 50 received no treatment and showed improvement, and 15 received no treatment and showed no improvement. The subjects are asked to indicate the degree of effectiveness of the treatment. Many subjects think that the treatment in question is effective, and a considerable number of subjects think that the treatment has substantial effectiveness. They focus on the large number of cases (200) in the cell indicating people who received treatment and showed improvement. Secondarily, they focus on the fact that more people who received treatment showed improvement (200) than showed no improvement (75).

In fact, the particular treatment tested in this experiment is completely *ineffective*. In order to understand why the treatment is ineffective, it is necessary to concentrate on the two cells that represent the outcome for the control group (the no-treatment group). There we see that 50 of 65 subjects in the control group, or 76.9 percent, improved when they got *no* treatment. This contrasts with 200 of 275, or 72.7 percent, who improved when they received the treatment. Thus, the percentage of improvement is actually larger in the no-treatment group, an indication that this treatment is totally ineffective. The tendency to ignore the outcomes in the no-treatment cells and focus on the large number in the treatment/improvement cell seduces many people into viewing the treatment as effective. In short, it is relatively easy to draw people's attention away from the fact that the outcomes in the control condition are a critical piece of contextual information in interpreting the outcome in the treatment condition.

Unfortunately, drawing people's attention away from the necessity of comparative information is precisely what our media often do. Psychology professor Peter Gray (2008) describes an article in *Time* magazine titled "The Lasting Wounds of Divorce" in which many case histories were reported of people who had divorced parents later living very troubled lives. A psychologist is quoted as saying that her "study" showed that "almost half of children of divorces enter adulthood as worried, underachieving, self-deprecating and sometimes angry young men and women" (p. 31). Of course, in the absence of a control group of individuals from nondivorced homes, we can conclude nothing from this. How do we know that individuals from divorced homes are *more* likely to display these negative outcomes? Only a matched control group would even begin to answer this question. This is particularly true given the "looseness" of the operational definitions in the so-called study. As Gray (2008) asks, "what does it mean to say that 'almost half' were 'sometimes angry'? Isn't everyone sometimes angry? And isn't everyone at least to some degree, at times, 'worried' and 'self-deprecating'? And, statistically, anywhere but in Lake Wobegon, wouldn't we expect half of the children (not just "almost half") to be under-achieving, if under-achieving means below the median in achievement?" (p. 31).

Despite examples such as this, both society and variety of applied disciplines are becoming more aware of the necessity of comparative information when evaluating evidence. This is a fairly recent development that is still underway in the medical field for instance (Groopman, 2007). Neurologist Robert Burton (2008) describes well the path that medicine has taken—from intuitive knowledge that hurt people to treatment based on truly useful knowledge obtained from comparative investigations: "For many years I have wondered why some bright, well-trained doctors would perform unnecessary surgeries, recommend the unproven, and tout the dangerous. My first inclination was to make accusations of greed, indifference, arrogance, or ignorance. Only since writing this book have I begun to understand how much of apparent malfeasance arises out of this same faulty belief that we can know with certainty when something unproven is correct. A powerful contradiction at the heart of medical practice is that we learn from experience, but without adequate trials we cannot know if our interpretation of the value of a particular treatment is correct. . . . But being a good doctor requires sticking with the best medical evidence, even if it contradicts your personal experience. We need to distinguish between gut feeling and testable knowledge, between hunches and empirically tested evidence" (pp. 160–161).

The intuitive "hunches" of other practical fields are increasingly being put to the test of controlled comparison. For example, credit card companies often send out letters with alternative terms to see which is most enticing to customers (Ayres, 2007). For example, one group of randomly assigned households will receive one combination of interest rate, yearly fee, and rewards program. Another group of randomly assigned households will receive letters with a different interest rate, yearly fee, and rewards program. If there is a different rate of acceptance in the two groups, then the company finds out which combination of terms is superior (from the point of view of drawing more customers). The point is, the credit card company has no way of knowing if its current terms are "working" (i.e., enticing as many customers as possible) unless it engages in some experimentation in which alternative sets of terms are compared.

Not only business but governments as well have turned to controlled experimentation to find out how to optimize their policies. One governmental experiment was called the Move to Opportunity Test, and it was conducted by the Department of Housing and Urban Development of the United States (Ayres, 2007). One group of randomly assigned low-income families was given housing vouchers that could be used anywhere. Another group of randomly assigned low-income families was given vouchers that were only usable in low-poverty (i.e., more middle-class) neighborhoods. The purpose was to see if there would be differences in a variety of outcome variables—educational outcomes, criminal behavior, health outcomes, etc.— when low-income families were not surrounded by other low-income families. This type of investigation is known as a *field experiment*—where a variable is manipulated in a nonlaboratory setting.

Another example of a government-sponsored field experiment is the Progressa Program for Education, Health and Nutrition in Mexico (Ayres, 2007). This program involves a *conditional* transfer of money to poor households. Mothers are paid cash if they get prenatal care. They are paid cash when their children attend school and pass nutrition checkups. The government ran a field experiment in 506 villages testing the efficacy of the program. Half of the villages were enrolled in Progressa and half were not. This enabled the government to test the cost effectiveness of the program when, two years later, the villages were checked for outcomes such as educational achievement, nutrition, and health. Without a control group, the government would have had no knowledge of what the education and health levels would have been *without* the program.

The Case of Clever Hans, the Wonder Horse

The necessity of eliminating alternative explanations of a phenomenon by the use of experimental control is well illustrated by a story that is famous in the annals of behavioral science: that of Clever Hans, the mathematical horse. More than 80 years ago, a German schoolteacher presented to the public a horse, Clever Hans, that supposedly knew how to solve mathematical problems. When Hans was given addition, subtraction, and multiplication problems by his trainer, he would tap out the answer to the problems with his hoof. The horse's responses were astoundingly accurate.

Many people were amazed and puzzled by Clever Hans's performance. Was the horse really demonstrating an ability thus far unknown in his species? Imagine what the public must have thought. Compelling testimonials to Hans's unique ability appeared in the German press. One Berlin newspaper reporter wrote that "this thinking horse is going to give men of science a great deal to think about for a long time to come" (Fernald, 1984, p. 30), a prediction that turned out to be correct, though not quite in the way the reporter expected. A group of "experts" observed Hans and attested to his abilities. Everyone was baffled. And bafflement was bound to remain as long as the phenomenon was merely observed in isolation—without controlled observations being carried out. The mystery was soon dispelled, however, when a psychologist, Oskar Pfungst, undertook systematic studies of the horse's ability (Spitz, 1997).

In the best traditions of experimental design, Pfungst systematically manipulated the conditions under which the animal performed, thus creating "artificial" situations (see Chapter 7) that would allow tests of alternative explanations of the horse's performance. After much careful testing, Pfungst found that the horse did have a special ability, but it was not a mathematical one. In fact, the horse was closer to being a behavioral scientist than a mathematician. You see, Hans was a very careful observer of human behavior. As it was tapping out its answer, it would watch the head of the trainer or other questioner. As Hans approached the answer, the trainer would involuntarily tilt his head slightly, and Hans would stop. Pfungst found that the horse was extremely sensitive to visual cues. It could detect extremely small head movements. Pfungst tested the horse by having the problems presented in such a way that the presenter did not know the answer to the problem or by having the trainer present the problem away from the horse's view. The animal lost its "mathematical abilities" when the questioner did not know the answer or when the trainer was out of view.

The case of Clever Hans is a good context in which to illustrate the importance of carefully distinguishing between the *description* of a phenomenon and the *explanation* of a phenomenon. That the horse tapped out the correct answers to mathematical problems presented by the trainer is not in dispute. The trainer was not lying. Many observers attested to the fact that the horse actually did tap out the correct answers to mathematical problems presented by the trainer. It is in the next step that the problem arises: making the inference that the horse was tapping out the correct answers *because* the horse had mathematical abilities. Inferring that the horse had mathematical abilities was a *hypothesized explanation* of the phenomenon. It did not follow logically—from the fact that the horse tapped out the correct answers to mathematical problems—that the horse had mathematical abilities. Positing that the horse had mathematical abilities was only one of many possible explanations of the horse's performance. It was an explanation that could be put to empirical test. When put to such a test, the explanation was falsified.

Before the intervention of Pfungst, the experts who looked at the horse had made this fundamental error: They had not seen that there might be alternative explanations of the horse's performance. They thought that, once they had observed that the trainer was not lying and that the horse actually did tap out the correct answers to mathematical problems, it necessarily followed that the horse had mathematical abilities. Pfungst was thinking more scientifically and realized that that was only one of many possible explanations of the horse's performance, and that it was necessary to set up controlled conditions in order to differentiate alternative explanations. By having the horse answer questions posed by the trainer from behind a screen, Pfungst set up conditions in which he would be able to differentiate two possible explanations: that the horse had mathematical abilities or that the horse was responding to visual cues. If the horse actually had such abilities, putting the trainer behind a screen should make no difference in its performance. On the other hand, if the horse was responding to visual cues, then putting the trainer behind a screen should disrupt its performance. When the latter happened, Pfungst was able to rule out the hypothesis that the horse had mathematical abilities (Spitz, 1997).

Note also the link here to the principle of parsimony discussed in Chapter 3—the principle that states that when two theories have the same explanatory power, the simpler theory (the one involving fewer concepts and conceptual relationships) is preferred. The two theories in contention here—that the horse had true mathematical abilities and that the horse was reading behavioral cues—are vastly different in parsimony. The latter requires no radical adjustments in prior psychological and brain theory. It simply requires us to adjust slightly our view of the potential sensitivity of horses to behavioral cues (which was already known to be high). The former theory—that horses can truly learn arithmetic—requires us to alter dozens of concepts in evolutionary science, cognitive science, comparative psychology, and brain science. It is unparsimonious in the extreme because it does not cohere with the rest of science and, thus, requires that many other concepts in science be altered if it is to be considered true (we shall discuss the so-called principle of connectivity in Chapter 8).

Clever Hans in the 1990s

The Clever Hans story is a historical example that has been used in methodology classes for many years to teach the important principle of the necessity of experimental control. No one ever thought that an *actual* Clever Hans could happen again—but it did. Throughout the early 1990s, researchers the world over watched in horrified anticipation—almost as if observing cars crash in slow motion—while a modern Clever Hans case unfolded before their eyes and had tragic consequences.

Autism is a developmental disability characterized by impairment in reciprocal social interaction, delayed and often qualitatively abnormal language development, and a restricted repertoire of activities and interests (Baron-Cohen, 2005). The extremely noncommunicative nature of many autistic children, who may be normal in physical appearance, makes the disorder a particularly difficult one for parents to accept. It is, therefore, not hard to imagine the excitement of parents of autistic children when, in the late 1980s and early 1990s, they heard of a technique coming out of Australia that enabled autistic children who had previously been totally nonverbal to communicate. This technique for unlocking communicative capacity in nonverbal autistic individuals was called facilitated communication, and it was uncritically trumpeted in such highly visible media outlets as *60 Minutes*, *Parade* magazine, and the *Washington Post* (see Gardner, 2001; Hines, 2003; Mulick, Jacobson, & Kobe, 1993; Offit, 2008; Twachtman-Cullen, 1997). The claim was made that autistic individuals and other children with developmental disabilities who had previously been nonverbal had typed highly literate messages on a keyboard when their hands and arms had been supported over the typewriter by a sympathetic "facilitator." Not surprisingly, these startlingly verbal performances on the part of autistic children who had previously shown very limited linguistic behavior spawned incredible hopes among frustrated parents of autistic children. It was also claimed that the technique worked for severely mentally retarded individuals who were nonverbal.

Although the excitement of the parents is easy to understand, the credulousness of many professionals is not so easy to accept. Unfortunately, claims for the efficacy of facilitated communication were disseminated to hopeful parents by many media outlets before any controlled studies had been conducted. Had the professionals involved had minimal training in the principles of experimental control, they should have immediately recognized the parallel to the Clever Hans case. The facilitator, almost always a sympathetic individual who was genuinely concerned that the child succeed, had numerous opportunities to consciously or unconsciously direct the child's hand to the vicinity of keys on the keyboard. That cuing by the facilitator was occurring should also have been suggested by the additional observation that the children sometimes typed out complicated messages while not even looking at the keyboard. Additionally, highly literate poetic English prose was produced by children who had not been exposed to the alphabet. For example, one child allegedly typed "Am I a slave or am I free? Am I trapped or can I be seen as an easy and rational spirit?" (Offit, 2008, p. 7).

A number of controlled studies have been reported that have tested the claims of facilitated communication by using appropriate experimental controls. Each study has unequivocally demonstrated the same thing: The autistic child's performance depended on tactile cuing by the facilitator (Jacobson, Foxx, & Mulick, 2004; Mostert, 2001; Offit, 2008; Spitz, 1997; Wegner, Fuller, & Sparrow, 2003). The controls used in several of the studies resembled those of the classic Clever Hans case. A controlled situation was set up in which both the child and the facilitator were presented with a drawing of an object but in which they could not see each other's drawing. When both child and facilitator were looking at the *same* drawing, the child typed the correct name of the drawing. However, when the child and the facilitator were shown *different* drawings, the child typed the name of the facilitator's drawing, not the one at which the child was looking. Thus, the responses were determined by the facilitator rather than the child. The conclusion that facilitated communication was a Clever Hans phenomenon and not a breakthrough therapeutic technique brought no joy to the investigators involved in conducting the studies. Psychologists Robert Cummins and Margot Prior (1992) concluded, "It is evident that some assistants through the use either of tactile/visual cues or through the actual imposition of movement, manipulate their clients' responses. This is the unpalatable and unavoidable conclusion drawn from the available empirical data" (p. 240).

But this sad story gets even worse. At some centers, during facilitated sessions on the keyboard, clients allegedly reported having been sexually abused by a parent in the past (Offit, 2008; Twachtman-Cullen, 1997). Children were removed from their parents' homes, only to be returned when the charges of abuse proved to be groundless: "Several court cases, most notably over criminal charges of abuse, have arisen from facilitated accusations. Court-ordered validations have found that the facilitator was unduly influencing the communications, and charges were subsequently dropped" (Smith & Belcher, 1993, p. 176). Hudson et al. (1993) reported a test of one 29-year-old female who lived at home with her parents and had been considered severely to profoundly mentally retarded. It was alleged that the woman, during a facilitated session, had made allegations of sexual assault by a significant person in her life. In the context of the legal proceedings, Hudson et al. tested the woman's communicative abilities in a facilitated session by using the logic that Pfungst had used in the Clever Hans case. Questions were read to the woman and to her facilitator through separate earphones. When the same question was read to her and to the facilitator, she answered correctly each time. When a different question was read to her and to the facilitator, she never answered correctly and 40 percent of the time gave the answer to the question that the facilitator had been asked.

As a result of these controlled studies, competent professional opinion finally began to be heard above the media din. Importantly, it is increasingly recognized that treatments that lack empirical foundation are not benignly neutral ("Oh, well, it might work, and so what if it doesn't?"). The implementation of unproven treatments has real costs. Howard Shane (1993), the director of the Communication Enhancement Center at Boston's Children's Hospital, said flatly,

> By all scientifically based indications, facilitated communication does not work. . . . Because of the potential harm inflicted by this method, it is hard to justify its continued use. For example, wrongful allegations of sexual abuse have been made through facilitated communication, inappropriate educational placements have been requested, and considerable training and research dollars have been appropriated to implement a technique that is ineffective. (p. 11)

James Mulick (see Mulick, Jacobson, & Kobe, 1993), professor of pediatrics and psychology at Ohio State University, was even more specific in detailing the costs of this educational fad:

> The promotion of FC [facilitated communication] diverts effort and funding from more plausible long-term strategies that have empirical support. The theoretical confusion gratuitously injected into the research and professional literature by FC proponents is damaging to accumulation of knowledge. . . . The popular confusion of FC with other nonspeech communication systems that have been used successfully with disabled people will discourage public support. . . . In our experience, people with handicaps can be valued members of their families and communities without resorting to appeals to miracle cures. There is effective help available, help that makes scientific sense. The genuine efforts of scientifically trained and compassionate professionals surpass all fad treatments, and always will. Advances in treatment and understanding come at the price of rigorous training, dedication to accuracy and scientific standards, and objective verification of all treatment claims. (pp. 278–279)

Here we have another example of the harm done by reliance on testimonial evidence and the fallacy of the idea that therapeutic fads and pseudoscience do no harm (see Chapter 4). We can also see that there is simply no substitute for the control and manipulation of the experimental method when we want to explain behavior.

Note again the link to the principle of parsimony. That the severe linguistic difficulties of autistic children could be solved by a single "magic bullet" (see Chapter 9) intervention flies in the face of decades of work on the cognitive, neuropsychological, and brain characteristics of autistic children (Baron-Cohen, 2005; Frith, 2003; Oberman & Ramachandran, 2007; Rajendran & Mitchell, 2007; Tager-Flusberg, 2007; Wellman, Cross, & Watson, 2001). It would require that too much else that we know about cognition and neurology be altered. The existence of facilitated communication would show no connectivity with the rest of science (see Chapter 8).

Prying Variables Apart: Special Conditions

The Goldberger pellagra example illustrates a very important lesson that can greatly aid in dispelling some misconceptions about the scientific process, particularly as it is applied in psychology. The occurrence of any event in the world is often correlated with many other factors. In order to separate, to pry apart, the causal influence of many simultaneously occurring events, we must create situations that will never occur in the ordinary world. Scientific experimentation breaks apart the natural correlations in the world to isolate the influence of a single variable.

Psychologists operate in exactly the same manner: by isolating variables via manipulation and control. For example, cognitive psychologists interested in the reading process have studied the factors that make word perception easier or more difficult. Not surprisingly, they have found that longer words are more difficult to recognize than shorter words. At first glance, we might think that the effect of word length would be easy to measure: Simply create two sets of words, one long and one short, and measure the difference in reader recognition speed between the two. Unfortunately, it is not that easy. Long words also tend to be less frequent in language, and frequency itself also affects perception. Thus, any difference between long and short words may be due to length, frequency, or a combination of these two effects. In order to see whether word length affects perception independently of frequency, researchers must construct special word sets in which length and frequency do not vary together.

Similarly, Goldberger was able to make a strong inference about causation because he set up a special set of conditions that does not occur naturally. (Considering that one manipulation involved the ingestion of bodily discharges, this is putting it mildly!) Recall that Oskar Pfungst had to set up some special conditions for testing Clever Hans, including trials in which the questioner did not know the answer. Dozens of people who merely observed the horse answer questions under normal conditions (in which the questioner knew the answer) never detected how the horse was accomplishing its feat. Instead, they came to the erroneous conclusion that the horse had true mathematical knowledge.

Likewise, note the unusual conditions that were necessary to test the claims of facilitated communication. The stimuli presented to the facilitator and the child had to be separated in a way that neither could see the stimulus presented to the other. Such unusual conditions are necessary in order to test the alternative hypotheses for the phenomenon.

Many classic experiments in psychology involve this logic of prying apart the natural relationships that exist in the world so that it can be determined which variable is the dominant cause. Psychologist Harry Harlow's famous experiments (Anderson & Anderson, 1996; Harlow, 1958) provide a case in point. Harlow wanted to test a prevailing hypothesis about infant–mother attachment: that the attachment resulted from the mother providing the infant's source of food. However, the problem was that, of course, mothers provide much more than nourishment (comfort, warmth, caressing, stimulation, etc.). Harlow (1958) examined the behavior of infant macaque monkeys in situations in which he isolated only one of the variables associated with attachment by giving the animals choices among "artificial" mothers. For example, he found that the contact comfort provided by a "mother" made of terrycloth was preferred to that provided by a "mother" made of wire mesh. After two weeks of age, the infant preferred a cold terrycloth mother to a warm wire one, a finding indicating that the contact comfort was more attractive than warmth (Harlow & Suomi, 1970). Finally, Harlow found that the infants preferred the terrycloth mother even when their nourishment came exclusively from a wire mother. Thus, the hypothesis that attachment was due solely to the nourishment provided by mothers was falsified. This was possible only because Harlow was able to pry apart variables that naturally covary in the real world.

Creating special conditions to test for actual causal relationships is a key tool we can use to prevent pseudoscientific beliefs from attacking us like a virus (Stanovich, 2004, 2009). Consider the case of therapeutic touch (TT)—a fad that swept the North American nursing profession in the 1990s. TT practitioners massage not the patient's body but instead the patient's so-called energy field. That is, they move their hands over the patient's body but do not actually massage it. Practitioners reported "feeling" these energy fields. Well, you guessed it. This ability to feel "energy fields" is tested properly by creating exactly the type of special conditions as in the Clever Hans and facilitated communication claims—that is, testing whether practitioners, when visually blinded, could still feel whether their hands were in proximity to a human body. Research has demonstrated the same thing as in the Clever Hans and facilitated communication cases—when vision is occluded, this ability to feel at a distance is no greater than chance (Hines, 2003; Rosa, Rosa, Sarner, & Barrett, 1998; Shermer, 2005). This example actually illustrates something that was mentioned in chapter—that the logic of the true experiment is really so straightforward that a child could understand it. This is because one of the published experiments showing that TT is ineffective was done as a school science project (Dacey, 2008).

In short, it is often necessary for scientists to create special conditions that will test a particular theory about a phenomenon. Merely observing the event in its natural state is rarely sufficient. People observed falling and moving objects for centuries without arriving at accurate principles and laws about motion and gravity. Truly explanatory laws of motion were not derived until Galileo and other scientists set up some rather artificial conditions for the observation of the behavior of moving objects. In Galileo's time, smooth bronze balls were rarely seen rolling down smooth inclined planes. Lots of motion occurred in the world, but it was rarely of this type. However, it was just such an unnatural situation, and others like it, that led to our first truly explanatory laws of motion and gravity. Speaking of laws of motion, didn't you take a little quiz at the beginning of this chapter?

Intuitive Physics

Actually, the three questions posed at the beginning of this chapter were derived from the work of Michael McCloskey, a psychologist at Johns Hopkins University. McCloskey (1983) has studied what he calls "intuitive physics," that is, people's beliefs about the motion of objects. Interestingly, these beliefs are often at striking variance from how moving objects actually behave (Kozhevnikov & Hegarty, 2001; Riener, Proffitt, & Salthouse, 2005).

For example, in the first problem, once the string on the circling ball is cut, the ball will fly in a straight line at a 90-degree angle to the string (tangent to the circle). McCloskey found that one-third of the college students who were given this problem thought, incorrectly, that the ball would fly in a curved trajectory. About half of McCloskey's subjects, when given problems similar to the bomber pilot example, thought that the bomb should be dropped directly over the target, thus displaying a lack of understanding of the role of an object's initial motion in determining its trajectory. The bomb should actually be dropped *five miles* before the plane reaches the target. The subjects' errors were not caused by the imaginary nature of the problem. When subjects were asked to walk across a room and, while moving, drop a golf ball on a target on the floor, the performance of more than half of them indicated that they did not know that the ball would move forward as it fell. Finally, many people are not aware that a bullet fired from a rifle will hit the ground at the same time as a bullet dropped from the same height.

You can assess your own performance on this little quiz. Chances are that you missed at least one if you have not had a physics course recently. "Physics course!" you might protest. "Of course I haven't had a physics class recently. This quiz is unfair!" But hold on a second. Why should you *need* a physics course? You have seen literally hundreds of falling objects in your lifetime. You have seen them fall under *naturally occurring* conditions. Moving objects surround you every day, and you are seeing them in their "real-life" state. You certainly cannot claim that you have not experienced moving and falling objects. Granted, you have never seen anything quite like the bullet example. But most of us have seen children let go of whirling objects, and many of us have seen objects fall out of planes. And besides, it seems a little lame to protest that you have not seen these exact situations. Given your years of experience with moving and falling objects, why can not you accurately predict what will happen in a situation only slightly out of the ordinary?

McCloskey's work demonstrates something of fundamental importance in understanding why scientists behave as they do. Despite extensive experience with moving and falling objects, people's intuitive theories of motion are remarkably inaccurate. It is critical to understand that the layperson's beliefs are inaccurate precisely because his or her observations are "natural," rather than controlled in the manner of the scientist's. Thus, if you missed a question on the little quiz at the beginning of the chapter, don't feel ignorant or inadequate. Simply remember that some of the world's greatest minds observed falling objects for centuries without formulating a physics of motion any more accurate than that of the modern high-school sophomore. In an article in *Scientific American,* McCloskey (1983) observed that many of his subjects held an incorrect theory about motion that was very similar to one held to be true some three centuries before Newton. McCloskey's modern subjects and medieval philosophers had something in common: Both groups had had much exposure to the motion of objects in the ordinary world, but none under the artificially created conditions of scientific manipulation, control, and comparison.

Even large amounts of personal experience are insufficient to prevent misconceptions about the nature of physical motion. Writing about the history of the development of knowledge about banked turns in aircraft, writer William Langewiesche (1993) noted that pilots in the early part of the twentieth century resisted the use of instrumentation such as gyroscopes because they believed in "instinctive balance." However, these "instincts" failed to uncover the existence of unfelt banks in clouds. Enough crashes and near crashes finally taught pilots a sobering lesson: No amount of instinct would substitute for knowledge of the actual physics of flight (Langewiesche, 1993).

Personal experience is likewise no guarantee against incorrect beliefs about human psychology. Behavioral economist Dan Ariely (2008) tells the story of suffering burns over 70 percent of his body as the result of an accident when he was 18 years old. He describes many months of subsequent treatment in which bandages that were removed quickly caused him great pain. The theory held by the nurses was that a quick removal (which caused a sharp pain) was preferable to slow removal which would cause a longer—although less intense—pain. After leaving the hospital and beginning his career as a psychology student, Ariely conducted experiments to test the nurses' belief. To his surprise, Ariely found that the slower procedure—lower pain intensity over a longer period—would have reduced the pain perception in such situations. He says that "by the time I had finished, I realized that the nurses in the burn unit were kind and generous individuals with a lot of experience in soaking and removing bandages, but they still didn't have the right theory about what would minimize their patients pain. How could they be so wrong, I wondered, considering their vast experience?" (p. xvi).

As discussed in Chapter 4, reliance on testimonials, case study evidence, and "common practice" can often obscure the need for a control group to check the veracity of a conclusion derived from informal observation. For example, Dingfelder (2006) describes how many medical professionals believe that they should not advise individuals with Tourette's syndrome (described in Chapter 2) to suppress their tics (involuntary vocal expressions). The physicians believed that this caused a so-called rebound effect—a higher rate of tics occurring after the suppression. This belief, though, is based on informal observation rather than controlled experimentation. When the proper experimentation was done—observing the number of tics systematically by comparing a period of suppression to a period of nonsuppression—it appeared that there was no "rebound" effect at all following tic suppression.

Intuitive Psychology

Philosopher Paul Churchland (1988) has argued that, if our intuitive (or "folk") theories about objects in motion are inaccurate, it is hard to believe that our folk theories in the more complex domain of human behavior could be correct:

> Our early folk theories of motion were profoundly confused, and were eventually displaced entirely by more sophisticated theories. Our early folk theories of the structure and activity of the heavens were wildly off the mark, and survive only as historical lessons in how wrong we can be. Our folk theories of the nature of fire, and the nature of life, were similarly cockeyed. And one could go on, since the vast majority of our past folk conceptions have been similarly exploded. . . . But the phenomenon of conscious intelligence is surely a more complex and difficult phenomenon than any of those just listed. So far as accurate understanding is concerned, it would be a miracle if we had got that one right the very first time, when we fell down so badly on all the others. (p. 46)

When we look at the actual literature on people's theories of behavior, we find that Churchland's speculation turns out to be right. In Chapter 1, we illustrated that a number of commonsense (or folk) beliefs about human behavior are wrong, and this was just a small sample. For example, it turns out that there is no strong evidence indicating that highly religious people are more altruistic than less religious people (Paloutzian & Park, 2005; Smith, Wheeler, & Diener, 1975). Studies have indicated that there is no simple relationship between degree of religiosity and the tendency to engage in charitable acts, to aid other people in distress, or to abstain from cheating other people.

Incorrect beliefs about human behavior can have very practical conse-quences. Keith and Beins (2008) mention that among their students, typical views about cell phones and driving are captured by statements such as "Talking doesn't impair my driving" and "I talk on the phone to keep myself from falling asleep." The students seem completely oblivious to the fact that driving while using a cell phone (even a hands-free phone) seriously impairs concentration and attention (Kunar, Carter, Cohen, & Horowitz, 2008; Strayer & Drews, 2007) and is a cause of accidents and deaths (Conkle & West, 2008; McEvoy et al., 2005; Parker-Pope, 2009).

The list of popular beliefs that are incorrect is long. For example, many people believe that a full moon affects human behavior. It doesn't (Byrnes & Kelly, 1992; Foster & Roenneberg, 2008). Some people believe that "opposites attract." They don't (Gaunt, 2006). Some people believe that "familiarity breeds contempt." It doesn't (Claypool, Hall, Mackie, & Garcia-Marques, 2008; Zebrowitz, White, & Wieneke, 2008). And the list goes on and on and on. For example, the rate of distress among women after an abortion is about equal to the rate of distress among women who have given birth (Clay, 2008; Dvoskin, 2008).

The many inadequacies in people's intuitive theories of behavior illus-trate why we need the controlled experimentation of psychology: so that we can progress beyond our flat-earth conceptions of human behavior to a more accurate scientific conceptualization.

Summary

The heart of the experimental method involves manipulation and control. This is why an experiment allows stronger causal inferences than a correla-tional study. In a correlational study, the investigator simply observes whether the natural fluctuation in two variables displays a relationship. By contrast, in a true experiment the investigator manipulates the variable hypothesized to be the cause and looks for an effect on the variable hypothe-sized to be the effect while holding all other variables constant by control and randomization. This method removes the third-variable problem present in correlational studies. The third-variable problem arises because, in the natural world, many different things are related. The experimental method may be viewed as a way of prying apart these naturally occurring relation-ships. It does so because it isolates one particular variable (the hypothesized cause) by manipulating it and holding everything else constant. However, in order to pry apart naturally occurring relationships, scientists often have to create special conditions that are unknown in the natural world.

CHAPTER 7

"But It's Not Real Life!" The "Artificiality" Criticism and Psychology

Having covered the basics of experimental logic in the previous two chapters, we are now in a position to consider some often heard criticisms of the field of psychology. In particular, we will discuss at length the criticism that scientific experiments are useless because they are artificial and not like "real life." Understanding why this is not a valid criticism will aid in thinking straight about psychology because the criticism is often aimed at psychological experimentation.

Why Natural Isn't Always Necessary

From the discussion in Chapter 6, it should already be fairly clear why this criticism is invalid. As was illustrated in that chapter, the artificiality of scientific experimentation is not a weakness but actually the very thing that gives the scientific method its unique power to yield explanations about the nature of the world. Contrary to common belief, the artificiality of scientific experiments is not an accidental oversight. It is intentionally sought. Scientists *deliberately* set up conditions that are unlike those that occur naturally because this is the only way to separate the many inherently correlated variables that determine events in the world. To use a phrase from Chapter 6, scientists set up special conditions in order to *pry variables apart*.

Sometimes the necessary conditions already exist naturally, as in the example of Snow and cholera. More often, this is not the case. The scientist must manipulate events in new and sometimes strange ways, as in the example of Goldberger and pellagra. In many instances, these manipulations cannot be accomplished in natural environments, and the scientist finds it necessary to bring the phenomenon into the laboratory, where more precise control is possible. Early studies of gravity and motion used specially constructed objects that were designed for no other reason than to create a set of special conditions for the observation of moving objects. It is often necessary to create increasingly *unreal* and extreme conditions in order to separate the many potential causes of a phenomenon.

Indeed, some phenomena would be completely impossible to discover if scientists were restricted totally to observing "natural" conditions. Physicists probing the most fundamental characteristics of matter build gigantic mile-long accelerators that induce collisions between elementary particles. Some of the by-products of these collisions are new particles that exist for less than a billionth of a second. The properties of these new particles, however, have implications for theories of atomic structure. Many of these new particles would not ordinarily exist on earth, and even if they did, there certainly would be no chance of observing them naturally. Yet few people doubt that this is how physicists should conduct their research—that probing nature in unusual and sometimes bizarre ways is a legitimate means of coming to a deeper understanding of the universe. Somehow, though, practices that seem reasonable for physicists are often viewed as invalid when used by psychologists.

Although the actions of all scientists are misunderstood when the public fails to realize the importance of creating special conditions in the laboratory, the work of psychologists is probably most subject to this type of misunderstanding. Many psychologists who have presented experimental evidence on behavior to an audience of laypersons have heard the lament "But it's not real life!" The remark reflects the belief that studying human psychology in the laboratory is somehow strange. This objection also contains the assumption that knowledge cannot be obtained unless natural conditions are studied.

It is not commonly recognized that many of the techniques used by the psychologist that are viewed as strange by the public are in no way unique to psychology; instead, they are manifestations of the scientific method as applied to behavior. Actually, similar bizarre ways of acquiring knowledge about the world can be observed in the investigations conducted by every science. Psychology ends up with the worst of both worlds. The same ignorance of the scientific method that supports the belief that psychology just can't be a science leads to the denigration of psychologists when they, like all other scientists, create the special conditions necessary to uncover more powerful and precise explanations of their phenomena.

Restriction to real-life situations would prevent us from discovering many things. For example, biofeedback techniques are now used in a variety of areas such as migraine and tension headache control, hypertension treatment, and relaxation training (deCharms et al., 2005; Maizels, 2005; Miller, 1985a). These techniques developed out of research indicating that humans could learn partial control of their internal physiological processes if they could monitor the ongoing processes via visual or auditory feedback. Of course, because humans are not equipped to monitor their physiological functions via external feedback, the ability to control such processes does not become apparent *except* under special conditions. Observations under natural conditions would never have uncovered the ability.

The "Random Sample" Confusion

Sometimes, however, the "it's not real life" complaint arises from a different type of confusion about the purposes of psychological experimentation, one that is actually quite understandable. Through media exposure, many people are familiar with survey research, particularly in the form of election and public opinion polling. There is now a growing awareness of some of the important characteristics of election polling. In particular, the media have given more attention to the importance of a random, or representative, sample for the accuracy of public opinion polls. This attention has led many people to believe, mistakenly, that random samples and representative conditions are an essential requirement of all psychological investigations. Because psychological research seldom uses random samples of subjects, the application of the random sample criterion by the layperson seems to undermine most psychological investigations and to reinforce the criticism that the research is invalid because it doesn't reflect real life.

Again, a moment's thought about the nature of other sciences should go a long way toward exposing the fallaciousness of this belief. Chemists make no attempt to draw random samples of compounds. Biologists do not experiment on random samples of cells or organisms. The rats and monkeys in a medical research facility are not at all representative of their species. The organisms in such laboratories are often studied under conditions that are vastly different from their natural environments. Indeed, these conditions are often utterly unique. Yet they yield insights that help shed great light on human biology. The same is true of most psychological investigations. This is because it is actually *not* necessary for every psychological investigation to employ a random sample of participants. And this is a good time to stress an important point: that random sampling and random assignment (discussed in Chapter 6) are not the same thing.

The Random Assignment Versus Random Sample Distinction

Because they both have the term *random* in them, many people come to think that random assignment and random sampling refer to the same thing. Actually they are very different concepts—similar only in that they make use of the properties of random number generation. But they are used for very different purposes.

Random sampling refers to how subjects are chosen to be part of a study. As noted previously, random sampling is not a requirement for all research, but when it does become necessary (in survey research, consumer research, or election polling, for example), it refers to drawing a sample from the population in a manner that ensures that each member of the population has an equal chance of being chosen for the sample. The sample that is drawn then becomes the subject of the investigation. And it is important to understand that that investigation could be either a correlational study or a true experiment. It is not a true experiment unless random assignment is *also* used.

Random assignment is a requirement of a true experiment in which an experimental group and a control group are formed by the experimenter. Random assignment is achieved when each subject is just as likely to be assigned to the control group as to the experimental group. This is why a randomizing device such as a coin flip (more often, a specially prepared table of random numbers) is employed—because it displays no bias in assigning the subjects to groups.

The best way to keep in mind that random assignment and random sampling are not the same thing is always to be clear that any of the four combinations can occur: nonrandom sampling without random assignment, nonrandom sampling with random assignment, random sampling without random assignment, and random sampling with random assignment. Most psychological research does not employ random sampling because it is not necessary. The research involves theory testing, as we will see in the next section, and a convenience sample is all that is necessary. If random assignment is employed in the study, then it becomes a true experiment. If random assignment is not employed, then the study is a correlational investigation. Many studies that do use random sampling do not employ random assignment because they are surveys and are only looking for associations—that is, they are correlational investigations. However, some studies using random samples do employ random assignment and they, of course, are true experiments.

Theory-Driven Research Versus Direct Applications

Douglas Mook (1983, 1989, 2001), a psychologist at the University of Virginia, discusses the different types of goals that characterize different types of investigation. In many kinds of applied research, the goal is to relate the results of the study directly to a particular situation. Election polling is an example of directly applied research. The goal is to predict a specific behavior in a very specific setting—in this case, voting on election day. Here, where the nature of the application is direct, questions of the randomness of the sample and the representativeness of the conditions are important because the findings of the study are going to be applied directly.

However, it would be a mistake to view this class of research as typical. The vast majority of research studies in psychology (or any other science, for that matter) are conducted with a very different purpose in mind. Their purpose is to advance theory. The findings of most research are applied only *indirectly* through modifications in a theory that, in conjunction with other scientific laws, is then applied to some practical problem (Nickerson, 1999). In short, most theory-driven research seeks to test theories of psychological processes rather than to generalize the findings to a particular real-world situation.

Research that focuses primarily on theory testing is often termed *basic research*. Whereas in applied research the purpose of the investigation is to go from data directly to a real-world application, basic research focuses on theory testing. However, it is probably a mistake to view the basic-versus-applied distinction solely in terms of whether a study has practical applications, because this difference often simply boils down to a matter of time. Applied findings are of use immediately. However, there is nothing so practical as a general and accurate theory. The history of science is filled with examples of theories or findings that eventually solved a host of real-world problems even though the scientists who developed the theories and/or findings did not intend to solve a specific practical problem.

Seymour Kety (1974) described how a seemingly unrelated set of scientific findings led up to the discovery of chlorpromazine, a drug of immense usefulness in treating schizophrenia. Kety made the point that virtually *none* of the precursor discoveries of this treatment for schizophrenia would have been recognized as having anything to do with schizophrenia! Time and time again, attempts to control the direction of science (by trying to tell scientists to solve a particular practical problem) turn out to impede rather than facilitate progress. Ironically, the urge to have scientists solve only practical problems and not bother with the "other stuff" (basic research) turns out to be wildly impractical and shortsighted.

The road to many practical applications is remarkably tortuous and unpredictable. A group of researchers at the University of Texas Southwestern Medical Center was seeking to genetically engineer a population of rats with arthritis in order to study that inflammatory disease. Unexpectedly, their rats also developed inflammation of the intestines (Fackelman, 1996). The research team "had serendipitously created rats with ulcerative colitis, thus giving scientists an animal model in which to study the human disease" (Fackelman, 1996, p. 302). Whether these scientists make any progress on arthritis (their original problem), it now looks as if they have made a substantial contribution to the eventual treatment of ulcerative colitis and Crohn's disease.

These indirect links between basic research and applications are often difficult to appreciate. Indeed, the seemingly remote relation between basic research and real-life concerns makes basic research easy to ridicule and mock. In the 1970s and 1980s, U.S. Senator William Proxmire made a sport of singling out odd-sounding titles of basic research studies and holding them out as examples of government waste (Benson, 2006a). But time after time, the joke turned out to be on Senator Proxmire rather than the researcher. It was repeatedly found that studies that Senator Proxmire had singled out because they sounded silly when boiled down to a single sentence ("Why Monkeys Clench Their Jaws") actually had led to important theoretical advances or practical applications. For example, the study of monkey jaw clenching helped to operationalize the concept of stress. This was helpful to government agencies who wanted to objectively assess the amount of stress present when people had to operate in close quarters for extended periods of time such as in outer space or in a submarine (Benson, 2006a).

Another study that Proxmire mocked ("Why Bowlers Smile") "provided a fundamental insight into one of the cross-cultural universals in human behavior, and that, in the process, it was among the first precursors to the field today known as evolutionary psychology. The senator was looking for research that to voters might appear silly with the right description. . . . [The study of smiling actually] uncovered a phenomenon that applies to interactions between mothers and their babies, therapists and their clients, workers and their bosses. . . . [It] provided a foundation for later research, both in the laboratory and the field, that provided increased understanding of how people communicate through facial expressions" (Diener, 2006, p. 15).

Senator Proxmire's tradition of mocking research studies that later turned out to be of real benefit was revived in the 2008 presidential campaign when candidate John McCain mocked a study of the DNA of bears in Montana by quipping "I don't know if it was a paternity issue or criminal, but it was a waste of money" (Krauss, 2008). His running-mate, Sarah Palin, criticized studies that have "little or nothing to do with the public good. Things like fruit fly research in Paris, France" (Krauss, 2008). Referring to these studies may have successfully pandered to the public's view that research is a waste of money, but they were particularly poor choices. It turned out that the bear study was mandated by the Federal Endangered Species Act, on the recommendation of scientists from the U.S. Geological Survey, the U.S. Fish and Wildlife Service, and the Montana Fish, Wildlife and Parks service. All of these agencies saw the study as essential to preserving a threatened species by allowing researchers to pinpoint bear numbers and locations.

Palin's choice of study was even worse—indeed, ironically poor. First, the lab in France was supported by the U.S. Department of Agriculture because France had had olive fruit fly infestation for decades before this infestation hit California (Krauss, 2008). It is of immediate economic benefit to the United States to be able to control olive fruit fly infestation. Even more ironically, Palin's speech in part concerned the federal Individuals with Disabilities Education Act and she herself has an intellectually disabled child. The fruit fly was (and continues to be) a critical organism in the field of genetics—a field of direct relevance to the diagnosis and treatment of a number of the disabilities that fall under the Individuals with Disabilities Education Act.

We must recognize that, although some research is designed to predict events directly in a specific environmental situation, much scientific research is basic research designed to test theory. Researchers who conduct applied and basic research have completely different answers to the question, how do these findings apply to real life? The former answers, "Directly, provided that there is a reasonably close relationship between the experimental situation and the one to which the findings are to be applied." Thus, questions of the random sampling of subjects and the representativeness of the experimental situation are relevant to the applicability of the results. However, the investigator in a theory-testing study answers that his or her findings do not apply *directly* to real life, and that the reason for conducting the study is not to produce findings that would be applicable to some specific environmental situation. Therefore, this scientist is not concerned with questions of how similar the subjects of the study are to some other group or whether the experimental situation mirrors some real-life environment. Does this mean, then, that these findings have no implications for the real world? No. These findings apply directly not to a particular situation but to a theory. The theory may, at some later date, in conjunction with other scientific laws, be applied to a particular problem.

This type of indirect application through theory has become quite common in some areas of psychology. For example, years ago when cell phones were first introduced, many cognitive psychologists immediately began to worry about the implications for safety when people began to use them while driving automobiles. The psychologists immediately expected that cell phone use would cause additional accidents—and not just because the phone would take a hand off the wheel. Instead, what they were worried about was the attentional requirements of talking on the cell phone. What is important to realize was that the psychologists became worried about cell phone use in cars long before there was a single experimental study of actual cell phone use and its relation to accidents (see Strayer & Johnston, 2001, 2007). The psychologists made their prediction of accident problems with cell phones through *theory*, in this case theories of limited-capacity attention that were decades old (e.g., Broadbent, 1958; Kahneman, 1973). Cell phone use in a car clearly falls within the domain of those theories, which had been established through voluminous experimentation (literally hundreds of laboratory studies). When in fact the actual studies of real cell phone use were done, they confirmed the prediction from the psychological theories of attention: Cell phone use is indeed a cause of motor vehicle accidents—and hands-free phones do not solve the attentional problem, which is the main cause of the accidents (Conkle & West, 2008; Insurance Institute for Highway Safety, 2005; Kunar, Carter, Cohen, & Horowitz, 2008; Levy, Pashler, & Boer, 2006; McEvoy et al., 2005; Redelmeier & Tibshirani, 1997, 2001; Strayer & Drews, 2007).

Douglas Mook (1983) discussed an example that illustrates the ideas of theory-testing experimentation and the nature of indirect application in psychology. In the 1930s, Selig Hecht published a series of studies of visual sensitivity in the *Handbook of General Experimental Psychology* (Murchison, 1934). These studies concerned the phenomenon of dark adaptation. You have probably experienced the temporary blindness that occurs when you walk into a darkened movie theater. As you wait in your seat, however, you probably notice that chairs, people, and other objects begin to become visible. If you keep concentrating on this phenomenon, you will observe that the visibility of objects in the theater continues to increase for several minutes.

This phenomenon is called *dark adaptation*, and it occurs in two phases: a rather quick but fairly small increase in visual sensitivity on entering a darkened room, followed by a delayed but much larger increase in sensitivity. Hecht linked this two-part adaptation curve to the two different types of receptor cells in the retina of the eye. The cones are receptor cells that are densely packed in the center of the fovea (the part of the retina where incoming light is focused) and are very sensitive to red light. The rods are located outside the foveal area, are much less densely packed, and are not very sensitive to red light. Hecht used these facts to establish that the initial phase of dark adaptation (a small, rapid increase in visual sensitivity) is due to the adaptation of the cones and that the second phase (a larger increase in sensitivity taking place over a longer period of time) is due to rod adaptation.

Mook (1983) urged us to consider the complete unnaturalness of Hecht's experimental situation. Subjects (who were not randomly chosen) were in a dark room responding, "Yes, I see it" or "No, I don't," depending on whether or not they detected a tiny red light that was flashed at them. We normally do not respond to little red lights in this way in everyday life. Hecht, however, was not concerned about generalizing his findings to individuals in dark rooms responding "yes" or "no" to tiny red lights, so whether such a situation ever actually occurs is irrelevant. Hecht was interested in establishing facts and testing theories about the basic processes that characterize the visual system, such as dark adaptation. He was not concerned about whether his experimental situation was realistic but about whether it adequately isolated the specific visual process he was interested in studying.

Hecht's findings gain generalizability not through the nature of the setting in which they occurred, but by their ability to establish a theory of basic visual processes that are implicated in many tasks. His research uncovered the basic functional relationships that characterize the human visual system, precisely because his situation was controlled and artificial. If the theoretical model for the relationships is correct, then it should have wide applicability and should account for performance in a variety of situations much different from the one in which it was derived. In other words, Hecht's findings have indirect applications through their influence on theory. For example, the basic understanding of the visual system promoted by Hecht's findings has helped in the treatment of night blindness and in the problem of reading X-rays (Leibowitz, 1996; Mook, 1982). And more dramatically, while awaiting the night raids of Hitler's bombers during the blitz in World War II, the British fighter pilots who were to engage the German planes wore red goggles (so that the rods—not being sensitive to red light—would stay dark-adapted; see Mook, 1982). The leap from subjects judging little red dots in a laboratory to the dangerous sky over London was made through *theory*, not through a redesign of Hecht's lab to resemble a Spitfire airplane.

Applications of Psychological Theory

Once we understand that the purpose of most research is to develop theory rather than to predict events in a specific environment and that the findings of most research are applied indirectly, through theory, rather than directly in a specific environmental situation, we can legitimately ask how much application through theory has been accomplished in psychology. That is, have psychology's theories been put to this test of generality?

On this point, we must admit that the record is mixed. But it is wise to keep psychology's diversity in mind here. It is true that some areas of research have made only modest progress along these lines. However, other areas have quite impressive records of experimentally derived principles of considerable explanatory and predictive power (see Adler & Rips, 2008; Buss, 2007; Gazzaniga, 2008; Hilton, 2003; Thaler & Sunstein, 2008; Zimbardo, 2004). For example, even applied areas like counseling psychology, school psychology, clinical psychology, and psychotherapy have benefited from theory-driven basic research (Gutkin & Reynolds, 2008; Lilienfeld, Lynn, & Lohr, 2003; Mahrer, 2000; Siegert & Ward, 2002).

Consider the basic behavioral principles of classical and operant conditioning. These principles and their elaborating laws were developed almost entirely from experimentation on nonhuman subjects, such as pigeons and rats, in highly artificial laboratory settings. Yet these principles have been successfully applied to a wide variety of human problems, including the treatment of autistic children, the teaching of large amounts of factual material, the treatment of alcoholism and obesity, the management of residents in psychiatric hospitals, and the treatment of phobias, to name just a few.

The principles from which these applications were derived were identified precisely because the laboratory experimentation allowed researchers to specify the relationships between environmental stimuli and behavior with an accuracy not possible in a natural situation, in which many behavioral relationships may operate simultaneously. As for the use of nonhuman subjects, in many cases theories and laws derived from their performance have provided good first approximations to human behavior (Vazire & Gosling, 2003). When humans were examined, their behavior often followed laws that were very similar to those derived from other animals. Findings such as these should hardly surprise anyone today, when just about every medical advance in the treatment of human illness has involved data from animal studies. For example, research with animals has contributed to developments in behavioral medicine, stress reduction, psychotherapy, the rehabilitation of injured and handicapped individuals, the effects of aging on memory, methods to help people overcome neuromuscular disorders, drug effects on fetal development, substance abuse, memory loss, traffic safety, and the treatment of chronic pain (Domjan & Purdy, 1995; Gosling, 2001; Kalat, 2007; Michaels, 2008; Miller, 1985b; Zimbardo, 2004). Recent research with monkeys has led to some real advances in understanding the underlying basis of phobias and anxiety disorders (Mineka & Zinbarg, 2006).

In fact, the it's-not-real-life argument has been used misleadingly to denigrate the results of animal research—often for political reasons. For example, lobbyists for polluting companies often put forth the argument that the evaluation of the human risk of cancer-causing agents is invalid if based on animal studies. However, in a 1988 study of 23 carcinogenic agents (benzene, asbestos, etc.) by a team of scientists, it was found that estimated death rates from animal studies were quite close to estimates from epidemiological studies of humans (Finkel, 1996).

Psychologists studying perceptual processes have made impressive theoretical progress, and the laws and theories they have derived have been applied to problems as diverse as radar monitoring, street lighting, and airplane cockpit design (Durso et al., 2007; Swets, Dawes, & Monahan, 2000; Wickens et al., 2003). Much is now known about the cognitive effects of aging (Salthouse, 2004), and this new knowledge has direct implications for efforts to design systems that will help people to compensate for cognitive loss (Dixon & Backman, 1995).

Psychological studies of judgment and decision making have had implications for medical decision making, educational decision making, and economic decision making (Gigerenzer et al., 2007; Gilovich, Griffin, & Kahneman, 2002; Hilton, 2003; Kahneman & Tversky, 2000; Tetlock, 2005; Thaler & Sunstein, 2008; Zweig, 2008). The famous obedience to authority studies of Stanley Milgram were used in officer training schools of the military (Blass, 2004; Cohen, 2008). An exciting new development is the increasing involvement of cognitive psychologists in the legal system, in which problems of memory in information collection, evidence evaluation, and decision making present opportunities to test the applicability of cognitive theories (Kassin, Tubb, Hosch, & Memon, 2001; Koehler & Thompson, 2006; Wells, Memon, & Penrod, 2006; Zimbardo, 2004). In recent decades, theory and practice in the teaching of reading have begun to be affected by research in cognitive psychology (Pressley, 2005; Snowling & Hulme, 2005; Stanovich, 2000; Vellutino, Fletcher, Snowling, & Scanlon, 2004; Wolf, 2007).

Psychologists have played an important role in providing scientific evidence to inform the public debate about the status of children's testimony in legal proceedings (Bruck & Ceci, 2004) and about the validity of "recovered" memories of child abuse (Brainerd & Reyna, 2005; Bremner, Shobe, & Kihlstrom, 2000; Gardner, 2006; Lynn, Loftus, Lilienfeld, & Lock, 2003;

McNally, 2003). Cognitive psychologist Barbara Tversky studies spatial cognition, and spinoffs from her work have been used in the design of computer map route generators and in writing the instructions for do-it-yourself furniture (Benson, 2006b). The potential applications of psychology are well illustrated in the career of Judi See, who received her doctoral degree in perception and experimental psychology and works on applying psychology to the problems of the military (See, 2006). In a varied and fascinating career, she has assessed the quality of surveillance in Global Hawk unmanned aerial vehicles, evaluated eyeglass inserts for Air Force gas masks, helped B-2 pilots schedule sleep and wake periods to counter fatigue during missions, evaluated the use of handheld translation devices in Iraq, and applied signal detection theory to the neutralization of explosive devices (See, 2006).

The American Psychological Association maintains a website where you can read about many more of the practical applications of psychological knowledge: http://www.psychologymatters.org/. The Association for Psychological Science sponsors a blog called "We're Only Human" written by Wray Herbert where many applications of psychological research are discussed: http://www.psychologicalscience.org/onlyhuman/. The magazine *Scientific American Mind* also reports on many applications of psychology.

The "College Sophomore" Problem

The concerns of many people who question the "representativeness" of psychological findings focus on the subjects of the research rather than on the intricacies of the experimental design. However, in many areas of psychology such as the study of basic perceptual and cognitive processes, conflicting results are more often due to the latter than to the former. The basic information-processing operations, the functional organization of the brain, and the nature of the visual systems of people in Montana tend to be very similar to those of people in Florida (or Argentina, for that matter). In addition, these characteristics of humans also depend very little on whether one's parents are tinkers, tailors, or professors.

All sciences assume that certain factors are so tangential that they will make no difference in the final results. Biologists do not generally worry that the slightly different thickness of petri dishes will significantly affect the bacteria in them. These differences, of course, may have an effect—every assumption in science is tentative—but biologists must expend their effort investigating possibilities with a higher probability. Similarly, Hecht assumed that dark adaptation did not depend on a person's religious affiliation, so he did not ask his subjects whether they were Lutherans or Roman Catholics.

We are confronting here what is sometimes called the *college sophomore problem*; that is, the worry that, because college sophomores are the subjects in an extremely large number of psychological investigations, the generality of the results is in question. Psychologists are concerned about the college sophomore issue because it is a real problem in certain areas of research. Nevertheless, it is important to consider the problem in perspective and to understand that psychologists have several legitimate responses to this criticism. Here are three:

1. The college sophomore criticism does not *invalidate* results but simply calls for *more* findings that will allow assessment of the theory's generality. Adjustments in theory necessitated by contrary data from other groups can be made accurately only because we have the college sophomore data. The worst case, a failure to replicate, will mean that theories developed on the basis of college sophomore data are not necessarily wrong but merely incomplete.
2. In many areas of psychology, the college sophomore issue is simply not a problem because the processes investigated are so basic (the visual system, for example) that virtually no one would believe that their fundamental organization depends on the demographics of the subject sample.
3. Replication of findings ensures a large degree of geographic generality and, to a lesser extent, generality across socioeconomic factors, family variables, and early educational experience. As opposed to studies conducted 50 years ago, when the sample of university subjects participating would have come from an extremely elite group, research now goes on in universities that serve populations from a great variety of backgrounds.

It would be remiss, however, not to admit that the college sophomore issue is a real problem in certain areas of research in psychology (Peterson, 2001). Nevertheless, psychologists are now making greater efforts to correct the problem. For example, developmental psychologists are almost inherently concerned about this issue. Each year hundreds of researchers in this area test dozens of findings and theories that were developed from studies of college subjects by performing the same research on subjects of different ages.

The results from subject groups of different ages do not always replicate those from college students. Developmental psychology would be starkly boring if they did. But this sizable group of psychologists is busy building an age component into psychological theories, demonstrating the importance of this factor, and ensuring that the discipline will not end up with a large theoretical superstructure founded on a thin database derived from college students.

Developmental psychologists also conduct cross-cultural research in order to assess the generality of the developmental processes uncovered by researchers working only with North American children. For example, Stevenson et al. (1985) gave a large battery of cognitive tasks to Chinese, Japanese, and American children and concluded, "The organization of cognitive abilities tapped in these tasks was very similar among the children in the three cultures" (p. 727). Other comparisons of cognitive abilities across racial and cultural groups have shown the same thing (Demetriou et al., 2005; McBride-Chang & Kail, 2002). With regard to other psychological characteristics, there are many other instances in which cross-cultural comparisons have shown similar trends across cultures (e.g., Day & Rounds, 1998; Rozin, Lowery, Imada, & Haidt, 1999), but there are others in which cross-cultural research does not replicate the trends displayed by American college sophomores (e.g., Buchtel & Norenzayan, 2009; Nisbett, 2003). However, when these discrepancies occur, they provide important information about the contextual dependence of theories and outcomes (Buchtel & Norenzayan, 2009; Henrich et al., 2004; Medin & Atran, 2004; Nisbett, 2003).

As previously mentioned, findings in cognitive psychology have met the basic test of replicability. Many of the fundamental laws of information processing have been observed in dozens of laboratories all over the world. It is often not realized that if a psychologist at the University of Michigan obtains a finding of true importance, similar experiments will almost immediately be attempted at Stanford, Minnesota, Ohio State, Cambridge, Yale, Toronto, and elsewhere. Through this testing, we will soon know whether the finding is due to the peculiarities of the Michigan subjects or the study's experimental setting.

Educational psychologists have also addressed the college sophomore problem. For example, in conjunction with developmental psychologists and other educational researchers, educational psychologists have constructed measures of basic cognitive skills that predict future educational achievements, such as the rate of reading acquisition, with a moderate degree of accuracy. The predictive accuracy of these measures has been shown to be very similar for children of different socioeconomic status and race and from different geographic regions and school districts.

The college sophomore problem and criticisms of representativeness are most often aimed at social psychology, which makes frequent use of college subjects in laboratory paradigms in an attempt to develop theories of social interaction, group behavior, and information processing in social situations (Myers, 2006). However, even in this area of psychology, evidence has indicated that the laboratory-derived relationships and theories do in fact predict behavior in a variety of other situations involving different types of individuals.

For example, several years ago, Leonard Berkowitz, a psychologist at the University of Wisconsin, demonstrated the so-called weapons effect— the fact that the mere presence of a weapon in a person's environment increases the probability of an aggressive response. This finding originated in the laboratory and is a perfect example of an unrepresentative situation. The results were strongly criticized as misleading because they were products of a contrived situation. Yet the fact remains that the finding has been replicated in experiments using different measures of aggression, has been obtained in Europe as well as the United States, has been found to hold for children as well as adults, and has been found outside the laboratory in field studies in which the subjects did not know they were part of an experiment (Berkowitz & Donnerstein, 1982; Turner, Simons, Berkowitz, & Frodi, 1977). Researchers have even isolated the cognitive mechanism behind the weapons effect. It is a process of automatic priming in semantic memory (see Meier, Robinson, & Wilkowski, 2007; Wilkowski & Robinson, 2008).

Cognitive, social, and clinical psychologists have also studied various human decision-making strategies. Most of the original studies in this research area were done in laboratories, used college students as subjects, and employed extremely artificial tasks. However, the principles of decision-making behavior derived from these studies have been observed in a variety of nonlaboratory situations, including the prediction of closing stock prices by bankers, actual casino betting, the prediction of patient behavior by psychiatrists, economic markets, military intelligence analysis, betting on NFL football games, the estimation of repair time by engineers, the estimation of house prices by realtors, business decision making, and diagnoses by physicians—and these principles are also now being applied in the very practical domain of personal financial counseling (Bazerman, 2001; Gilovich, Griffin, & Kahneman, 2002; Hilton, 2003; Taleb, 2007; Thaler & Sunstein, 2008; Zweig, 2008).

Birnbaum (1999, 2004) has demonstrated that the Internet provides a way for psychology to deal with the college sophomore problem. He ran a series of decision-making experiments in the laboratory and by recruiting participants over the Internet. The laboratory findings all replicated on the Internet sample even though the latter was vastly more diverse—including 1,224 participants from 44 different countries (see also Jaffe, 2005; Johnson, 2001; McGraw, Tew, & Williams, 2000). Gosling et al. (2004) studied a large Internet sample of participants (361,703 people) and compared them with the participants in 510 traditional samples in published studies. They found that the Internet sample was more diverse with respect to gender, socioeconomic status, geographic region, and age. Importantly, they found that findings in many areas of psychology, such as personality theory, were similar on the Internet when compared to traditional methods.

These few examples illustrate that the degree of consistency and generality of the findings of psychological research is often underestimated (Gage, 1996; Rosenthal, 1990; Rosnow & Rosenthal, 2003). Anderson, Lindsay, and Bushman (1999) have reported the most systematic examination of the relation between experimental effects found in laboratory and field studies. Across a variety of studies examining diverse topics such as aggression, leadership, and depression, Anderson et al. (1999) found a high level of convergence—almost always the different research settings led to similar conclusions.

Of course, not all psychological findings replicate. On the contrary, replication failures do happen, and they are often more instructive than confirmations. However, in cognitive psychology, replication failures are rarely due to the peculiarities of the subjects. Instead, most are due to subtle differences in experimental stimuli and methods. By closely examining exactly what experimental conditions are necessary for the demonstration of a phenomenon, scientists come to a more precise understanding of the phenomenon and lay the foundation for a more precise theory about its occurrence.

But how can any psychological findings be applied if replication failures sometimes occur? How can applications be justified if knowledge and theories are not established with certainty, when there is not complete agreement among scientists on all the details? This particular worry about the application of psychological findings is common because people do not realize that findings and theories in other sciences are regularly applied before they are firmly established. Of course, Chapter 2 should have made it clear that all scientific theories are subject to revision. If we must have absolutely certain knowledge before we can apply the results of scientific investigations, then no applications will ever take place. Applied scientists in all fields do their best to use the most accurate information available, realizing at the same time that the information is fallible.

The Real-Life and College Sophomore Problems in Perspective

Several issues have been raised in this chapter, and it is important to be clear about what has, and what has not, been said. We have illustrated that the frequent complaint about the artificiality of psychological research arises from a basic misunderstanding not only of psychology but also of basic principles that govern all sciences. Artificial conditions are not an accident that represents a drawback. They are deliberately created so that we can pry variables apart. We have also seen why people are concerned that psychologists do not use random samples in all their research and also why this worry is often unfounded. Finally, we have seen that a legitimate concern, the college sophomore problem, is sometimes overstated, particularly by those who are unfamiliar with the full range of activities and the diverse types of research that go on in psychology (see Chapter 1).

Nevertheless, psychologists should always be concerned that their experimental conclusions not rely too heavily on any one method or particular subject population. The next chapter deals with this very point. Indeed, some areas of psychology *are* plagued by a college sophomore problem (Jaffe, 2005; Peterson, 2001; Wintre, North, & Sugar, 2001). Cross-cultural psychology, an antidote to the college sophomore problem, is a very underdeveloped field. However, there is reason for optimism because self-criticism is valued highly by research psychologists (see Chapter 12; Baumeister, Vohs, & Funder, 2007; Henriques, 2004, 2005; Jaffe, 2005; Mischel, 2008; Rozin, 2006, 2007). In fact, there are many psychologists who are well known because they have made a career of criticizing the field (Leary, 2001; Robinson, 2001). Not a year goes by without many articles in scientific journals warning psychologists of flaws in their methods and pointing out the college sophomore problem. The latter has been an issue of great concern within psychology, and no psychologist is unaware of it. So, although we should not ignore the issue, we must also keep it in perspective.

Summary

Some psychological research is applied work in which the goal is to relate the results of the study directly to a particular situation. In such applied research, in which the results are intended to be extrapolated directly to a naturalistic situation, questions of the randomness of the sample and the representativeness of the conditions are important because the findings of the study are going to be applied directly. However, most psychological research is not of this type. It is basic research designed to test theories of the underlying mechanisms that influence behavior. In most basic research, the findings are applied only indirectly through modifications in a theory that will at some later point be applied to some practical problem. In basic research of this type, random sampling of subjects and representative situations are not an issue because the emphasis is on testing the universal prediction of a theory. In fact, artificial situations are deliberately constructed in theory-testing basic research because (as described in the previous chapter) they help to isolate the critical variable for study and to control extraneous variables. Thus, the fact that psychology experiments are "not like real life" is a strength rather than a weakness.

CHAPTER 8

Avoiding the Einstein Syndrome: The Importance of Converging Evidence

"Biological Experiment Reveals the Key to Life," "New Breakthrough in Mind Control," "California Scientist Discovers How to Postpone Death"—as you can see, it is not difficult to parody the "breakthrough" headlines of the tabloid press and electronic media. Because such headlines regularly come from the most irresponsible quarters of the media, it should not be surprising that most scientists recommend that they be approached with skepticism. The purpose of this chapter, though, is not only to warn against the spread of misinformation via exaggeration or to caution that the source must be considered when evaluating reports of scientific advances. In this chapter, we also want to develop a more complex view of the scientific process than was presented in earlier chapters. We shall do this by elaborating on the ideas of systematic empiricism and public knowledge that were introduced in Chapter 1.

The breakthrough headlines in the media obscure an understanding of psychology and other sciences in many ways. One particular misunderstanding that arises from breakthrough headlines is the implication that all problems in science are solved when a single, crucial experiment completely decides the issue, or that theoretical advance is the result of a single critical insight that overturns all previous knowledge. Such a view of scientific progress fits in nicely with the operation of the news media, in which history is tracked by presenting separate, disconnected events in bite-sized units. It is also a convenient format for the Hollywood entertainment industry, where events must have beginnings and satisfying endings that resolve ambiguity. However, this is a gross caricature of scientific progress and, if taken too seriously, leads to misconceptions about scientific advance and impairs the ability to evaluate the extent of scientific knowledge concerning a given issue. In this chapter, we will discuss two principles of science—the connectivity principle and the principle of converging evidence—that describe scientific progress much more accurately than the breakthrough model.

The Connectivity Principle

In denying the validity of the "great-leap" or crucial-experiment model of all scientific progress, we do not wish to argue that such critical experiments and theoretical advances never occur. On the contrary, some of the most famous examples in the history of science represent just such occurrences. The development of the theory of relativity by Albert Einstein is by far the most well known. Here, a reconceptualization of such fundamental concepts as space, time, and matter was achieved by a series of remarkable theoretical insights.

However, the monumental nature of Einstein's achievement has made it the dominant model of scientific progress in the public's mind. This dominance is perpetuated because it fits in nicely with the implicit "script" that the media use to report most news events. More nonsense has been written about, and more unwarranted conclusions have been drawn from, relativity theory than perhaps any other idea in all of history (no, Einstein did *not* prove that "everything is relative"—see Holton, 1996; Randall, 2005). Of course, our purpose is not to deal with all of these fallacies here. There is one, however, that will throw light on our later discussions of theory evaluation in psychology.

The reconceptualization of ideas about the physical universe contained in Einstein's theories is so fundamental that popular writing often treats it as if it were similar to conceptual changes in the arts (a minor poet is reevaluated and emerges with the status of a genius; an artistic school is declared dead). Such presentations ignore a basic difference between conceptual change in the arts and in the sciences.

Conceptual change in science obeys a principle of *connectivity* that is absent or, at least, severely limited in the arts (see Bronowski, 1977; Dobzhansky, 1973; Haack, 2007). That is, a new theory in science must make contact with previously established empirical facts. To be considered an advance, it must not only explain new facts but also account for old ones. The theory may explain old facts in a way quite different from that of a previous theory, but explain them it must. This requirement ensures the cumulative progress of science. Genuine progress does not occur unless the realm of our explanatory power has been widened. If a new theory accounts for some new facts but fails to account for a host of old ones, it will not be considered a complete advance over the old theories and, thus, will not immediately replace them. Instead, the old and new theories will exist as contending theories until a new synthesis is achieved.

Despite the startling reconceptualizations in Einstein's theories (clocks in motion running slower, mass increasing with velocity, and so on), they did maintain the principle of connectivity. In rendering Newtonian mechanics obsolete, Einstein's theories did not negate or render meaningless the facts about motion on which Newton's ideas were based. On the contrary, at low velocities the two theories make essentially the same predictions. Einstein's conceptualization is superior because it accounts for a wide variety of new, sometimes surprising, phenomena that Newtonian mechanics cannot accommodate. Thus, even Einstein's theories, some of the most startlingly new and fundamental reconceptualizations in the history of science, maintain the principle of connectivity.

A Consumer's Rule: Beware of Violations of Connectivity

The breakthrough model of scientific progress—what we might call the Einstein syndrome—leads us astray by implying that new discoveries violate the principle of connectivity. This implication is dangerous because, when the principle of connectivity is abandoned, the main beneficiaries are the purveyors of pseudoscience and bogus theories. Such theories derive part of their appeal and much of their publicity from the fact that they are said to be startlingly new. "After all, wasn't relativity new in its day?" is usually the tactic used to justify novelty as a virtue. Of course, the data previously accumulated in the field that the pseudoscientists wish to enter would seem to be a major obstacle. Actually, however, it presents only a minor inconvenience because two powerful strategies are available to dispose of it. One strategy that we have already discussed (see Chapter 2) is to explain the previous data by making the theory unfalsifiable and, hence, useless.

The second strategy is to dismiss previous data by declaring them irrelevant. This dismissal is usually accomplished by emphasizing what a radical departure the new theory represents. The phrases "new conception of reality" and "radical new departure" are frequently used. The real sleight of hand, though, occurs in the next step of the process. The new theory is deemed so radical that experimental evidence derived from the testing of other theories is declared irrelevant. Only data that can be conceptualized within the framework of the new theory are to be considered; that is, the principle of connectivity is explicitly broken. Obviously, because the theory is so new, such data are said not yet to exist. And there you have it: a rich environment for the growth of pseudoscience. The old, "irrelevant" data are gone, and the new, relevant data do not exist. The scam is easily perpetrated because the Einstein syndrome obscures the principle of connectivity, the importance of which is ironically illustrated by Einstein's theories themselves.

University of California paleontologist Kevin Padian provides another example of how the nature of science is misunderstood by the public when people fail to appreciate the importance of the connectivity principle. Referring to the decision of the Kansas Board of Education to remove mention of evolution from its required curriculum, Padian pointed out that "we are talking about a complete misunderstanding of how the sciences are integrated. . . . It's so absurd to pretend that you can rope off one part of science—especially one such as evolution, which is the central organizing theory of biology—and think that it won't have ramifications" (Carpenter, 1999, p. 117). Philosopher of biology Michael Ruse (2008) notes that evolutionary theory displays connectivity with such disparate areas of science as paleontology, embryology, morphology, biogeography, neuroscience, and others. Likewise, Shermer (1997) points out that "if the universe and Earth are only about ten thousand years old, then the modern sciences of cosmology, astronomy, physics, chemistry, geology, paleontology, paleoanthropology, and early human history are all invalid" (p. 143). Stephen J. Gould, the noted science writer and paleontologist, agreed when he noted that "teaching biology without evolution is like teaching English but making grammar optional" (Wright, 1999, p. 56).

Ruse (1999) illustrates an example of Darwin himself using the connectivity principle and abandoning an idea when it failed to display the necessary continuity with the rest of science. The example concerns Darwin's search for a mechanism of heredity to go with his theory of natural selection. Darwin tried to formulate a theory of so-called pangenesis, "in which little gemmules, given off by all of the body parts, circulate around the body and eventually collect in the sex organs, from where they are ready to start the next generation" (p. 64). One problem was that this theory did not cohere with cell theory. Second, Darwin could not explain how the gemmules were transported because transfusion experiments had already proven that it could not be via the blood. For these and other reasons pangenesis faded from science "because it did not cohere with the rest of biology" (p. 64).

It is likewise with psychology. A new theory that denied the existence of classical and operant conditioning would never develop in psychology because it would not connect with what else is known in behavioral science. Recall the discussion of facilitated communication in Chapter 6. It is suspect as a "cure" for the language problems of autism because it breaks the principle of connectivity—if that treatment worked, it would require that we overturn basic knowledge in fields as diverse as neurology, genetics, and cognitive psychology. This hypothesized cure shows no connectivity with the rest of science. It is likewise with creationist arguments against evolution. Creationism shows no connectivity with anything else in science—in biology, geology, ecology, chemistry, and genetics. By contrast, evolution shows extreme connectivity with all the other sciences. As biologist Sean Carroll (2005) notes, "evolution is much more than just a topic in biology, it is the foundation of the entire discipline. Biology without evolution is like physics without gravity" (p. 52).

Consider an example from psychology. Imagine two treatments have been developed to remediate the problems of children with extreme reading difficulties. No direct empirical tests of efficacy have been carried out using either treatment. The first, Treatment A, is a training program to facilitate the awareness of the segmental nature of language at the phonological level. The second, Treatment B, involves giving children training in vestibular sensitivity by having them walk on balance beams while blindfolded. Treatments A and B are equal in one respect—neither has had a direct empirical test of its efficacy, which reflects badly on both. Nevertheless, one of the treatments has the edge when it comes to the principle of connectivity. Treatment A makes contact with a broad consensus in the research literature that children with extraordinary reading difficulties are hampered because of insufficiently developed awareness of the segmental structure of language (Snowling & Hulme, 2005; Vellutino et al., 2004). Treatment B is not connected to any corresponding research literature consensus. This difference in connectivity dictates that Treatment A is a better choice, even though neither has been directly tested.

The "Great-Leap" Model Versus the Gradual-Synthesis Model

The tendency to view the Einsteinian revolution as typical of what science is tempts us to think that all scientific advances occur in giant leaps. The problem is that people tend to generalize such examples into a view of the way all scientific progress *should* take place. In fact, many areas in science have advanced not by single, sudden breakthroughs but by series of fits and starts that are less easy to characterize.

There is a degree of fuzziness in the scientific endeavor that most of the public is unaware of. Experiments rarely completely decide a given issue, supporting one theory and ruling out all others. New theories are rarely clearly superior to all previously existing competing conceptualizations. Issues are most often decided not by a critical experiment, as movies about science imply, but when the community of scientists gradually begins to agree that the preponderance of evidence supports one alternative theory rather than another. The evidence that scientists evaluate is not the data from a single experiment that has finally been designed in the perfect way. Instead, scientists most often must evaluate data from literally dozens of experiments, each containing some flaws but providing part of the answer. This alternative model of scientific progress has been obscured because the Einstein syndrome creates in the public a tendency to think of all science by reference to physics, to which the great-leap model of scientific progress is perhaps most applicable.

Consider the rapid advances in genetics and molecular biology that have occurred in the last hundred years. These advances have occurred not because one giant, Einstein, came onto the scene at the key moment to set everything straight. Instead, dozens of different insights based on hundreds of flawed experiments have contributed to the modern synthesis in biology. These advances occurred not by the instantaneous recognition of a major conceptual innovation, but by long, drawn-out haggling over alternative explanations, each of which had partial support. It took over 10 years of inconclusive experimentation, along with much theoretical speculation, argument, and criticism, for scientists to change their view about whether genes were made of protein or nucleic acid. The consensus of opinion changed, but not in one great leap.

Ernest Rutherford, discoverer of the atom's nucleus, stressed that "Scientists are not dependent on the ideas of a single person, but on the combined wisdom of thousands" (Holton & Roller, 1958, p. 166). Rutherford's point emphasizes another consumer rule for separating scientific from pseudoscientific claims. Science—a cumulative endeavor that respects the principle of connectivity—is characterized by the participation of many individuals, whose contributions are judged by the extent to which they further our understanding of nature. No single individual can dominate discourse simply by virtue of his or her status. Science rejects claims of "special knowledge" available to only a few select individuals. This rejection, of course, follows from our discussion of the public nature of science in Chapter 1. By contrast, pseudosciences often claim that certain authorities or investigators have a "special" access to the truth.

We have presented two ideas here that provide a useful context for understanding the discipline of psychology. First, no experiment in science is perfectly designed. There is a degree of ambiguity in the interpretation of the data from any one experiment. Scientists often evaluate theories not by waiting for the ideal or crucial experiment to appear, but by assessing the overall trends in a large number of partially flawed experiments. Second, many sciences have progressed even though they are without an Einstein. Their progress has occurred by fits and starts, rather than by discrete stages of grand Einsteinian syntheses. Also like psychology, many other sciences are characterized instead by growing mosaics of knowledge that lack a single integrating theme.

Converging Evidence: Progress Despite Flaws

The previous discussion has led to a principle of evidence evaluation of much importance in psychology. This idea is sometimes called the *principle of converging evidence* (or *converging operations*). Scientists and those who apply scientific knowledge must often make a judgment about where the preponderance of evidence points. When this is the case, the principle of converging evidence is an important tool. The principle of converging evidence is also a very useful tool for the lay consumer of scientific information and is particularly useful in evaluating psychological claims. Although a full technical discussion of the idea of converging evidence would soon take us far afield, the aspects most useful in the practical application of the concept are actually easy to understand. We will explore two ways of expressing the principle, one in terms of the logic of flawed experiments and the other in terms of theory testing.

There are always a number of ways in which an experiment can go wrong (or become *confounded*, to use the technical term). However, a scientist with much experience in working on a particular problem usually has a good idea of what the most likely confounding factors are. Thus, when surveying the research evidence, scientists are usually aware of the critical flaws in each experiment. The idea of converging evidence, then, tells us to examine the pattern of flaws running through the research literature because the nature of this pattern can either support or undermine the conclusions that we wish to draw.

For example, suppose the findings from a number of different experiments were largely consistent in supporting a particular conclusion. Given the imperfect nature of experiments, we would go on to evaluate the extent and nature of the flaws in these studies. If all the experiments were flawed in a similar way, this circumstance would undermine confidence in the conclusions drawn from them because the consistency of the outcome may simply have resulted from a particular flaw that all the experiments shared. On the other hand, if all the experiments were flawed in different ways, our confidence in the conclusions would be increased because it is less likely that the consistency in the results was due to a contaminating factor that confounded all the experiments. As Anderson and Anderson (1996) noted, "Different methods are likely to involve different assumptions. When a conceptual hypothesis survives many potential falsifications based on different sets of assumptions, we have a robust effect" (p. 742).

Each experiment helps to correct errors in the design of other experiments and is itself bolstered by other studies that examine its flaws. When evidence from a wide range of experiments, each flawed in a somewhat different way or carried out with techniques of differing strengths and weaknesses, points in a similar direction, then the evidence has converged. A reasonably strong conclusion is justified even though no one experiment was perfectly designed. Thus, the principle of converging evidence urges us to base conclusions on data that arise from a number of slightly different experimental sources. The principle allows us to draw stronger conclusions because consistency that has been demonstrated in such a context is less likely to have arisen from the peculiarities of a single type of experimental procedure.

The principle of converging evidence can also be stated in terms of theory testing. Research is highly convergent when a series of experiments consistently supports a given theory while collectively eliminating the most important competing explanations. Although no single experiment can rule out all alternative explanations, taken collectively a series of partially diagnostic experiments can lead, if the data patterns line up in a certain way, to a strong conclusion.

For example, suppose that five different theoretical accounts (call them A, B, C, D, and E) of a given set of phenomena exist at one time and are investigated in a series of experiments. Suppose that one experiment represents a strong test of theories A, B, and C, and that the data largely refute theories A and B and support C. Imagine also that another experiment is a particularly strong test of theories C, D, and E, and that the data largely refute theories D and E and support C. In such a situation, we would have strong converging evidence for theory C. Not only do we have data supportive of theory C, but we have data that contradict its major competitors. Note that no one experiment tests all the theories, but taken together, the entire set of experiments allows a strong inference. The situation might be depicted like this:

	Theory A	Theory B	Theory C	Theory D	Theory E
Experiment 1	refuted	refuted	supported	untested	untested
Experiment 2	untested	untested	supported	refuted	refuted

	Theory A	Theory B	Theory C	Theory D	Theory E
Overall Conclusion	refuted	refuted	supported	refuted	refuted

By contrast, if *both* experiments represented strong tests of B, C, and E, and the data of both experiments strongly supported C and refuted B and E, the overall support for theory C would be less strong than in our previous example. The reason is that, although data supporting theory C have been generated, there is no strong evidence ruling out two viable alternative theories (A and D). The situation would be something like the following:

	Theory A	Theory B	Theory C	Theory D	Theory E
Experiment 1	untested	refuted	supported	untested	refuted
Experiment 2	untested	refuted	supported	untested	refuted

	Theory A	Theory B	Theory C	Theory D	Theory E
Overall Conclusion	untested	refuted	supported	untested	refuted

Thus, research is highly convergent when a series of experiments consistently supports a given theory while collectively eliminating the most important competing explanations. Although no single experiment can rule out all alternative explanations, taken collectively a series of partially diagnostic experiments can lead to a strong conclusion if the data converge in the manner of our first example.

Finally, the introduction of the idea of converging evidence allows us to dispel a misconception that may have been fostered by our oversimplified discussion of falsifiability in Chapter 2. That discussion may have seemed to imply that a theory is falsified when the first piece of evidence that disconfirms it comes along. This is not the case, however. Just as theories are confirmed by converging evidence, they are also disconfirmed by converging results.

Converging Evidence in Psychology

The reason for stressing the importance of convergence is that conclusions in psychology are often based on the principle of converging evidence. There is certainly nothing unique or unusual about this fact (conclusions in many other sciences rest not on single, definitive experimental proofs, but on the confluence of dozens of fuzzy experiments). But there are reasons that this might be especially true of psychology. Experiments in psychology are usually of fairly low diagnosticity. That is, the data that support a given theory usually rule out only a small set of alternative explanations, leaving many additional theories as viable candidates. As a result, strong conclusions are usually possible only after data from a very large number of studies have been collected and compared.

It should not be surprising that experiments in psychology have a high fuzzy factor, given the enormous complexity of the problems concerning behavior. Better public understanding will come about if psychologists openly acknowledge this fact and then take pains to explain just what follows from it. Psychologists should admit that, although a science of psychology exists and is progressing, progress is slow, and our conclusions come only after a sometimes excruciatingly long period of research amalgamation and debate. Media claims of breakthroughs should always engender skepticism, but this is especially true of psychological claims.

In psychology we have to walk a very fine line. For example, we must resist the temptation to regard a particular psychological hypothesis as "proven" when the evidence surrounding it is still ambiguous. This skeptical attitude has been reinforced in several chapters of this book. The cautions against inferring causation from correlation and against accepting testimonial evidence have served as examples. At the same time, we should not overreact to the incompleteness of knowledge and the tentativeness of conclusions by doubting whether firm conclusions in psychology will ever be reached. Nor should we be tempted by the irrational claim that psychology cannot be a science. From this standpoint, the principle of converging evidence can be viewed as a counterweight to the warnings against overinterpreting tentative knowledge. Convergence allows us to reach many reasonably strong conclusions despite the flaws in all psychological research.

The best way to see the power of the principle of converging evidence is to examine some areas in psychology where conclusions have been reached by an application of the principle. Let's consider an example.

A research problem that illustrates the importance of the principle of converging evidence is the question of whether exposure to violent television programming increases children's tendencies toward aggressive behavior. There is now a scientific consensus on this issue: The viewing of violent programming (on television, in movies, or in streaming video) does appear to increase the probability that children will engage in aggressive behavior. The effect is not extremely large, but it is real. Again, the confidence that scientists have in this conclusion derives not from a single definitive study, but from the convergence of the results of dozens of different investigations (e.g., Anderson, Berkowitz, Donnerstein, Huesmann, Johnson, Linz, Malamuth, & Wartella, 2003; Anderson & Huesmann, 2005; Bushman & Anderson, 2002; Carnagey, Anderson, & Bartholow, 2007; Feshbach & Tangney, 2008). This research conclusion holds for violent video games as well as television and movies (Anderson & Bushman, 2001; Carnagey et al., 2007; Sheese & Graziano, 2005). The general research designs, subject populations, and specific techniques used in these investigations differed widely, and as should now be clear, these differences are a strength of the research in this area, not a weakness.

Television network executives and video game industry executives, naturally resistant to hard evidence of the negative effects of their industry on children, have carried on a campaign of misinformation that capitalizes on the public's failure to realize that research conclusions are based on the convergence of many studies rather than on a single critical demonstration that decides the issue. The television networks continually single out individual studies for criticism and imply that the general conclusion is undermined by the fact that each study has demonstrated flaws. Although social science researchers may contest particular criticisms of a specific study, it is not commonly recognized that researchers often candidly admit the flaws in a given study. The critical difference is that researchers reject the implication that admitting a flaw in a given study undermines the general scientific consensus on the effects of televised violence on aggressive behavior. The reason is that the general conclusion derives from a convergence. Research without the specific flaws of the study in question has produced results pointing in the same direction. This research may itself have problems, but other studies have corrected for these and have also produced similar results.

For example, very early in the investigation of this issue, evidence of the correlation between the amount of violent programming viewed and aggressive behavior in children was uncovered. It was correctly pointed out that this correlational evidence did not justify a causal conclusion. Perhaps a third variable was responsible for the association, or perhaps more aggressive children chose to watch more violent programming (the directionality problem).

But the conclusion of the scientific community is not based on this correlational evidence alone. There are more complex correlational techniques than the simple measurement of the association between two variables, and these correlational techniques allow some tentative conclusions about causality (one, that of partial correlation, was mentioned in Chapter 5). One of these techniques involves the use of a longitudinal design in which measurements of the same two variables—here, television violence and aggression—are taken at two different times. Certain correlational patterns suggest causal connections. Studies of this type have been conducted, and the pattern of results suggested that viewing televised violence did tend to increase the probability of engaging in aggressive behavior later in life.

Again, it is not unreasonable to counter that these longitudinal correlational techniques are controversial, because they are. The important point is that the conclusion of a causal connection between televised violence and aggressive behavior does not depend entirely on correlational evidence, either simple or complex, because numerous laboratory studies have been conducted in which the amount of televised violence was manipulated rather than merely assessed. In Chapter 6, we discussed how the manipulation of a variable, used in conjunction with other experimental controls such as random assignment, prevents the interpretation problems that surround most correlational studies. If two groups of children, experimentally equated on all other variables, show different levels of aggressive behavior, and if the only difference between the two is that one group viewed violent programming and one did not, then we are correct in inferring that the manipulated variable (televised violence—the independent variable) caused the changes in the outcome variable (aggressive behavior—the dependent variable). This result has occurred in the majority of studies.

These studies have prompted some to raise the "it's-not-real-life" argument discussed in the previous chapter and to use the argument in the fallacious way discussed in that chapter. In any case, the results on the effects of television violence are not peculiar to a certain group of children because these results have been replicated in different regions of the United States and in several countries around the world. The specific laboratory setup and the specific programs used as stimuli have varied from investigation to investigation, yet the results have held up.

Importantly, the same conclusions have been drawn from studies conducted in the field rather than in the laboratory. A design known as the *field experiment* has been used to investigate the televised-violence/aggressive-behavior issue. The existence of this type of design reminds us to avoid assuming a necessary link between experimental design and experimental setting. People sometimes think that studies that manipulate variables are conducted only in laboratories and that correlational studies are conducted only in the field. This assumption is incorrect. Correlational studies are often conducted in laboratories, and variables are often manipulated in nonlaboratory settings. Although they sometimes require considerable ingenuity to design, field experiments (several of which were mentioned in Chapter 6), in which variables are manipulated in nonlaboratory settings, are becoming more common in psychology.

For example, a recent field experiment tested the so-called "broken windows" theory of crime incidence (Keizer, Lindenberg, & Steg, 2008). The theory posits that seemingly incidental indicators of social disorder (broken windows, graffiti, etc.) can actually increase crime by sending signals that transgressions are the norm in a particular area. Kees Keizer and colleagues created two conditions in alleys where bikes were parked. In the control condition, a sign prohibiting graffiti was put in an alley with no graffiti. In the experimental condition, a sign prohibiting graffiti was put in an alley with lots of graffiti on the walls. A paper flyer was put on the handlebars of each bike in the alley. Keizer and colleagues found that 69 percent of the subjects in the experimental group littered with their flyer (threw it on the ground) compared with only 33 percent in the control group.

Of course, field experiments themselves have weaknesses, but many of these weaknesses are the strengths of other types of investigation. In summary, the evidence linking the viewing of televised violence to increased probabilities of aggressive behavior in children does not rest only on the outcome of one particular study or even one generic type of study.

The situation is analogous to the relationship between smoking and lung cancer. Smokers are 15 times more likely to die from lung cancer than nonsmokers (Gigerenzer et al., 2007). Cigarette company executives often attempted to mislead the public by implying that the conclusion that smoking causes lung cancer rested on some specific study, which they would then go on to criticize (Offit, 2008). Instead, the conclusion is strongly supported by a wealth of converging evidence. The convergence of data from several different types of research is quite strong and will not be changed substantially by the criticism of one study.

Actually it is appropriate to discuss here a medical problem like the causes of lung cancer. Most issues in medical diagnosis and treatment are decided by an amalgamation of converging evidence from many different types of investigations. For example, medical science is confident of a conclusion when the results of epidemiological studies (field studies of humans in which disease incidence is correlated with many environmental and demographic factors), highly controlled laboratory studies using animals, and clinical trials with human patients all converge. When the results of all these types of investigation point to a similar conclusion, medical science feels assured of the conclusion, and physicians feel confident in basing their treatment on the evidence.

However, each of the three different types of investigation has its drawbacks. Epidemiological studies are always correlational, and the possibility of spurious links between variables is high. Laboratory studies can be highly controlled, but the subjects are often animals rather than humans. Clinical trials in a hospital setting use human subjects in a real treatment context, but there are many problems of control because of placebo effects and the expectations of the medical treatment team that deals with the patients. Despite the problems in each type of investigation, medical researchers are justified in drawing strong conclusions when the data from all the different methods converge strongly, as in the case of smoking and lung cancer. Just such a convergence also justifies the conclusions that psychologists draw from the study of a behavioral problem like the effect of televised violence on aggressive behavior.

The principle of converging evidence is often a difficult one for the public to understand, however. For example, David Michaels (2008), an epidemiologist at George Washington University, describes a court case involving harm from toxic substances, *General Electric v. Joiner*, in which the judge found a flaw in each piece of scientific evidence presented and then proceeded to throw out the entire package of evidence. Michaels reminds us that "in the real world, scientists do not operate this way. They consider the strengths and weaknesses of each piece of evidence. It is entirely possible to draw a sound conclusion despite flaws or limitations in each and every test and study that constitute the evidence for that conclusion. This happens all the time" (p. 163).

Scientific Consensus

The problem of assessing the impact of televised violence is typical of how data finally accumulate to answer questions in psychology. Particularly in areas of pressing social concern, it is wise to remember that the answers to these problems emerge only slowly, after the amalgamation of the results from many different experiments. They are unlikely to be solved by a single breakthrough study. To put things in the form of a simple rule, when evaluating empirical evidence in the field of psychology, think in terms of *scientific consensus* rather than *breakthrough*—in terms of *gradual synthesis* rather than *great leap*.

The usefulness of applying the "consensus-rather-than-breakthrough" rule is illustrated by the controversy surrounding the effects of early-childhood compensatory-education programs. In the late 1960s and early 1970s, when debate over the efficacy of President Lyndon B. Johnson's Great Society programs was raging, the public was treated to headlines such as "Early Intervention Raises IQs by Thirty Points" and "Head Start a Failure." What was the concerned layperson to make of such contradictory information? In this case, the consensus-rather-than-breakthrough rule would clearly have provided some assistance, because it would suggest that both headlines were probably premature. In fact, it took another decade of research to arrive at a scientific consensus on this important social issue.

The consensus arose not from the results of a single critical study, but when a group of Cornell University researchers (Lazar, Darlington, Murray, Royce, & Sniper, 1982) combined the data from hundreds of subjects in 11 different early-education projects conducted in the 1960s and early 1970s. Although the results of individual programs were sometimes hard to interpret, the overall results were reasonably clear-cut when they were pooled. Brief programs of early-educational intervention did not routinely lead to IQ gains of 30 points. On the other hand, Head Start and programs like it were definitely not failures. Programs of early-education intervention did have concrete and replicable effects on the later educational histories of the children who had participated in them. Such children were less likely to be held back a grade, were less likely to be assigned to special-education classes, had more positive attitudes toward school and school achievement, and showed lasting academic achievement gains (see also Lee, Brooks-Gunn, Schnur, & Liaw, 1990; Ramey, 1999).

Scientific conclusions derive from a consensus based on a convergence of many studies rather than from a single definitive study. The failure to appreciate this fact impeded the public's understanding of the evidence that human activity is a contributor to global warming (Begley, 2007; Jordan, 2007; Nijhuis, 2008). Many political groups did not like the evidence that human energy consumption, gasoline usage, and carbon emission in the economy was having negative environmental effects. The evidence ran counter to their political agendas. Many of these groups would then attack individual studies and conduct a media campaign that gave their attacks wide publicity. They wished to create the impression that because a single study was in dispute, there was a great scientific controversy about the role of human activity in global warming (Manjoo, 2008; Michaels, 2008; Nijhuis, 2008). In fact, there was no great controversy, because the conclusion did not rest on a single study. There were over 900 global climate-change papers published between 1993 and 2003, and they overwhelmingly converged on the conclusion that human activity was involved in global warming (Oreskes, 2004). No single study was definitive in establishing the conclusion so, obviously, undermining a single study would not change the conclusion at all. Nevertheless, the political groups wished to create doubt among the public—and in this they were successful. In 2006, over 60 percent of the public thought that scientists were still debating the conclusion when it had long since been settled.

Unfortunately, the media, with their "he-said, she-said" orientation, played right into the hands of the global-warming deniers, because the media's "one-side, otherside" reporting suggested that there was great controversy when there was not. Late in the day, several media outlets stepped in to stop political groups from exploiting the public's failure to understand that scientific conclusions derive from convergence and consensus. On the cover of its August 13, 2007 issue, *Newsweek* magazine printed the large title "Global Warming is a Hoax" with an asterisk. In the lower left part of the cover, the asterisk explained the joke: "Or so claim well-funded naysayers who still reject the overwhelming evidence of climate change." The magazine contained a large feature article on, what they termed "the denial machine"—the political groups who had successfully convinced the public that there was doubt about global warming because a single study was flawed. The article noted that "There was an extraordinary campaign by the denial machine to find and hire scientists to sow dissent and make it appear that the research community was deeply divided" (Begley, 2007, p. 25). A former chief of the Environmental Protection Agency noted that "driven by notions of fairness and objectivity, the press qualified every mention of human influence on climate change with 'some scientists believe,' where the reality is that the vast preponderance of scientific opinion accepts that human-caused [greenhouse] emissions are contributing to warming . . . the pursuit of balance has not done justice to the science" (p. 25).

Science writers Barbara Kantrowitz and Claudia Kalb (2006) warn that the proliferation of media reports of medical studies is good in one sense but may have the potential to backfire and result in *less* public understanding if the public is not schooled in the convergence principle. They argue that "all this coverage would be fine, perhaps even beneficial, if medical progress were as straightforward as it's often reported. Unfortunately, it's not. Headlines and sound bites can't capture the complexity of research. Science works in small steps, and failure and mistakes are an integral part of the process" (p. 47). They quote leading cancer researcher Judah Folkman as reminding the public that "most science isn't a breakthrough. It's incremental, brick by brick" (p. 47).

Methods and the Convergence Principle

The convergence principle also implies that we should expect many different methods to be used in all psychological research areas. A relative balance among the methodologies used to arrive at a given conclusion is desirable because the various classes of research techniques have different strengths and weaknesses. Psychology has long been criticized for relying too heavily on laboratory-based experimental techniques. The validity of this criticism depends on the specific research area that is the focus of discussion. Nevertheless, an unmistakable trend in recent years has been to expand the variety of methods used in all areas of psychology. For example, social psychologists, who have perhaps received the most criticism for overreliance on laboratory techniques, have turned to increasingly imaginative field designs in search of converging evidence to support their theories.

The work of psychologists Bibb Latane and John Darley provides a good example. These investigators are well known for their work on what has been termed the *unresponsive bystander phenomenon*, that is, the failure of some people to respond with help when observing another individual in an emergency situation. Latane and Darley (1970) documented the fact that, in many emergency situations, the probability that a given bystander will respond with help is lower when other bystanders are present.

However, the investigators were well aware that their conclusions would be tenuous if they were based only on the responses of individuals who witnessed emergencies after reporting to a laboratory to participate in an experiment. Therefore, in an interesting study, Latane and Darley attempted to observe the phenomenon in another setting. They found a cooperative liquor store that agreed to have fake robberies occur in the store 96 different times. While the cashier was in the back of the store getting some beer for a "customer," who was actually an accomplice of the experimenter, the "customer" walked out the front door with a case of beer. This was done in the view of either one or two real customers who were at the checkout counter. The cashier then came back and asked the customers, "Hey, what happened to that man who was in here? Did you see him leave?" thus giving the customers a chance to report the theft. Consistent with the laboratory results, the presence of another individual inhibited the tendency to report the theft.

Many of the principles of probabilistic decision making to be discussed in Chapter 10 originated in the laboratory but have also been tested in the field. For example, researchers have examined the way that physicians, stock-brokers, jurors, economists, and gamblers reason probabilistically in their environments (Gilovich, Griffin, & Kahneman, 2002; Hilton, 2003; Thaler & Sunstein, 2008; Zweig, 2008). Principles of behavioral decision theory have been used in such applied situations as deciding the optimal type of bullet to be used by the Denver Police Department and deciding whether to build a dam in central Arizona (Hammond, Harvey, & Hastie, 1992).

The convergence of laboratory and nonlaboratory results has also characterized several areas of educational psychology. For example, both laboratory studies and field studies of different curricula have indicated that early phonics instruction facilitates the acquisition of reading skill (Ehri, Nunes, Stahl, & Willows, 2001; Pressley, 2005; Snowling & Hulme, 2005; Stanovich, 2000; Vellutino et al., 2004).

In summary, current research in psychology uses a wide variety of experimental techniques and settings. Although research on many problems has sometimes been overly focused on the use of certain techniques, the distribution of research methods in psychology is now much more balanced than it was just a few years ago.

The Progression to More Powerful Methods

Research on a particular problem often proceeds from weaker methods to ones that allow more powerful conclusions to be drawn. For example, interest in a particular hypothesis may originally stem from a particular case study of unusual interest. As we discussed in Chapter 4, this is the proper role of case studies: to suggest hypotheses for further study with more powerful techniques and to motivate scientists to apply more rigorous methods to a research problem. Thus, following the case studies, researchers undertake correlational investigations to verify whether the link between variables is real rather than the result of the peculiarities of a few case studies. If the correlational studies support the relationship between relevant variables, researchers will attempt experiments in which variables are manipulated in order to isolate a causal relationship between the variables. The progression, then, is from case studies, to correlational studies, to experiments with manipulated variables. Although this gradual progression toward more powerful research methods is not always followed in every research area (sometimes different types of investigations go on in parallel), the progression quite commonly occurs.

Discussing the idea of the progression through the more powerful research methods provides us with a chance to deal with a misconception that some readers may have derived from Chapter 5—that is, that correlational studies are not useful in science. It is true that, when a causal hypothesis is at issue, studies with true experimental manipulation are preferred. However, this does not mean that correlational studies cannot contribute to knowledge. First, many scientific hypotheses are stated in terms of correlation or lack of correlation, so that such studies are directly relevant to these hypotheses. Second, although correlation does not imply causation, causation does imply correlation. That is, although a correlational study cannot definitively prove a causal hypothesis, it may rule one out. Third, correlational studies are more useful than they may seem, because some of the recently developed complex correlational designs allow for some very limited causal inferences. We discussed in Chapter 5 the complex correlational technique of partial correlation, in which it is possible to test whether a particular third variable is accounting for a relationship.

Perhaps most important, however, some variables simply cannot be manipulated for ethical reasons (for instance, human malnutrition or physical disabilities). Other variables, such as birth order, sex, and age, are inherently correlational because they cannot be manipulated, and, therefore, the scientific knowledge concerning them must be based on correlational evidence. This circumstance, again, is not unique to psychology. Astronomers obviously cannot manipulate all the variables affecting the objects they study, yet they are able to arrive at conclusions.

An example of the evolution of research methods in health psychology is the work concerning the link between the type A behavior pattern and coronary heart disease (Chida & Hamer, 2008; Curtis & O'Keefe, 2002; Matthews, 2005; Smith, 2003; Suls & Bunde, 2005). The original observations that led to the development of the concept of the type A behavior pattern occurred when two cardiologists thought they noticed a pattern in the behavior of some of their coronary patients that included a sense of time urgency, free-floating hostility, and extremely competitive striving for achievement. Thus, the idea of the type A personality originated in a few case studies made by some observant physicians. These case studies suggested the concept, but they were not taken as definitive proof of the hypothesis that a particular type of behavior pattern is a partial cause of coronary heart disease. Proving the idea required more than just the existence of a few case studies. It involved decades of work by teams of cardiologists and psychologists.

The research quickly moved from merely accumulating case studies, which could never establish the truth of the hypothesis, to more powerful methods of investigation. Researchers developed and tested operational definitions of the type A concept. Large-scale epidemiological studies established a correlation between the presence of type A behavior and the incidence of coronary heart disease. The correlational work then became more sophisticated. Researchers used complex correlational techniques to track down potential third variables. The relation between type A behavior and heart attacks could have been spurious because the behavior pattern was also correlated with one of the other traditional risk factors (such as smoking, obesity, or serum cholesterol level). However, results showed that type A behavior was a significant independent predictor of heart attacks. When other variables were statistically partialed out, there was still a link between the type A behavior pattern and coronary heart disease.

Finally, researchers undertook experimental studies with manipulated variables to establish whether a causal relationship could be demonstrated. Some of the studies attempted to test models of the physiological mechanisms that affected the relationship and used animals as subjects—what some might call "not real life." Another experimental study used human subjects who had had a heart attack. These subjects were randomly assigned to one of two groups. One group received counseling designed to help them avoid traditional risky behavior such as smoking and eating fatty foods. The other group received this counseling and were also given a program designed to help them reduce their type A behavior. Three years later, there had been significantly fewer recurrent heart attacks among the patients given the type A behavior counseling.

In short, the evidence converged to support the hypothesis of the type A behavior pattern as a significant causal factor in coronary heart disease. The investigation of this problem provides a good example of how research gradually moves from interesting case studies, to correlational techniques, to more complex correlational techniques, and finally to studies in which variables are manipulated.

A final lesson we can draw from this example is that scientific concepts evolve, an issue first raised in Chapter 3 when we discussed operational definitions. Recent research seems to indicate that it is oversimplifying to talk about the connection between heart attacks and the type A behavior pattern *as a whole*. The reason is that only certain components of the pattern (particularly antagonistic hostility) appear to be linked to coronary heart disease (Chida & Hamer, 2008; Curtis & O'Keefe, 2002; Matthews, 2005; Suls & Bunde, 2005). Thus, we have an example of how science uncovers increasingly specific relationships as it progresses and how theoretical concepts become elaborated.

A Counsel Against Despair

One final implication of the convergence principle is that we should not despair when the initial results of studies on a problem appear to be contradictory. The process of evidence amalgamation in science is like a projector slowly bringing an unknown slide into focus. At first, the blur on the screen could represent just about anything. Then, as the slide is focused a bit more, many alternative hypotheses may be ruled out even though the image cannot be identified unambiguously. Finally, an identification can be made with great confidence. The early stages of the evidence amalgamation process are like the beginning of the focusing process. The ambiguous blur of the slide corresponds to contradictory data or to data that support many alternative hypotheses.

Thus, contradictory data obtained at the beginning of an investigation should not drive us to despair of ever finding the truth. Nor is such a situation unique to psychology. It also occurs in more mature sciences. Indeed, the public is usually unaware that contradictory data are obtained often in science. Such contradictory data are simply the result of our current inadequate understanding of the problem. The contradictions may be simply chance occurrences (something we will discuss at length in Chapter 11), or they may be due to subtle methodological differences between experiments.

Many other sciences have endured confusing periods of uncertainty before a consensus was achieved (Ioannidis, 2004; Simonton, 2004). Medical science certainly displays this pattern all the time. For example, research has confirmed that taking a daily baby aspirin helps prevent cardiovascular disease. However, research into aspirin's role as a cancer preventative has been extremely confusing, uncertain, and nonconverging. Aspirin fights inflammation by inhibiting substances known as cyclooxygenase, or COX, enzymes. Because COX enzymes also are involved in the formation of some cancerous tumors, it was thought that daily aspirin might also inhibit this effect. But actual research on this speculation has produced inconsistent results. Some researchers think that the inconsistency has to do with the fact that the optimal dosage level has not yet been found. Regardless of how this issue is finally resolved, it is illustrative of the uncertainty that often precedes the resolution of a scientific problem. Dr. Michael Thun, of the American Cancer Society, acknowledged the feeling of frustration that the public might have if they do not understand how science works and how conclusions only gradually emerge from a slow-developing convergence: "A general perspective that people have is, 'Why is it so difficult to get a clear answer on a pill that costs a few pennies and is available over-the-counter and taken by millions of people?'" (Associated Press, 2007). But it is difficult. Arriving at causal conclusions is not easy, as we have seen throughout this book. Psychology is not alone in having long periods of uncertainty that precede a firm conclusion.

Consider another example from medicine. Writer Malcolm Gladwell (1996) describes the evolution of thinking about the proper immediate treatment to give to victims of traumatic brain injury. He describes a victim in New York who was lucky enough to be treated by one of the world's leading experts, Dr. Jam Ghajar, who had tried to reorient the thinking of practitioners in this area of medicine. Gladwell describes how several years ago, when Ghajar and five other researchers had done a survey of trauma centers, they found that steroids were being given to over 75 percent of the coma patients even though it had repeatedly been shown that steroids were of no use in reducing intracranial pressure (and could potentially do harm). He noted,

> part of the problem is that in the field of neurosurgery, it has been difficult to reach hard, scientific conclusions about procedures and treatments. . . . The complexity and mystery of the brain has, moreover, led to a culture that rewards intuition, and has thus convinced each neurosurgeon that their own experience is as valid as anyone else's. (p. 39)

Speaking of his colleagues' views a few years ago, Ghajar noted, "It wasn't that the neurosurgeons were lazy, it was just that there was so much information out there it was confusing" (p. 39).

In short, just as in many areas of psychology, there was research out there, but it had not been focused and conceptualized in a way that allowed a convergence to be discerned. Thus, in 1994, Ghajar participated in a long series of meetings with several of his colleagues in which they attempted to synthesize the evidence in a way that would reveal any convergence. The meetings were sponsored by the Brain Trauma Foundation, and the researchers examined over 4,000 scientific papers on 14 aspects of brain injury management. The executive director of the Brain Trauma Foundation described how the neurosurgeons went about their task: "What they did was argue the evidence of the scientific documents, and as soon as someone said, 'It's been my experience,' everyone would say, 'Oh, no, that won't cut it. We want to know what the evidence is'" (Gladwell, 1996, p. 40). The final result proved to be fruitful:

> The group did find convergence in the literature and published a book laying out the scientific evidence and state-of-the-art treatment in every phase of brain-trauma care. The guidelines represent the first successful attempt by the neurosurgery community to come up with a standard treatment protocol, and if they are adopted by anything close to a majority of the country's trauma centers they could save more than ten thousand lives a year. (Gladwell, 1996, p. 40)

The guidelines are already being used to save lives, but interestingly, when Ghajar himself discusses this part of medical history, he stresses the value of converging evidence and the public nature of scientific knowledge (a principle from Chapter 1 of this book): "People want to personalize this. . . . I guess that's human nature. They want to say, 'It's Ghajar's protocol. He's a wonderful doctor.' But that's not it. These are standards developed according to the best available science. These are standards that everyone can use" (Gladwell, 1996, p. 40).

As is clear from this example, psychology is not the only science with research areas in which the findings are all over the map. There is no shortage of instances in other sciences in which reaching conclusions is difficult because of "fuzziness" in the data patterns. Gladwell (2004), in an article titled "The Picture Problem," discusses how people have difficulty understanding why the medical profession still has disagreements about the degree of benefit derived from mammograms. This is because a mammography picture seems so "concrete" to most people that they think it should be determinative. They fail to understand that human judgment is necessarily involved, and that mammography assessment and disease prediction are inherently probabilistic (Gigerenzer et al., 2007). Gladwell notes that "the picture promises certainty, and it cannot deliver on that promise. Even after forty years of research, there remains widespread disagreement over how much benefit women in the critical fifty-to-sixty-nine age bracket receive from breast X-rays, and further disagreement about whether there is enough evidence to justify regular mammography in women under fifty and over seventy" (p. 81). However, Gladwell, goes on to note that in this area of medicine—just as in psychology—knowledge can be useful even when it is not certain: "The answer is that mammograms do not have to be infallible to save lives. . . . Mammography isn't as a good as we'd like it to be. But we are still better off than we would be without it" (p. 81).

In psychology and many other sciences, the combining of evidence from disparate studies to form a conclusion is now being done more formally by the use of the statistical technique termed meta-analysis (Borenstein, Hedges, Higgins, & Rothstein, 2009). In a medical context, meta-analysis

> involves adding together the data from many clinical trials to create a single pool of data big enough to eliminate much of the statistical uncertainty that plagues individual trials. . . . The great virtue of meta-analysis is that clear findings can emerge from a group of studies whose findings are scattered all over the map. (Plotkin, 1996, p. 70)

The use of meta-analysis for determining the research validation of psychological conclusions is just the same as in medicine. The effects obtained when one experimental group is compared with another are expressed in a common statistical metric that allows comparison of effects across studies. The findings are then statistically amalgamated in some standard ways and a conclusion about differential effects is reached if the amalgamation process passes certain statistical criteria. In some cases, of course, no conclusion can be drawn with confidence, and the result of the meta-analysis is inconclusive.

More and more commentators are calling for a greater emphasis on meta-analysis as a way of dampening the contentious disputes about conflicting studies in the behavioral sciences. The method is useful for ending disputes that seem to be nothing more than a "he-said, she-said" debate. An emphasis on meta-analysis has often revealed that we actually have more stable and useful findings than is apparent from a perusal of the conflicts in our journals.

The National Reading Panel (2000; Ehri, Nunes, Stahl, & Willows, 2001) found just this in their meta-analysis of the evidence surrounding several issues in reading education. For example, they concluded that the results of a meta-analysis of the results of 38 different studies indicated "solid support for the conclusion that systematic phonics instruction makes a bigger contribution to children's growth in reading than alternative programs providing unsystematic or no phonics instruction" (p. 2–84). In another section of their report, the National Reading Panel reported that a meta-analysis of 52 studies of phonemic awareness training indicated that "teaching children to manipulate the sounds in language helps them learn to read. Across the various conditions of teaching, testing, and participant characteristics, the effect sizes were all significantly greater than chance and ranged from large to small, with the majority in the moderate range" (p. 2–5).

It is likewise in the domain of health psychology. Chida and Hamer (2008) meta-analyzed data from a whopping 281 studies relating the hostility and aggression aspects of the Type A behavior pattern to cardiovascular reactivity (heart rate and blood pressure) in order to establish that there was indeed a relationship. As another example, Currier, Neimeyer, and Berman (2008) meta-analyzed 61 controlled studies of psychotherapeutic interventions for bereaved persons. Their meta-analysis had a disappointing outcome, however. Psychotherapeutic intervention had an immediate effect after bereavement, but had no positive effect at follow-up.

A statement by a task force of the American Psychological Association (Wilkinson, 1999) on statistical methods in psychology journals provides an apt summary for this section. The task force stated that investigators should not "interpret a single study's results as having importance independent of the effects reported elsewhere in the relevant literature" (p. 602). Science progresses by convergence upon conclusions. The outcomes of one study can only be interpreted in the context of the present state of the convergence on the particular issue in question.

Summary

In this chapter, we have seen how the breakthrough model of scientific advance is a bad model for psychology and why the gradual-synthesis model provides a better framework for understanding how conclusions are reached in psychology. The principle of converging operations describes how research results are synthesized in psychology: No one experiment is definitive, but each helps us to rule out at least some alternative explanations and, thus, aids in the process of homing in on the truth. The use of a variety of different methods makes psychologists more confident that their conclusions rest on a solid empirical foundation. Finally, when conceptual change occurs, it adheres to the principle of connectivity: New theories not only must account for new scientific data but must also provide an explanation of the previously existing database.

CHAPTER 9

The Misguided Search for the "Magic Bullet": The Issue of Multiple Causation

In Chapter 8, we focused on the importance of converging operations and the need to progress to more powerful research methods in order to establish a single connection between variables. In this chapter, we go beyond a simple connection between two variables to highlight an important point: Behavior is multiply determined.

Any particular behavior is caused not by one variable but by a large number of different variables. To conclude that there is a significant causal connection between variable A and behavior B does not mean that variable A is the *only* cause of behavior B. For example, researchers have found a negative relationship between amount of television viewing and academic achievement, but they do not claim that the amount of television viewed is the *only* thing that determines academic achievement. That, of course, would be silly, because academic achievement is partially determined by a host of other variables (home environment, quality of schooling, and the like). In fact, television viewing is only a minor determinant of academic achievement when compared with these other factors. Similarly, the amount of television violence viewed by children is not the only reason that they may display aggressive behavior. It is one of many contributing factors.

But often people forget that behavior is multiply determined. They seem to want to find the so-called magic bullet—the *one* cause of the behavioral outcome that interests them. Psychologist Theodore Wachs (2000) uses as an example the way that people tried to explain the wave of school shootings that took place in the United States in 1998 and 1999. He points out that people argued that the causes involved were the easy availability of guns, low parental involvement with their children, information on the Internet,

145

violence on television and the movies, peer influences, and mental illness. Wachs noted that "rarely was the possibility considered that the increase in school shootings was the result of a convergence among a number of the above factors, and that any solution must go beyond dealing with a single potential cause" (p. x).

Like so many of the other principles discussed in this book, it is important to put the idea of multiple causes in perspective. On the one hand, this idea warns us not to overinterpret a single causal connection. The world is complicated, and the determinants of behavior are many and complex. Just because we have demonstrated a cause of behavior does not mean that we have uncovered the only cause or even the most important cause. To provide a thorough explanation of a particular behavior, researchers must study the influence of many different variables and amalgamate the results of these studies to give a complete picture of all the causal connections.

On the other hand, to say that a variable is only one of many determinants and that it explains only a small portion of the variability in a given behavior is not to say that the variable is unimportant. First, the relationship may have far-reaching theoretical implications. Second, the relationship may have practical applications, particularly if the variable can be controlled, as is the case with television violence, for example. Few would argue that a variable that could reduce the number of acts of physical violence by as much as 1 percent annually is not of enormous importance. In short, if the behavior in question is of great importance, then knowing how to control only a small proportion of it can be extremely useful.

Rosenthal (1990) provides an example of a study of heart attack survival in which a treatment accounted for less than 1 percent of the variability in the outcome, yet the results were considered so startlingly positive that the study was terminated prematurely for ethical considerations: The outcome of the experiment was considered so strong that it was deemed unethical to withhold the treatment from the placebo group. Likewise, any factor that could cut motor vehicle deaths by just 1 percent would be immensely important— it would save over 450 lives each year. Reducing the homicide rate by just 1 percent would save over 170 lives each year. In short, the fact that an outcome is determined by many different variables does not reduce the importance of any one variable that is causally related to the outcome—even if the variable accounts for only a small portion of the outcome.

The Concept of Interaction

The idea of multiple causation leads to an important concept that is often discussed at length in methodology texts, although we can only mention it here: A factor that influences behavior may have different effects when operating in conjunction with another factor compared to when it is acting alone. This is called the concept of *interaction*: The magnitude of the effect that one variable has may depend on the level of another variable. Research conducted by Simmons, Burgeson, Carlton-Ford, and Blyth (1987) provides an example. These investigators examined the academic grade point averages of a group of adolescents as a function of life changes (school transition, pubertal development, early dating behavior, residential mobility, and family disruption). They found that the combination of life changes was the critical factor in cases of negative outcome. No single factor had a huge effect, but when several of the factors were conjoined together there was a sizeable effect.

A similar example occurs in Michael Rutter's (1979) review of the factors related to psychiatric disorders in children, in which he stated:

> The first very striking finding is that single isolated chronic stresses carry no appreciable psychiatric risk. . . . None of these risk factors, when they occurred in isolation, was associated with disorder in the children; the risk was no higher than that for children without any family stresses. However, when any two stresses occurred together, the risk went up no less than fourfold. With three and four concurrent stresses, the risk went up several times further still. It is clear that the combination of chronic stresses provided very much more than an additive effect. There was an interactive effect such that the risk which attended several concurrent stresses was much more than the sum of the effects of the stresses considered individually. (p. 295)

To understand the logic of what is happening when an interaction occurs such as that described by Rutter, imagine a risk scale where a score of 80–110 represents low risk, 110–125 moderate risk, and 125–150 high risk. Imagine that we had found an average risk score of 82 for children with no stressors, an average risk score of 84 for children with stress factor A, and an average risk score of 86 for children with stress factor B. An interaction effect would be apparent if, when studying children with both risk factor A *and* risk factor B, we found an average risk score of 126. That is, the joint risk when two risk factors were conjoined was much greater than what would be predicted from studying each risk factor separately.

Developmental psychology contains many examples like the one described by Rutter. Researchers Bonnie Breitmeyer and Craig Ramey (1986) studied two groups of infants, one of a nonoptimal perinatal status and the other of normal status. One-half of the members of each group were randomly assigned at birth either to a day-care program designed to prevent mild mental retardation or to a control group that did not receive special treatment. The results indicated that when the children reached four years of age, the children who were at risk perinatally and the normal children were at the same level of cognitive maturity when *both* were given the day-care program. However, when *neither* group was given the day-care program, the children with nonoptimal perinatal scores showed slower cognitive development. Thus, biology interacted with environment in this situation to illustrate that a complex outcome (cognitive development) is determined by a multitude of factors. A negative cognitive outcome occurred only when nonoptimal perinatal status was combined with the absence of a day-care program. The researchers concluded, "The results provide support for a framework stressing initial biological vulnerability and subsequent environmental insufficiency as cumulative risk factors in the development of children from low SES [socioeconomic status] families" (p. 1151).

Many negative behavioral and cognitive outcomes have a similar logic to them—including many situations where biological and environmental variables have been found to be in interactive relationships. For example, variations in the so-called *5-HTT* gene have been found to be related to major depression in humans (Hariri & Holmes, 2006). People with one variant (the S allele) are more likely to suffer from major depression than people with the other variant of the gene (the L allele). However, this greater risk for those with the S allele is *only* true for those who have *also* suffered multiple traumatic life events, such as child abuse or neglect, job loss, and/or divorce.

It is likewise with the variants of the monoamine oxidase A (*MAOA*) gene and anti-social behavior. One variant of the gene increases the probability of anti-social behavior, but only if other risk factors are present such as child abuse, birth complications, or negative home environments (Raine, 2008). A final example is provided by research on the link between rumination and depression. The tendency to ruminate does predict the duration of depressive symptoms, but it interacts with cognitive styles—rumination predicts lengthened periods of depressive symptoms only when conjoined with negative cognitive styles (Nolen-Hoeksema, Wisco, Lyubomirsky, 2008).

Positive outcomes also have the characteristic that they are explained by multiple, interactive factors. In a study of prosocial behavior on the part of six- to nine-year-old children, Knight, Johnson, Carlo, and Eisenberg (1994) examined the psychological factors that were associated with children's tendency to help other children (which was operationalized as donating money to children in need). They found that certain variables, such as levels of sympathy, affective reasoning, and knowledge about money—when taken alone—were only weakly related to prosocial behavior (donating more money to help others). However, in combination, these variables were much more potent predictors of prosocial behavior. For example, children high in sympathy, affective reasoning, and knowledge about money donated four times as much as the children low in all of these variables.

Developmental psychologist Dan Keating (2007) has reviewed the literature on the consequences of states' Graduated Driver Licensing programs on teen driver safety. These programs work—they lower the rate of teen auto crashes and teen auto fatalities. However, the programs are all different from state to state, each state having somewhat different subsets of several basic components: required driver education, passenger restrictions, night driving restrictions, extended legal age, minimum practice driving requirements, and extended learner's permit time. Thus, the question becomes whether each of these components is causally effective and whether they have any interactive effects. Research indicates that no *one* of the components lowers teen crash or fatality rates. However, in *combination* they can lower the number of teen fatalities by over 20 percent.

Thus, the concept of multiple causes involves even more complexities than you might have thought at first. Not only is it necessary to track down and measure the many factors that may influence the behavior in question, but it is also necessary to investigate how these factors operate together.

Clinical psychologist Scott Lilienfeld (2006) discusses the continuum of causal influence for variables—from strong to weak (see Rutter, 2007). Only at the very strongest end of the continuum does a variable act in isolation. The strongest form of causal influence is one where a variable is necessary *and* sufficient for producing an effect on dependent variable. The variable must be present for the effect to occur (it is necessary) and when it is, by itself, it is sufficient to produce the effect. Weaker forms of causation, however, all involve the contextualization of a variable's effect by other variables. A causal variable might be necessary (it must be there for the dependent variable to display an effect) but not sufficient (it depends on the presence of another variable for its effect). Finally, a weak causal variable might be *neither* necessary nor sufficient—its presence just increases the overall statistical probability of the effect.

The Temptation of the Single-Cause Explanation

It seems that the basic idea that complex events in the world are multiply determined should be an easy one to grasp. In fact, the concept *is* easy to grasp and to apply when the issues are not controversial. However, when our old nemesis, preexisting bias (see Chapter 3), rears its head, people have a tendency to ignore the principle of multiple causation. How many times do we hear people arguing about such emotionally charged issues as the causes of crime, the distribution of wealth, the causes of terrorism, the treatment of women and minorities, the causes of poverty, the effect of capital punishment, and the level of taxation in a way that implies that these issues are simple and unidimensional and that outcomes in these areas have a single cause? These examples make it clear that, as Nisbett and Ross (1980) argued, "Although people sometimes acknowledge the existence of multiple causes, it is clear that they frequently act in ways far more consistent with beliefs in unitary causation. In a sense, they behave as if causation were 'hydraulic' or as if causal candidates competed with one another in a zero-sum game" (p. 128).

A zero-sum game—in which one person's gain is another's loss—often characterizes our discussions of emotionally charged issues. Under emotional influence, we tend to forget the principle of multiple causation. For example, consider discussions of crime by people on opposite ends of the political spectrum. Liberals may argue that people of low-socioeconomic status who commit crimes may themselves be victims of their circumstances (e.g., job-lessness, poor housing, poor education, and lack of hope about the future). Conservatives may reply that a lot of poor people do not commit crimes; therefore, economic conditions are not the cause. Instead, the conservative may argue, it is personal values and personal character that determine crimi-nal behavior. Neither side in the debate ever seems to acknowledge that both individual factors and environmental factors may contribute to criminal behavior.

Political writer Richard Cohen has noted how we often turn our "single-cause" explanations around 180 degrees, depending on the direction of our preexisting biases. He cited the case of a 63-year-old farmer who was deep in debt and losing his farm because of the severe farm recession in Iowa. The man shot the banker to whom he was hopelessly in debt and then shot his wife and himself. The conventional wisdom of neighbors and of the media regarding this event was that the man simply "snapped" because of his immense financial difficulties. Media coverage was highly favorable. As Cohen described it, the farmer was presented as a "hard-working entrepre-neur, up against nature, the bank, and the vagaries of traders in places such as Chicago. He is honest, thrifty and the embodiment of almost every American virtue—self-employed, self-reliant and God-fearing" (Cohen, 1985, p. 11).

But Cohen wondered why, if this man could simply "snap" because of economic difficulties, do we not invoke this same (single-cause) theory when explaining the behavior of the ghetto resident who shoots someone? "If this is the case when it comes to farmers on besieged farms, why is it not also the case with the ghetto resident? Why is it that even to suggest that poverty, lack of opportunity, lousy schools and brutality contribute to crime, brings nothing but scorn?" (p. 11). Cohen was, of course, pointing out a further absurdity in our tendency toward single-cause explanations: We use them in ways that conveniently fit in with our biases. He argued that we might be less apt to do this if, from the beginning, we recognized that both of these cases were probably multiply determined. The actions of the Iowa farmer who killed someone and the ghetto resident who kills someone are both influenced by their individual psychological-biological characteristics and environmental pressures. There is no one explanation of crime. Criminal behavior is determined by a multitude of factors, some of which are environ-mental and some of which are characteristics of the individual.

Consider also discussions of the causes of complex economic outcomes. These outcomes are hard to predict precisely because they are multiply deter-mined. For example, economic debate has focused on a problem of the last several decades with important social implications: the growing inequality of wealth in the United States (Bartels, 2008; Bilmes & Stiglitz, 2009; Brooks, 2008; Gelman, 2008; Karger, 2005; Madrick, 2006). Just as in the Clever Hans case discussed in Chapter 6, the facts are not in dispute. It is the *explanation* of the facts that is the subject of contentious argument. The facts are these. Since

1979, the real (that is, adjusted for inflation) income of all male workers in the United States has been quite stagnant. That is, middle-Americans and lower-income Americans have barely been holding their own in income. In contrast, the incomes of the top 1 percent of the population have gone up over 100 percent in the same period (in real terms, adjusted for inflation). Another way to put this is that over 80 percent of all of the income gains in America from 1980 to 2005 went to the richest 1 percent of taxpayers (Bartels, 2008). In 1977, the richest 20 percent of the population earned four times what the poorest 20 percent earned. By 2006, they earned over ten times as much.

The social consequences of this massive transfer of wealth from one class of citizens to another have set off a contentious political debate about its cause. The debate has been notable for its focus on single causes. Each side in the political debate picks a single cause and then tries to denigrate all others. In fact, quantitative economic studies (Bartels, 2008; Bilmes & Stiglitz, 2009; Cassidy, 1995; Gelman, 2008; Madrick, 2006) have focused on four variables (many more than four have been proposed, but these four have been the most extensively studied). One factor discussed is that the rising immigration of unskilled workers into the United States puts downward pressure on the wages of the lower-paid workers because it creates an oversupply of unskilled labor. A second argument is that globalization increases income disparity because corporations can outsource labor to countries with lower wage rates, thus putting downward pressure on wages in the United States. A third factor is the declining power of labor unions and the increasing power of large corporations. A fourth factor is that tax cuts enacted in the 1980s and in 2001 disproportionately eased the tax burden on the rich.

What have economic studies found with respect to these four variables? You guessed it. All four are factors contributing to the rising inequality in our society. This example also illustrates the concept of interaction mentioned previously. Cassidy (1995) notes indications that "some of the factors probably interacted and reinforced each other. The rise of global competition may have encouraged managers to break unions. . . . Similarly, the threat of corporate relocation and the growth of cheap immigrant labor may have contributed to the weakness of labor unions" (p. 122).

Like economic problems, virtually all of the complex problems that psychologists investigate are multiply determined. Take the problem of learning disabilities, for example, which educational psychologists, cognitive psychologists, and developmental psychologists have investigated extensively. Research has revealed that there are brain anomalies associated with learning disabilities (Price & McCrory, 2005; Shaywitz & Shaywitz, 2004; Wolf, 2007). Studies have also indicated that there is a genetic component in learning disabilities (Olson, 2004; Pennington & Olson, 2005). These two findings may seem to suggest the conclusion that learning disabilities are solely biological-brain problems. This conclusion would be wrong. The reason it would be wrong is that research has also revealed that learning disabilities are caused partly by the lack of certain instructional experiences in early schooling (Pressley, 2005) and by poor home environments (Dickinson & Neuman, 2005; Senechal, 2006). There is no single cause of learning disabilities; instead, there is a confluence of biological predispositions and environmental causes.

A similar situation characterizes the causes and treatment of depression. Depression is multiply determined by genetic propensities and environmental risk factors. Likewise, a multiplicity of treatments combined—medication plus psychotherapy—seems to result in the best therapeutic outcome (Hollon, Thase, & Markowitz, 2002).

Summary

The single lesson of this chapter is an easy one but an important one. When thinking about the causes of behavior, think in terms of multiple causes. Do not fall into the trap of thinking that a particular behavior must have a single cause. Most behaviors of any complexity are multiply determined. A variety of factors act to cause their occurrence. Sometimes these factors interact when in combination. That is, the effect of the variables acting together is different than what one would have expected from simply studying them in isolation.

CHAPTER 10

The Achilles' Heel of Human Cognition: Probabilistic Reasoning

Question:
Men are taller than women, right?

Answer:
"Right."

Question:
All men are taller than all women, right?

Answer:
"Wrong."

Correct. Believe it or not, we are going to devote part of this chapter to something that you just demonstrated you knew by answering the previous two questions. But don't skip this chapter just yet, because there are some surprises waiting in the explanation of what seems like a very simple principle.

You answered affirmatively to the first question because you did not interpret "Men are taller than women" to mean what the second statement said: "All men are taller than all women." You correctly took the first statement to mean *"There is a tendency for* men to be taller than women," because everyone knows that not all men are taller than all women. You correctly interpreted the statement as reflecting a probabilistic trend rather than a fact that holds in every single instance. By *probabilistic trend,* we simply mean that it is more likely than not but does not hold true in all cases. That is, the relationship between sex and height is stated in terms of likelihoods and probabilities rather than certainties. Many other relationships in nature are probabilistic: It tends to be warmer near the equator. Families tend to have fewer than eight children. Most parts of the earth tend to have more insects than humans. These are all statistically demonstrable trends, yet there are exceptions to every one of them. They are probabilistic trends and laws, not relationships that hold true in every single case.

Medical scientists are acutely aware that they deal in probabilities and not certainties. In an interview, James Evans, a physician and a genetic counselor, answered the question "Isn't that what you do—work with probabilities?" by saying that "Yes, that's what a geneticist does. We're all about probability. In my medical genetics clinic, when I counsel someone who's had a gene test, I might say: 'The BRCA2 mutation you were found to carry confers about a 50 to 85 percent risk of breast cancer and a 25 percent risk of ovarian cancer'" (Evans, 2008, p. D2).

Americans received a sad lesson in the probabilistic nature of medical knowledge in the summer of 2008 when much-loved political broadcaster Tim Russert died of a heart attack at age 58. Russert took cholesterol pills and aspirin, rode an exercise bike, and had yearly stress tests, yet he still died of a heart attack (Grady, 2008). The fact that he had been fairly vigilant toward his health led many readers of the *New York Times* to write in saying that the doctors must have missed something. These readers did not understand that medical knowledge is probabilistic. Every failure to predict is not a mistake. In fact, his doctors missed nothing. They applied their probabilistic knowledge as best they could—but this does not mean that they could predict individual cases of heart attack. Science writer Denise Grady (2008) tells us that, based on his stress test and many other state-of-the art diagnostics that Mr. Russert was given in his last exam, the doctors estimated—from a widely used formula—that Mr. Russert's probability of a heart attack in the next ten years was 5 percent. This means that 95 out of 100 people with Mr. Russert's medical profile should not have a heart attack in the next ten years. Mr. Russert was just one of the unlucky five—and medical science, being probabilistic, cannot tell us in advance who those unlucky five will be.

People have a hard time accepting the reality of probabilistic prediction— that they do not live in a world of certainties. Science writer Natalie Angier (2007) discusses how some people think that seismologists really *can* predict individual earthquakes, but that they do not make these predictions public so as "not to create a panic." One seismologist received a letter from a woman asking him to tell her if he ever sent his children to see out-of-town relatives. From this example, Angier notes that people seem to prefer to believe that authorities are engaged in monstrous lying than to simply admit that there is uncertainty in science. A formal study by Gigerenzer and colleagues (Gigerenzer et al., 2007) confirms Angier's fears. Gigerenzer et al. found that 44 percent of a sample of German citizens thought (wrongly) that mammography tests give an "absolutely certain" result and 63 percent thought (wrongly) that fingerprinting gave an "absolutely certain" result.

Virtually all the facts and relationships that have been uncovered by the science of psychology are stated in terms of probabilities. There is nothing unique about this. Many of the laws and relationships in other sciences are stated in probabilities rather than certainties. The entire subdiscipline of population genetics, for example, is based on probabilistic relationships. Physicists tell us that the distribution of the electron's charge in an atom is described by a probabilistic function. It is true that many of the probabilistic trends uncovered in psychology are weak. However, the fact that behavioral relationships are stated in probabilistic form does not distinguish them from those in many other sciences.

Many writers have made the point that "people seem to be in a land of sometimes and perhaps, and they had hoped to go on living with always and with certainty" (Bronowski, 1978a, p. 94). In this chapter, we will try to make you more comfortable in the "land of sometimes and perhaps," because to understand psychology one must be comfortable with the subject of this chapter: probabilistic reasoning.

"Person-Who" Statistics

Most of the public is aware that many of the conclusions of medical science are statements of probabilistic trends and are not predictions of absolute certainty. Smoking causes lung cancer and a host of other health problems. Voluminous medical evidence documents this fact (Gigerenzer et al., 2007). Yet will everyone who smokes get lung cancer, and will everyone who refrains from smoking be free of lung cancer? Most people know that these implications do not follow. The relationship is probabilistic. Smoking vastly increases the probability of contracting lung cancer but does not make it a certainty. Medical science can tell us with great confidence that more people in a group of smokers will die of lung cancer than in an equivalent group of nonsmokers. It cannot tell us which ones will die, though. The relationship is probabilistic; it does not hold in every case. We are all aware of this—or are we? How often have we seen a nonsmoker trying to convince a smoker to stop by citing the smoking—lung-cancer statistics, only to have the smoker come back with "Oh, get outta here! Look at old Joe Ferguson down at the store. Three packs of Camels a day since he was sixteen! Eighty-one years old and he looks great!" The obvious inference that one is supposed to draw is that this single case somehow invalidates the relationship.

It is surprising and distressing how often this ploy works. Too frequently, a crowd of people will begin to nod their heads in assent when a single case is cited to invalidate a probabilistic trend. This agreement reflects a failure to understand the nature of statistical laws. If people think a single example can invalidate a law, they must feel the law should hold in every case. In short, they have failed to understand the law's probabilistic nature.

There will always be a few "people who" go against even the strongest of trends. Consider our smoking example. Only 5 percent of men who live to the age of 85 are smokers (University of California, Berkeley, 1991). Or to put it another way, 95 percent of men who live to age 85 are either nonsmokers or have smoked for a period and then quit. Continuous smoking without quitting markedly shortens lives. Yet a few smokers do make it to 85.

Adapting the terminology of psychologists Richard Nisbett and Lee Ross (1980), we will call instances like the "old Joe Ferguson" story examples of the use of "person-who" statistics: situations in which well-established statistical trends are questioned because someone knows a "person who" went against the trend. For example, "You say job opportunities are expanding in service industries and contracting in heavy industry? No way. I know a man who got a job in a steel mill just last Thursday"; "You say families are having fewer children than they did 30 years ago? You're crazy! The young couple next door already has three and they're both under 30"; "You say children tend to adopt the religious beliefs of their parents? Well, I know a man at work whose son converted to another religion just the other day."

The ubiquitous "person who" is usually trotted out when we are confronted with hard statistical evidence that contradicts a previously held belief. Thus, it could be argued that people actually know better and simply use the "person who" as a technique to invalidate facts that go against their opinions. However, the work of psychologists who have studied human decision making and reasoning suggests that the tendency to use the "person who" comes not simply from its usefulness as a debating strategy. Instead, it appears that this fallacious argument is used so frequently because people experience great difficulty in dealing with probabilistic information. Much research into the nature of human thinking has indicated that probabilistic reasoning may well be the Achilles' heel of human cognition.

Probabilistic Reasoning and the Misunderstanding of Psychology

Probabilistic thinking is involved in many areas of science, technology, and human affairs. Thus, there is no necessary reason why this type of thinking is more important to an understanding of psychology than of any other science. However, the findings of psychology are often misunderstood because of the problems people have in dealing with probabilistic information. We all understand "men are taller than women" as a statement of probabilistic tendency. We realize that it is not invalidated by a single exception (one man who is shorter than a woman). Most people understand the statement "smoking causes lung cancer" in the same way (although old "Joe Ferguson" can be convincing to some smokers who do not want to believe that their habit may be killing them!). However, very similar probabilistic statements about behavioral trends cause widespread disbelief and are often dismissed by many people with the first appearance of a single "person who." Most psychology instructors have witnessed a very common reaction when they discuss the evidence on certain behavioral relationships. For example, the instructor may present the fact that children's scholastic achievement is related to the socioeconomic status of their households and to the educational level of their parents. This statement often prompts at least one student to object that he has a friend who is a National Merit Scholar and whose father finished only eighth grade. Even those who understood the smoking—lung-cancer example tend to waver at this point.

People who would never think of using "person-who" arguments to refute the findings of medicine and physics routinely use them to refute psychological research. Most people understand that many treatments, theories, and facts developed by medical science are probabilistic. They understand that, for example, a majority of patients, but not all of them, will respond to a certain drug. Medical science, however, often cannot tell in advance which patients will respond. Often all that can be said is that if 100 patients take treatment A and 100 patients do not, after a certain period the 100 patients who took treatment A will *collectively* be better off. I mentioned in an earlier chapter that I take a medication called Imitrex (sumatriptan succinate) for relief from migraine headaches. The information sheet accompanying this drug tells me that controlled studies have demonstrated that, at a particular dosage level, 57 percent of patients taking this medication receive relief in two hours. I am one of the lucky 57 percent—but neither the drug company nor my physician could give me a guarantee that I would not be one of unlucky 43 percent. The drug does not work in every case.

No one would doubt the worth of medical knowledge just because it is probabilistic and does not apply in every case. Yet this is exactly what happens in the case of many psychological findings and treatments. The fact that a finding or treatment does not apply in every case often engenders profound disappointment and denigration of psychology's progress. When the issues are psychological, people tend to forget the fundamental principle that knowledge does not have to be certain to be useful—that even though individual cases cannot be predicted, the ability to forecast *group* trends accurately is often very informative. The prediction of outcomes based on group characteristics is often called *aggregate* or *actuarial prediction* (we will discuss actuarial prediction in more detail in the next chapter).

Consider an unhealthy person going to a physician. The person is told that unless he or she exercises and changes diet, he or she has a high risk of heart attack. We are not tempted to say that the doctor has no useful knowledge because he or she cannot tell the person that without a change of diet he or she will have a heart attack on September 18, 2014. We tend to understand that the physician's predictions are probabilistic and cannot be given with that level of precision. It is likewise when geologists tell us that there is an 80 percent probability of a magnitude 8.0 or greater earthquake in a certain area in the next 30 years. We do not denigrate their knowledge because they cannot say that there will be an earthquake exactly *here* on July 5, 2016. Science writer Elizabeth Kolbert (2005) describes how a group of prominent climatologists posted an essay on their Website titled, "Could New Orleans be the first major U.S. city ravaged by human-caused climate change?" In an attempt to educate the public, they pointed out that this is entirely the wrong question to ask. Their point was that "the science of global warming has nothing to say about any particular hurricane (or drought or heat wave or flood), only about the larger statistical pattern" (p. 36).

When a school psychologist recommends a program for a child with learning disabilities, of course he or she is making a probabilistic prediction—that the child has a higher probability of good academic achievement if in a certain program. It is likewise when a clinical psychologist recommends a program for a child with self-injurious behavior. The psychologist judges that there is a higher probability of a good outcome if a certain approach is followed. But unlike the heart attack and earthquake examples, the psychologist is often confronted with questions like "but *when* will my child be reading at grade level?" or "exactly how long will he have to be in this program?" These are unanswerable questions—in the same way that the questions about exactly when the earthquake or the heart attack will occur are also unanswerable questions. They are unanswerable because in all these cases—the heart attack, the learning disabled child, the earthquake, the child with self-injurious behavior—the prediction being made is probabilistic.

For these reasons, a thorough understanding of probabilistic reasoning is critical to an understanding of psychology. There is a profound irony here. Psychology probably suffers the most from the general public's inability to think statistically. Yet psychologists have done the most research into the nature of probabilistic reasoning abilities.

Psychological Research on Probabilistic Reasoning

In the past three decades, the research of psychologists such as Daniel Kahneman of Princeton University (winner of the Nobel Prize in 2002, see MacCoun, 2002) and the late Amos Tversky has revolutionized the way we think about people's reasoning abilities. In the course of their studies, these investigators have uncovered some fundamental principles of probabilistic reasoning that are absent or, more commonly, insufficiently developed in many people. As has often been pointed out, it should not be surprising that they are insufficiently developed. As a branch of mathematics, probability theory is a very recent development (Hacking, 1990). Games of chance existed centuries before the fundamental laws of probability were discovered. Here is another example of how personal experience does not seem to be sufficient to lead to a fundamental understanding of the world (see Chapter 7). It took formal study of the laws of probability to reveal how games of chance work. Thousands of gamblers and their "personal experiences" were insufficient to uncover the underlying nature of games of chance.

The problem is that as society becomes more complex, the need for probabilistic thinking becomes greater for everyone. If ordinary citizens are to have a basic understanding of the society in which they live, they must possess at least a rudimentary ability to think statistically.

"Why did they raise my insurance rate," you might wonder, "and why is John's rate higher than Bill's? Is Social Security going broke? Is our state lottery crooked? Is crime increasing or decreasing? Why do doctors order all those tests? Why can people be treated with certain rare drugs in Europe and not in the United States? Do women really make less than men in comparable jobs? Do international trade deals cost Americans jobs and drive down wages? Is educational achievement in Japan really higher than here? Is Canadian health care better than that in the United States and cheaper as well?" These are all good questions—concrete, practical questions about our society and how it works. To understand the answers to each of them, one must think statistically.

Clearly, a complete discussion of statistical thinking is beyond the scope of this book. We will, however, briefly discuss some of the more common pitfalls of probabilistic reasoning. A good way to start developing the skill of probabilistic thinking is to become aware of the most common fallacies that arise when people reason statistically. In addition, many are particularly relevant to understanding the importance of psychological findings and theories.

Insufficient Use of Probabilistic Information

One finding that has been much replicated is that there is a tendency for concrete single-case information to overwhelm more abstract probabilistic information in people's judgments (the vividness problem discussed in Chapter 4). The tendency to give insufficient weight to probabilistic information is not limited to the scientifically unsophisticated layperson. Casscells, Schoenberger, and Graboys (1978) gave a variant of the following problem to 20 medical students, 20 attending physicians, and 20 house officers at four Harvard Medical School teaching hospitals: Imagine that the virus (HIV) that causes AIDS occurs in 1 in every 1,000 people. Imagine also that there is a test to diagnose the disease that always indicates correctly that a person who has HIV actually has it. Finally, imagine that the test has a false-positive rate of 5 percent. This means that the test wrongly indicates that HIV is present in 5 percent of the cases in which the person does not have the virus. Imagine that we choose a person randomly and administer the test and that it yields a positive result (indicates that the person is HIV-positive). What is the probability that the individual actually has the HIV virus, assuming that we know nothing else about the individual's personal or medical history?

The most common answer was 95 percent. The correct answer is approximately 2 percent. The physicians vastly overestimated the probability that a positive result truly indicated the disease because of the tendency to overweight the case information and underweight the base rate information (that only 1 in 1,000 people are HIV-positive). A little logical reasoning can help to illustrate the profound effect that base rates have on probabilities. Of 1,000 people, 1 will actually be HIV-positive. If the other 999 (who do not have the disease) are tested, the test will indicate incorrectly that approximately 50 of them have the virus (0.05 multiplied by 999) because of the 5 percent false-positive rate. Thus, of the 51 patients testing positive, only 1 (approximately 2 percent) will actually be HIV-positive. In short, the base rate is such that the vast majority of people do not have the virus (only 1 in 1,000). This fact, combined with a substantial false-positive rate, ensures that, in absolute numbers, the vast majority of positive tests will be of people who do not have the virus.

Although all the physicians in the Casscells et al. study would have immediately recognized the correctness of this logic, their initial tendency was to discount the base rates and overweight the clinical evidence. In short, the physicians actually knew better but were initially drawn to an incorrect conclusion. Psychologists have termed problems like these cognitive illusions (see Kahneman & Frederick, 2005; Pohl, 2004). In *cognitive illusions,* even when people know the correct answer, they may be drawn to an incorrect conclusion by the structure of the problem.

In this problem, the case evidence (the laboratory test result) seems tangible and concrete to most people, whereas the probabilistic evidence seems, well—probabilistic. This reasoning, of course, is fallacious because case evidence itself is always probabilistic. A clinical test misidentifies the presence of a disease with a certain *probability.* The situation is one in which two probabilities—the probable diagnosticity of the case evidence and the prior probability (base rate)—must be combined if one is to arrive at a correct decision. There are right and wrong ways of combining these probabilities, and more often than not—particularly when the case evidence gives the illusion of concreteness (recall our discussion of the vividness problem in Chapter 4)—people combine the information in the wrong way. This particular failure of probabilistic reasoning may very well hinder the use of psychological knowledge, which is often stated in the form of probabilistic relationships among behaviors.

Science writer K. C. Cole (1998) asks us to imagine two situations. One is the standard one in which we try to convey the dangers of smoking to an individual by stating a probability of death—say, for example, a probability of death of 0.000055. The second way is more vivid. It asks the smoker to imagine that one pack in every 18,250 packs of cigarettes is different—it is filled with explosives. When a smoker opens it, the package explodes and the smoker dies. There is little doubt which case is more effective—yet they both are conveying the same fact.

Failure to Use Sample Size Information

Consider these two problems, developed by Tversky and Kahneman (1974):

1. A certain town is served by two hospitals. In the larger hospital, about 45 babies are born each day, and in the smaller hospital, about 15 babies are born each day. As you know, about 50 percent of all babies are boys. However, the exact percentage varies from day to day. Sometimes it is higher than 50 percent, sometimes lower. For a period of one year, each hospital recorded the days on which more than 60 percent of the babies born were boys. Which hospital do you think recorded more such days?
   a. The larger hospital
   b. The smaller hospital
   c. About the same
2. Imagine an urn filled with balls, two-thirds of which are of one color and one-third of which are of another. One individual has drawn 5 balls from the urn and found that 4 are red and 1 is white. Another individual has drawn 20 balls and found that 12 are red and 8 are white. Which of the two individuals should feel more confident that the urn contains two-thirds red balls and one-third white balls, rather than vice versa? What odds should each individual give?

In problem 1, the majority of people answer "about the same." People not choosing this alternative pick the larger and the smaller hospital with about equal frequency. Because the correct answer is the smaller hospital, approximately 75 percent of subjects given this problem answer incorrectly. These incorrect answers result from an inability to recognize the importance of sample size in the problem. Other things being equal, a larger sample size always more accurately estimates a population value. Thus, on any given day, the larger hospital, with its larger sample size, will tend to have a proportion of births closer to 50 percent. Conversely, a small sample size is always more likely to deviate from the population value. Thus, the smaller hospital will have more days on which the proportion of births displays a large discrepancy from the population value (60 percent boys, 40 percent boys, 80 percent boys, etc.).

In problem 2, most people feel that the sample of 5 balls provides more convincing evidence that the urn is predominantly red. Actually, the probabilities are in the opposite direction. The odds are 8 to 1 that the urn is predominantly red for the 5-ball sample, but they are 16 to 1 that the urn is predominantly red for the 20-ball sample. Even though the proportion of red balls is higher in the 5-ball sample (80 percent versus 60 percent), this is more than compensated for by the fact that the other sample is four times as large and, thus, is more likely to be an accurate estimate of the proportions in the urn. The judgment of most subjects, however, is dominated by the higher proportion of red in the 5-ball sample and does not take adequate account of the greater reliability of the 20-ball sample.

An appreciation of the influence of sample size on the reliability of information is a basic principle of evidence evaluation that applies in many different areas but, again, is particularly relevant to understanding research in the behavioral sciences. Whether we realize it or not, we all hold generalized beliefs about large populations. What we often do not realize is how tenuous the database is on which our most steadfast beliefs rest. Throw together some observations about a few neighbors and a few people at work, add some anecdotes from the TV news, and we are all too ready to make statements about human nature or "the American people."

The Gambler's Fallacy

Please answer the following two problems:

> Problem A: Imagine that we are tossing a fair coin (a coin that has a 50/50 chance of coming up heads or tails) and it has just come up heads five times in a row. For the sixth toss, do you think that
> _____It is more likely that tails will come up than heads?
> _____It is more likely that heads will come up than tails?
> _____Heads and tails are equally probable on the sixth toss?
>
> Problem B: When playing slot machines, people win something one out of every 10 times. Julie, however, has just won on her first three plays. What are her chances of winning the next time she plays?
> _____out of_____

These two problems probe whether a person is prone to the so-called gambler's fallacy—the tendency for people to see links between events in the past and events in the future when the two are really independent. Two outcomes are independent when the occurrence of one does not affect the probability of the other. Most games of chance that use proper equipment have this property. For example, the number that comes up on a roulette wheel is independent of the outcome that preceded it. Half the numbers on a roulette wheel are red, and half are black (for purposes of simplification, we will ignore the green zero and double zero), so the odds are even (0.50) that any given spin will come up red. Yet after five or six consecutive reds, many bettors switch to black, thinking that it is now more likely to come up. This is the gambler's fallacy: acting as if previous outcomes affect the probability of the next outcome when the events are independent. In this case, the bettors are wrong in their belief. The roulette wheel has no memory of what has happened previously. Even if 15 reds in a row come up, the probability of red coming up on the next spin is still 0.50.

In problem A, some people think that it is more likely that either heads or tails will come up after five heads, and they are displaying the gambler's fallacy by thinking so. The correct answer is that heads and tails are equally probable on the sixth toss. Likewise, for problem B any answer other than 1 out of 10 indicates the gambler's fallacy.

The gambler's fallacy is not restricted to the inexperienced. Research has shown that even habitual gamblers, who play games of chance over 20 hours a week, still display belief in the gambler's fallacy (Petry, 2005; Wagenaar, 1988). In fact, research has shown that individuals in treatment for pathological gambling problems were *more* likely to believe in the gambler's fallacy compared to control subjects (Toplak et al., 2007).

It is important to realize that the gambler's fallacy is not restricted to games of chance. It operates in any domain in which chance plays a substantial role, that is, in almost *everything*. The genetic makeup of babies is an example. Psychologists, physicians, and marriage counselors often see couples who, after having two female children, are planning a third child because "We want a boy, and it's *bound* to be a boy this time." This, of course, is the gambler's fallacy. The probability of having a boy (approximately 50 percent) is exactly the same after having two girls as it was in the beginning. The two previous girls make it *no more likely* that the third baby will be a boy.

The gambler's fallacy stems from many mistaken beliefs about probability. One is the belief that if a process is truly random, no sequence—not even a small one (six coin flips, for instance)—should display runs or patterns. People routinely underestimate the likelihood of runs (HHHH) and patterns (HHTTHHTTHHTT) in a random sequence. For this reason, people cannot generate truly random sequences when they try to do so. The sequences that they generate tend to have too few runs and patterns. When generating such sequences, people alternate their choices too much in a mistaken effort to destroy any structure that might appear (Nickerson, 2002; Olivola & Oppenheimer, 2008).

Those who claim to have psychic powers can easily exploit this tendency. Consider a demonstration sometimes conducted in college psychology classes. A student is told to prepare a list of 200 numbers by randomly choosing from the numbers 1, 2, and 3 over and over again. After it is completed, the list of numbers is kept out of view of the instructor. The student is now told to concentrate on the first number on the list, and the instructor tries to guess what the number is. After the instructor guesses, the student tells the class and the instructor the correct choice. A record is kept of whether the instructor's guess matched, and the process continues until the complete record of 200 matches and nonmatches is recorded. Before the procedure begins, the instructor announces that she or he will demonstrate "psychic powers" by reading the subject's mind during the experiment. The class is asked what level of performance—that is, percentage of "hits"—would constitute empirically solid evidence of psychic powers. Usually a student who has taken a statistics course volunteers that, because a result of 33 percent hits could be expected purely on the basis of chance, the instructor would have to achieve a larger proportion than this, probably at least 40 percent, before one should believe that she or he has psychic powers. The class usually understands and agrees with this argument. The demonstration is then conducted, and a result of more than 40 percent hits is obtained, to the surprise of many.

The students then learn some lessons about randomness and about how easy it is to fake psychic powers. The instructor in this example merely takes advantage of the fact that people do not generate enough runs: They alternate too much when producing "random" numbers. In a truly random sequence of numbers, what should the probability of a 2 be after three consecutive 2s? One-third, the same as the probability of a 1 or a 3. But this is not how most people generate such numbers. After even a small run, they tend to alternate numbers in order to produce a representative sequence. Thus, on each trial in our example, the instructor merely picks one of the two numbers that the student did not pick on the previous trial. Thus, if on the previous trial the student generated a 2, the instructor picks a 1 or a 3 for the next trial. If on the previous trial the subject generated a 3, the instructor picks a 1 or a 2 on the next trial. This simple procedure usually ensures a percentage of hits greater than 33 percent—greater than chance accuracy without a hint of psychic power.

The tendency for people to believe that if a sequence is random then it should display no runs or patterns was illustrated humorously in the controversy over the iPod's "shuffle" feature that broke out in 2005 (Levy, 2005). This feature plays the songs loaded into the iPod in a random sequence. Of course, knowing the research I have just discussed, many psychologists and statisticians chuckled to themselves when the inevitable happened—users complained that the shuffle feature could not be random because they often experienced sequences of songs from the same album or genre. Technical writer Steven Levy (2005) described how he had experienced the same thing. His iPod seemed always to have a fondness for Steely Dan in the first hour of play! But Levy was smart enough to accept what the experts told him: that truly random sequences will often not seem random to people because of our tendency to see patterns everywhere. After conducting his research into the issue, Levy concluded that "life may indeed be random, and the iPod probably is, too. But we humans will always provide our own narratives and patterns to bring chaos under control. The fault, if there is any, lies not in shuffle but in ourselves" (p. 10).

A Further Word About Statistics and Probability

These, then, are just a few of the shortcomings in statistical reasoning that obscure an understanding of psychology. More complete and detailed coverage is provided in the book *Heuristics and Biases: The Psychology of Intuitive Judgment* (2002), edited by Gilovich, Griffin, and Kahneman. Introductions to many of these ideas (and good places to start for those who lack extensive statistical training) are contained in Gigerenzer's *Calculated*

Risks: How to Know When Numbers Deceive You (2002), Hastie and Dawes's *Rational Choice in an Uncertain World* (2001), Baron's *Thinking and Deciding* (2008), and Nickerson's *Cognition and Chance: The Psychology of Probabilistic Reasoning* (2004).

The probabilistic thinking skills discussed in this chapter are of tremendous practical significance. Because of inadequately developed probabilistic thinking abilities, physicians choose less effective medical treatments (Groopman, 2007); people fail to assess accurately the risks in their environment (Margolis, 1996); information is misused in legal proceedings (Gigerenzer, 2002; Gigerenzer et al., 2007); animals are hunted to extinction (Baron, 1998); unnecessary surgery is performed (Gigerenzer et al., 2007; Groopman, 2007); and costly financial misjudgments are made (Zweig, 2008).

Of course, a comprehensive discussion of statistical reasoning cannot be carried out in a single chapter. Our goal was much more modest: to emphasize the importance of statistics in the study and understanding of psychology. Unfortunately, there is no simple rule to follow when confronted with statistical information. Unlike some of the other components of scientific thinking that are more easily acquired, functional reasoning skills in statistics probably require some type of formal study. Fortunately, most universities and community colleges now offer introductory-level statistics courses that require no previous university-level mathematics.

Although many scientists sincerely wish to make scientific knowledge accessible to the general public, it is intellectually irresponsible to suggest that a deep understanding of a particular subject can be obtained by the layperson when that understanding is crucially dependent on certain technical information that is available only through formal study. Such is the case with statistics and psychology. Psychologist Alan Boneau (1990) surveyed authors of psychology textbooks, asking them to list the most important terms and concepts that students need to learn in psychology. Approximately 40 percent of the 100 terms and concepts that were listed most frequently were in the areas of statistics and methodology. No one can be a competent contemporary psychologist without being fully conversant with statistics and probability (Evans, 2005; Friedrich, Buday, & Kerr, 2000). The president of the Association for Psychological Science, Morton Ann Gernsbacher (2007), derived a list of 10 things of intellectual value that she thinks psychological training specifically instills, and 4 of her 10 were in the domains of statistics and methodology.

The National Council of Education has warned that "the world of the twenty-first century is a world awash in numbers" (Lutsky, 2006, p. 35). Psychology professor Neil Lutsky (2006) reinforces this point by reminding us that "data-based claims are nonetheless a staple of policy debates, advertisements, medical news, educational assessments, financial decision-making, and everyday conversation" (p. 35). Like Gernsbacher, Lutsky argues that the study of psychology has a unique ability to inculcate statistical instincts and insights. That probability and statistics are so central to so *many* sciences is apparent in a popular book on the essential discoveries in science by writer Natalie Angier (2007). Her book covered *all* of the sciences, yet very early in her book—at the very beginning in Chapter 2—was a chapter on probability and statistics.

Clearly, one of the goals of this book is to make research in the discipline of psychology more accessible to the general reader. However, the empirical methods and techniques of theory construction in psychology are so intertwined with statistics (as is the case in many other fields, such as economics, sociology, and genetics) that it would be wrong to imply that one can thoroughly understand the field without having some statistical knowledge. Thus, although this chapter has served as an extremely sketchy lesson in statistical thinking, its main purpose has been to highlight the existence of an area of expertise that is critical to a full understanding of psychology.

Summary

As in most sciences, the conclusions that are drawn from psychological research are probabilistic conclusions—generalizations that hold more often than not but that do not apply in every single case. The predictions derived from psychological findings and theories are still useful even though they are not 100 percent accurate (just as is the case in other sciences). One thing that prevents the understanding of much psychological research is that many people have difficulty thinking in probabilistic terms. In this chapter, we discussed several well-researched examples of how probabilistic reasoning goes astray for many people: They make insufficient use of probabilistic information when they also have vivid testimonial evidence available; they fail to take into account the fact that larger samples give more accurate estimates of population values; and, finally, they display the gambler's fallacy (the tendency to see links among events that are really independent). The gambler's fallacy derives from a more general tendency that we will discuss in the next chapter: the tendency to fail to recognize the role of chance in determining outcomes.

CHAPTER 11

The Role of Chance in Psychology

In the last chapter, we discussed the importance of probabilistic trends, probabilistic thinking, and statistical reasoning. In this chapter, we will continue that discussion with an emphasis on the difficulties of understanding the concepts of randomness and chance. We will emphasize how people often misunderstand the contribution of research to clinical practice because of a failure to appreciate how thoroughly the concept of chance is integrated within psychological theory.

The Tendency to Try to Explain Chance Events

Our brains have evolved in such a way that they engage in a relentless search for patterns in the world. We seek relationships, explanations, and meaning in the things that happen around us. Eric Wargo (2008) writes in the *APS Observer* that "the brain could be described as an 'acausal connecting organ'—an insatiable meaning maker" (p. 19).

This strong tendency to search for structure has been studied by psychologists. It is characteristic of human intelligence, and it accounts for many of the most astounding feats of human information processing and knowledge acquisition.

Nevertheless, this extremely adaptive aspect of human cognition sometimes backfires on us. The quest for conceptual understanding is maladaptive when it takes place in an environment in which there is nothing to conceptualize. What plays havoc with one of the most distinguishing features of human cognition? What confounds our quest for structure and obscures understanding? You guessed it: probability. Or, more specifically, chance and randomness.

Chance and randomness are integral parts of our environment. The mechanisms of biological evolution and genetic recombination are governed by laws of chance and randomness. Physics has taught us to explain the fundamental structure of matter by invoking statistical laws of chance. Many things that happen in nature are a complex result of systematic, explainable factors and chance. Again, recall a previous example: Smoking causes lung cancer. A systematic, explainable aspect of biology links smoking to this particular disease. But not all smokers contract lung cancer. The trend is probabilistic. Perhaps we will eventually be able to explain why some smokers do not contract cancer. However, for the time being, this variability must be ascribed to the multitude of chance factors that determine whether a person will contract a particular disease.

As this example illustrates, when we say that something is due to chance, we do not necessarily mean that it is *indeterminate,* only that it is currently *indeterminable.* A coin toss is a chance event, but not because it is in principle impossible to determine the outcome by measuring the angle of the toss, the precise composition of the coin, and many other variables. In fact, the outcome of a toss is determined by all these variables. But a coin toss is called a chance event because there is no easy way to measure all the variables in the event. The outcome of a toss is not in principle indeterminate, just currently indeterminable.

Many events in the world are not entirely explainable in terms of systematic factors, at least not currently. Often, however, when no systematic explanation of a particular phenomenon is currently available, our conceptualizing apparatus still grinds away, imposing meaningless theories on data that are inherently random. Psychologists have conducted experiments on this phenomenon. In one experimental situation, subjects view a series of stimuli that vary in many different dimensions. The subjects are told that some stimuli belong to one class and other stimuli belong to another. Their task is to guess which class each of a succession of stimuli belongs to. However, the researcher actually assigns the stimuli to classes randomly. Thus, there is no rule except randomness. The subjects, however, rarely venture randomness as a guess. Instead, they often concoct extremely elaborate and complicated theories to explain how the stimuli are being assigned.

Similarly, "conspiracy theories" of various types usually require layers and layers of complicated schemes to explain the sequence of random events that their adherents are desperately seeking to understand. This phenomenon is characteristic even of various authorities working in their area of expertise. For example, the thinking of many financial analysts illustrates this fallacy. They routinely concoct elaborate explanations for every little fluctuation in stock market prices. In fact, much of this variability is simply random fluctuation (Malkiel, 2008; Taleb, 2007). Nevertheless, stock market analysts continue to imply to their customers (and perhaps themselves believe) that they can "beat the market" when there is voluminous evidence that the vast majority of them can do no such thing. Throughout most of the last several decades, if you had bought all of the 500 stocks in the Standard and Poor's Index and simply held them (what we might call a no-brain strategy—a strategy you could carry out by buying a mutual fund that tracks that index), then you would have had higher returns than over two-thirds of the money managers on Wall Street (Egan, 2005; Hulbert, 2006; Malkiel, 2008). You would also have beaten 80 percent of the financial newsletters that subscribers buy at rates of up to $500 per year.

But what about the managers who *do* beat the no-brain strategy? You might be wondering whether this means that they have some special skill. We can answer that question by considering the following thought experiment. One hundred monkeys have each been given 10 darts, and they are each going to throw them at a wall containing the names of each of the Standard and Poor's 500 stocks. Where the darts land will define that monkey's stock picks for the year. How will they do a year later? How many will beat the Standard and Poor's 500 Index? You guessed it. Roughly half of the monkeys. Would you be interested in paying the 50 percent of the monkeys who beat the index a commission to make your picks for you next year?

The logic by which purely random sequences seem to be the result of predictable factors is illustrated by a continuation of this example of financial predictions (Paulos, 2001). Imagine that a letter comes in the mail informing you of the existence of a stock-market-prediction newsletter. The newsletter does not ask for money but simply tells you to test it out. It tells you that IBM stock is going to go up during the next month. You put the letter away, but you do notice IBM stock does go up the next month. Having read a book like this one, however, you know better than to make anything of this result. You chalk it up to a lucky guess. Subsequently, you receive *another* newsletter from the same investment-advice company telling you that IBM stock will go down the following month. When the stock does go down, you again chalk the prediction up to a lucky guess, but you do get a bit curious. When the third letter from the same company comes and predicts that IBM will go down again the next month, you do find yourself watching the financial pages a little more closely, and you confirm for the third time that the newsletter's prediction was correct. IBM has gone down this month. When the fourth newsletter arrives from the same company and tells you that the stock will rise the next month, and it actually does move in the predicted direction for the fourth time, it becomes difficult to escape the feeling that this newsletter is for real—difficult to escape the feeling that maybe you should send in the $29.95 for a year's worth of the newsletter. Difficult to escape the feeling, that is, unless you can imagine the cheap basement office in which someone is preparing next week's batch of 1,600 newsletters to be sent to 1,600 addresses: 800 of the newsletters predict that IBM will go up during the next month, and 800 of the newsletters predict that IBM will go down during the next month. When IBM does go up, that office sends out letters to *only* the 800 addressees who got the correct prediction the month before (400 predicting that the stock will go up in the next month and 400 predicting that it will go down, of course). Then you can imagine the "boiler room"—probably with telemarketing scams purring on the phones in the background—sending the third month's predictions to only the 400 who got the correct prediction the second week (200 predicting that the stock will go up in the next month and 200 predicting that it will go down). Yes, you were one of the lucky 100 who received four correct random predictions in a row! Many of these lucky 100 (and probably very impressed) individuals will pay the $29.95 to keep the newsletters coming.

Now this seems like a horrible scam to play on people. And indeed it is. But it is no less a scam than when "respectable" financial magazines and TV shows present to you the "money manager who has beaten more than half his peers four years in a row!" Again, think back to our monkeys throwing the darts. Imagine that they were money managers making stock picks year after year. By definition, 50 percent of them will beat their peers during the first year. Half of these will again—by chance—beat their peers in the second year, making a total of 25 percent who beat their peers two years in a row. Half of these will again—by chance—beat their peers in the third year, making a total of 12.5 percent who beat their peers *three* years in a row. And finally, half of these 12.5 percent (i.e., 6.25 percent) will again beat their peers in the fourth year. Thus, about 6 of the 100 monkeys will have, as the financial shows and newspapers say, "consistently beaten other money managers for four years in a row." These 6 monkeys who beat their dartboard peers (and, as we just saw, would beat a majority of *actual* Wall Street money managers; see Egan, 2005; Malkiel, 2008) certainly deserve spots on the financial television programs, don't you think?

Explaining Chance: Illusory Correlation and the Illusion of Control

The tendency to explain chance events is illustrated in a phenomenon psychologists have studied that is called *illusory correlation*. When people believe that two types of events should commonly occur together, they tend to think that they are seeing co-occurrences with great frequency, even when the two critical events are occurring randomly and, thus, do not co-occur more frequently than any other combination of events. In short, people tend to see their expected correlation even in random events (Kida, 2006; King & Koehler, 2000; Stanovich, 2004). They see structure where there is none.

Controlled studies have demonstrated that when people have a prior belief that two variables are connected, they tend to see that connection even in data in which the two variables are totally unconnected. Unfortunately, this finding generalizes to some real-world situations that adversely affect people's lives. For example, many psychological practitioners continue to believe in the efficacy of the Rorschach test. This is the famous inkblot test in which the subject responds to blotches on a white paper. Because the inkblots lack structure, the theory is that people will respond to them in the same style that they typically respond to ambiguity and, thus, reveal "hidden" psychological traits. The test is called *projective* because the subjects presumably project unconscious psychological thoughts and feelings in their responses to the inkblots. The problem with all of this is that there is no evidence that the Rorschach test provides any additional diagnostic utility when used as a projective test (Crews, 2004; Lilienfeld et al., 2000; Wood, Nezworski, Lilienfeld, & Garb, 2003). Belief in the Rorschach test arises from the phenomenon of illusory correlation. Clinicians see relationships in response patterns because they believe they are there, not because they are actually present in the pattern of responses being observed.

Many of the interpersonal encounters in our lives have a large amount of chance in them: the blind date that leads to marriage, the canceled appointment that causes the loss of a job, the missed bus that leads to a meeting with an old high-school friend. It is a mistake to think that each chance event of our lives requires an elaborate explanation. But when essentially chance events lead to important consequences, it is difficult to avoid constructing complicated theories to explain them.

The tendency to try to explain chance probably derives from a deep desire to believe that we can control such events. Psychologist Ellen Langer (1975) studied what has been termed the *illusion of control*, that is, the tendency to believe that personal skill can affect outcomes determined by chance. In one study, two employees of two different companies sold lottery tickets to their co-workers. Some people were simply handed a ticket, whereas others were allowed to choose their ticket. Of course, in a random drawing, it makes no difference whether a person chooses a ticket or is assigned one. The next day, the two employees who had sold the tickets approached each individual and attempted to buy the tickets back. The subjects who had chosen their own tickets demanded four times as much money as the subjects who had been handed their tickets! In several other experiments, Langer confirmed the hypothesis that this outcome resulted from an inability to accept the fact that factors of skill cannot affect chance events.

Evidence of the widespread nature of this fallacy comes from the experience of states in which lotteries have been instituted. These states are descended on by purveyors of bogus books advising people how to "beat" the lottery—books that sell because people do not understand the implications of randomness. In fact, the explosion in the popularity of state lotteries in the United States did not occur until the mid-1970s, when New Jersey introduced participatory games in which players could scratch cards or pick their own numbers (Clotfelter & Cook, 1989; Thaler, 1992, p. 138). These participatory games exploit the illusion of control investigated by Langer: people's mistaken belief that their behavior determines random events. This illusion is so strong in some people who like to gamble that they will pay $1495 for a "special course" that will supposedly teach them to control the outcomes of the dice that they throw (Schwartz, 2008). Such "courses" are of course entirely bogus.

Other psychologists have studied a related phenomenon known as the *just-world hypothesis,* that is, the fact that people tend to believe that they live in a world in which people get what they deserve (Hafer & Begue, 2005). Researchers have found empirical support for one corollary of the belief in a just world: People tend to derogate the victims of chance misfortune. The tendency to seek explanations for chance events contributes to this phenomenon. People apparently find it very hard to believe that a perfectly innocent or virtuous person can suffer misfortune purely because of chance. We long to believe that good things happen to good people and that bad things happen to the bad. Chance, though, is completely unbiased—it does not operate to favor "good people."

People's misunderstanding of chance that is reflected in their belief in a just world serves to support many other incorrect folk beliefs. It leads to the tendency to see illusory correlations. We mentioned in Chapter 6, for example, the incorrect belief that blind people are "blessed" with supersensitive hearing, a folk myth probably perpetuated because people desire to see a correlation that "evens things out."

Chance and Psychology

In psychology, the tendency to try to explain everything, to have our theories account for every bit of variability rather than just the systematic nonchance components of behavior, accounts for the existence of many unfalsifiable psychological theories, both personal theories and those that are ostensibly scientific. Practitioners of "psychohistory" are often guilty of committing this error. Every minor twist and turn in a famous individual's life is explained in these psychohistories, usually via psychoanalytic principles. The problem with most psychohistories is not that they explain too little but that they explain too much. Rarely do they acknowledge the many chance factors that determine the course of a person's life.

An understanding of the role of chance is critical to the lay consumer of psychological information. Legitimate psychologists admit that their theories account for a portion of the variability in human behavior but not for all of it. They openly acknowledge the chance factor. The *Oprah Winfrey Show* guest (Chapter 4) who has an answer for every single case, for every bit of human behavior, should engender not admiration but suspicion. True scientists are not afraid to admit what they do not know. In short, another consumer rule for evaluating psychological claims is this: Before accepting a complicated explanation of an event, consider what part chance may have played in its occurrence.

Coincidence

The tendency to seek explanations for essentially chance occurrences leads to much misunderstanding regarding the nature of coincidental events. Many people think that coincidences need special explanation. They do not understand that coincidences are bound to occur even if nothing other than chance is operating. Coincidences need no special explanation.

Webster's New World Dictionary defines *coincidence* as "an accidental remarkable occurrence of related or identical events." Because the same dictionary defines *accidental* as "occurring by chance," there is no problem here. A coincidence is merely an occurrence of related events that is due to chance. Unfortunately, this is not how many people interpret what is meant by coincidence. The tendency to seek patterns and meanings in events, combined with the "remarkable" aspect of coincidences, leads many to overlook chance as an explanation. Instead, they seek elaborate theories in order to understand these events. How many times have you heard stories like this: "You know, the other day I was sitting around thinking about how I hadn't called old Uncle Bill down in Texas in a long time. And guess what? The next thing that happens . . . ring, ring. Yeah, you guessed it! It's old Uncle Bill on the phone. There must be something to this telepathy stuff after all!" This is a fairly typical example of an elaborate explanation of a coincidental event. On any given day, most of us probably think about several different distant people. How often do these people call us after we think of them? Almost never. Thus, during a year, we probably think about hundreds of people who do not call. Eventually, in the course of these hundreds of "negative trials," which we never recognize as such, someone is going to call after we think of her or him. The event is rare, but rare events do happen—purely by chance. No other explanation is necessary.

If people truly understood what coincidence meant (a remarkable occurrence that is due to chance), they would not fall prey to the fallacy of trying to develop systematic, nonchance explanations for these chance events. Yet, completely contrary to the dictionary definition, coincidence has come to imply to many people something that needs an explanation rather than something that can be explained by chance. For example, most of us have heard statements like "My goodness, what a coincidence! I wonder *why* that happened!" This reflects a fundamental error—coincidences do not *need* an explanation.

Psychologist David Marks (2001) has suggested the neutral term *oddmatch* to signify two events whose co-occurrence strikes us as odd or strange. One thing that contributes to the tendency to search for explanations of coincidental events is the mistaken idea that rare events never happen, that oddmatches are never due to chance. Our belief in this fallacy is intensified because probabilities are sometimes stated in terms of odds and because of the connotations that such statements have. Think of how we phrase the following: "Oh, goodness, that's very unlikely. The odds are 100 to 1 against that happening!" The manner in which we articulate such a statement strongly implies that it will never happen. Of course, we could say the same thing in a very different way, one that has very different connotations: "In 100 events of this type, this outcome *will* probably happen once." This alternative phrasing emphasizes that, although the event is rare, in the long run rare events do happen. In short, oddmatches do occur purely because of chance.

In fact, the laws of probability guarantee that as the number of events increases, the probability that some oddmatch will occur becomes very high. Not only do the laws of chance allow oddmatches to happen, but they virtually *guarantee* them in the long run. Consider one of Marks's (2001) examples. If you flipped 5 coins all at once and they all came up heads, you would probably consider this result an oddmatch, an unlikely event. You would be right. The probability of this happening in any one flip of 5 coins is 1/32 or 0.03. But if you flipped the 5 coins 100 times and asked how likely it is that in at least 1 of those 100 trials the coins would all come up heads, the answer would be 0.96. That is, in 100 trials, this rare event, this oddmatch, is *very likely* to happen.

Since many states have instituted lotteries, in which the winning numbers are usually drawn randomly, either by a computer or by some mechanical randomizing device, many statisticians and behavioral scientists have had occasion to chuckle to themselves when the inevitable has happened—that is, when the same winning sequence of numbers are drawn twice. Such an outcome often provokes howls of protest from the public, who interpret the outcome as proof that the lottery is rigged or "crooked." The public's feeling that there is something wrong with this outcome arises from the mistaken view that something this odd or unlikely cannot happen by chance alone. Of course, the reason the statisticians are chuckling is that chance works in just the opposite way. If lotteries go on long enough, consecutive identical winning numbers are bound to be drawn eventually. For example, on June 21, 1995 in a German lottery called 6/49 (six numbers are picked out of forty-nine possible) the numbers drawn were 15-25-27-30-42-48—exactly the same set of numbers that had been drawn on December 20, 1986 (Mlodinow, 2008). Many people were surprised to learn that over that time period the chance that *some* set of numbers would repeat was as high as 28 percent.

Some years ago, Ann Landers popularized a series of "eerie" coincidences between Presidents Abraham Lincoln and John Kennedy:

1. Lincoln was elected president in 1860; Kennedy was elected in 1960.
2. Lincoln and Kennedy were both concerned with civil rights.
3. *Lincoln* and *Kennedy* have seven letters each.
4. Lincoln had a secretary named Kennedy, and Kennedy had a secretary named Lincoln.
5. Both were succeeded by southerners named Johnson.
6. Both were assassinated by men with three names (John Wilkes Booth and Lee Harvey Oswald).

7. Booth and Oswald both espoused unpopular political ideas.
8. Booth shot Lincoln in a theater and hid in a warehouse; Oswald shot Kennedy from a warehouse and hid in a theater.

Of course, being coincidences, these conjunctions of events are not eerie at all. This was clearly demonstrated by University of Texas computer programmer John Leavy (1992), who ran a "spooky presidential coincidences contest" to demonstrate just how easy it is to generate lists like this for virtually *any* two presidents. For example, the Leavy article contains parallels between William Henry Harrison and Zachary Taylor, Polk and Carter, Garfield and McKinley, Lincoln and Jackson, Nixon and Jefferson, Washington and Eisenhower, Grant and Nixon, and Madison and Wilson. Here, for example, are the eerie similarities between Garfield and McKinley:

1. McKinley and Garfield were both born and raised in Ohio.
2. McKinley and Garfield were both Civil War veterans.
3. McKinley and Garfield both served in the House of Representatives.
4. McKinley and Garfield both supported the gold standard and tariffs for the protection of American industry.
5. *McKinley* and *Garfield* both have eight letters.
6. McKinley and Garfield were both replaced by vice presidents from New York City (Theodore Roosevelt and Chester Alan Arthur).
7. *Chester Alan Arthur* and *Theodore Roosevelt* have 17 letters each.
8. Both of the vice presidents wore mustaches.
9. McKinley and Garfield were both shot in September, in the first year of their current terms.
10. Both of their assassins, Charles Guiteau and Leon Czolgosz, had foreign-sounding names.

The lists for many other conjunctions of presidents are similar. In short, given the complexity of the interactions and events in a life that lasts several decades, it would be surprising if there were *not* some parallels between virtually any two individuals in what is perhaps a sample space of tens of thousands of events (Martin, 1998).

It is practically useful to know when to refrain from concocting complicated explanations for events that simply reflect the operation of chance factors. Writer Atul Gawande (1999) described how during the Yom Kippur War in 1973 cognitive psychologist Daniel Kahneman was approached by the Israeli Air Force for advice. Two squads of aircraft had gone out and one squad had lost four aircraft and one had lost none. The Air Force wanted Kahneman to investigate whether there were factors specific to the different squadrons that might have contributed to this outcome. Instead of doing a study, Kahneman used the insights in this chapter and told the Israeli Air Force not to waste their time: "Kahneman knew that if Air Force officials investigated they would inevitably find some measurable differences between the squadrons and feel compelled to act on them" (Gawande, 1999, p. 37). But Kahneman knew that any such factors would most likely be spurious—the result of mere chance fluctuation.

Personal Coincidences

Oddmatches that happen in our personal lives often have special meaning to us and, thus, we are especially prone not to attribute them to chance. There are many reasons for this tendency. Some are motivational and emotional, but others are due to failures of probabilistic reasoning. We often do not recognize that oddmatches are actually just a small part of a much larger pool of "nonoddmatches." It may seem to some of us that oddmatches occur with great frequency. But do they?

Consider what an analysis of the oddmatches in your personal life would reveal. Suppose on a given day you were involved in 100 distinct events. This does not seem an overestimate, considering the complexity of life in a modern industrial society. Indeed, it is probably a gross underestimate. You watch television, talk on the telephone, meet people, negotiate the route to work or to the store, do household chores, take in information while reading, send and receive email, complete complex tasks at work, and so on. All these events contain several components that are separately memorable. One hundred, then, is probably on the low side, but we will stick with it. An oddmatch is a remarkable conjunction of two events. How many possible different pairs of events are there in the 100 events of your typical day? Using a simple formula to obtain the number of combinations, we calculate that there are 4,950 different pairings of events possible in your typical day. This is true 365 days a year. Now, oddmatches are very memorable. You would probably remember for several years the day Uncle Bill called. Assume that you can remember all the oddmatches that happened to you in a 10-year period. Perhaps, then, you remember six or seven oddmatches (more or less, people differ in their criteria for oddness). What is the pool of nonoddmatches from which these six or seven oddmatches came? It is 4,950 pairs per day multiplied by 365 days per year multiplied by 10 years, or 18,067,500. In short, six oddmatches happened to you in 10 years, but 18,067,494 things that could have been oddmatches also happened. The probability of an oddmatch happening in your life is 0.00000033. It hardly seems strange that 6 out of 18 million conjunctions of events in your life should be odd. Odd things do happen. They are rare, but they do happen. Chance guarantees it (recall the example of simultaneously flipping five coins). In our example, six odd things happened to you. They were probably coincidences: remarkable occurrences of related events that were due to chance.

Psychologists, statisticians, and other scientists have pointed out that many oddmatches are commonly thought to be more odd than they really are. The famous "birthday problem" provides a good example of this. In a class of 23 people, what is the probability that 2 of them will have their birthday on the same day? What is the probability in a class of 35 people? Most people think that the odds are pretty low. Actually, in the class with 23 people, the odds are better than 50–50 that 2 people will have birthdays on the same day. And in the class of 35 students, the odds are very high (the probability is over 0.80; see Martin, 1998). Thus, because there have been 43 presidents of the United States born, it is not surprising that 2 (James Polk and Warren Harding) were born on the same day (November 2). Nor is it surprising, because 38 presidents have died, that 2 (Millard Fillmore and William Howard Taft) have died on the same day (March 8) and, furthermore, that three *more* (John Adams, Thomas Jefferson, James Monroe) have all also died on the same day. And the day that Adams, Jefferson, and Monroe all died on was July 4! Isn't that amazing? No, not amazing—probabilistic.

Accepting Error in Order to Reduce Error: Clinical versus Actuarial Prediction

The reluctance to acknowledge the role of chance when trying to explain outcomes in the world can actually decrease our ability to predict real-world events. Acknowledging the role of chance in determining outcomes in a domain means that we must accept the fact that our predictions will never be 100 percent accurate, that we will always make some errors in our predictions. But interestingly, acknowledging that our predictions will be less than 100 percent accurate can actually help us to increase our overall predictive accuracy. It may seem paradoxical, but it is true that we must accept error in order to reduce error (Dawes, 1991; Einhorn, 1986).

The concept that we must accept error in order to reduce error is illustrated by a very simple experimental task that has been studied for decades in cognitive psychology laboratories. The subject sits in front of two lights (one red and one blue) and is told that she or he is to predict which of the lights will be flashed on each trial and that there will be several dozen such trials (subjects are often paid money for correct predictions). The experimenter has actually programmed the lights to flash randomly, with the provision that the red light will flash 70 percent of the time and the blue light 30 percent of the time. Subjects do quickly pick up the fact that the red light is flashing more, and they predict that it will flash on more trials than they predict that the blue light will flash. In fact, they predict that the red light will flash approximately 70 percent of the time. However, as discussed earlier in this chapter, subjects come to believe that there is a pattern in the light flashes and almost never think that the sequence is random. Instead, they switch back and forth from red to blue, predicting the red light roughly

70 percent of the time and the blue light roughly 30 percent of the time. Subjects rarely realize that—despite the fact that the blue light is coming on 30 percent of the time—if they stopped switching back and forth and predicted the red light every time, they would actually do better! How can this be?

Let's consider the logic of the situation. How many predictions will subjects get correct if they predict the red light roughly 70 percent of the time and the blue light roughly 30 percent of the time and the lights are really coming on randomly in a ratio of 70 to 30? We will do the calculation on 100 trials in the middle of the experiment—after the subject has noticed that the red light comes on more often and is, thus, predicting the red light roughly 70 percent of the time. In 70 of the 100 trials, the red light will come on and the subject will be correct on about 70 percent of those 70 trials (because the subject predicts the red light 70 percent of the time). That is, in 49 of the 70 trials (70 times 0.70), the subject will correctly predict that the red light will come on. In 30 of the 100 trials, the blue light will come on, and the subject will be correct in 30 percent of those 30 trials (because the subject predicts the blue light 30 percent of the time). That is, in 9 of the 30 trials (30 times 0.30), the subject will correctly predict that the blue light will come on. Thus, in 100 trials, the subject is correct 58 percent of the time (49 correct predictions on red light trials and 9 correct predictions on blue light trials). But notice that this is a poorer performance than could be achieved if the subject simply noticed which light was coming on more often and then predicted it in every trial—in this case, noticing that the red light came on more often and predicting it in every trial (let's call this the 100 percent red strategy). Of the 100 trials, 70 would be red flashes, and the subject would have predicted all 70 of these correctly. Of the 30 blue flashes, the subject would have predicted none correctly but still would have a prediction accuracy of 70 percent—12 percent better than the 58 percent correct that the subject achieved by switching back and forth.

The optimal strategy does have the implication though—that you will be wrong every time a blue occurs. And since blue light stimuli are occurring on at least *some* of the trials, it just does not seem right *never* to predict them. But this is just what correct probabilistic thinking requires. It requires accepting the errors that will be made on blue trials in order to attain the higher overall hit rate that will be obtained when predicting red each time. In short, we must *accept* the blue errors in order to make *fewer* errors overall. Predicting human behavior with some accuracy often involves accepting error in order to reduce error, that is, getting better prediction by relying on general principles but acknowledging that we cannot be right in every single case.

Accepting error in order to make fewer errors is a difficult thing to do, however, as evidenced by the 40-year history of research on clinical versus actuarial prediction in psychology. The term *actuarial prediction* refers to predictions based on group trends derived from statistical records, the type of group (i.e., aggregate) predictions that we discussed at the beginning of this chapter. A simple actuarial prediction is one that predicts the same outcome for all individuals sharing a certain characteristic. So, to take an imaginary example, predicting a life span of 77.5 years for people who do not smoke and a life span of 64.3 years for individuals who smoke would be an example of an actuarial prediction. More accurate predictions can be made if we take more than one group characteristic into account (using the complex correlational techniques mentioned in Chapter 5—specifically a technique known as *multiple regression*). For example, predicting a life span of 58.2 years for people who smoke, are overweight, and do not exercise would be an example of an actuarial prediction based on a set of variables (smoking behavior, weight, and amount of exercise), and such predictions are almost always more accurate than predictions made from a single variable.

Such actuarial predictions are common in economics, human resources, criminology, business and marketing, and the medical sciences. For example, in studies published in the *Journal of the American Medical Association* and in the *Annals of Internal Medicine* the following probabilistic trends were reported: people who are obese in middle age are four times more likely than nonobese people to have heart problems after age 65; overweight (but not obese) people are twice as likely to develop kidney problems; and obese people are seven times more likely to develop kidney problems (Seppa, 2006). But probabilistic prediction admits error. Not all obese people will have health problems. Recall the case (from Chapter 10) of the political broadcaster Tim Russert who died of a heart attack at age 58. Physicians determined that Mr. Russert's probability of a heart attack in the next ten years was only 5 percent. That is, *most* people (95 out of 100) with Mr. Russert's profile would be heart-attack free for 10 years. Mr. Russert was one of the unlucky 5 percent— he was an exception to the general trend.

People sometimes find it difficult to act on actuarial evidence, however, because doing so often takes mental discipline. For example, in 2003 the Food and Drug Administration issued a health-advisory warning of a potential link between a popular anti-depressant drug and teen suicide (Dokoupil, 2007). Many physicians worried that, on an actuarial basis, the warning would result in more suicides. They worried that perhaps fewer teenagers would die of suicide *because* of the drug but that *even more* children would die because of an increased hesitancy to prescribe the drug. This is indeed what happened. Treatment with this drug can put children at a temporary risk, but untreated depression is far worse. As one doctor put it, "You may induce two suicides by treatment, but by stopping treatment you're going to lose dozens to hundreds of kids. You're losing more than you're saving. That's the calculus" (p. 48). Or, perhaps we should say: that's the calculus of actuarial prediction. But it can be a hard calculus to follow when folk wisdom is saying things like "better to be safe than sorry." But in the domain of medical treatment "better to be safe than sorry" ignores one half of the equation. It focuses our attention on those who might be hurt by the treatment, but it totally ignores those who would be hurt if the treatment were unavailable.

Knowledge in most subareas of psychology, such as cognitive psychology, developmental psychology, organizational psychology, personality psychology, and social psychology, is stated in terms of actuarial predictions. In contrast, some subgroups of clinical psychological practitioners claim to be able to go beyond group predictions and to make accurate predictions of the outcomes of particular individuals. This is called *clinical*, or *case, prediction*. When engaged in clinical prediction, as opposed to actuarial prediction,

> professional psychologists claim to be able to make predictions about individuals that transcend predictions about "people in general" or about various categories of people. . . . Where professional psychologists differ is in their claim to understand the single individual as unique rather than as part of a group about which statistical generalizations are possible. They claim to be able to analyze "what caused what" in an *individual's* life rather than to state what is "in general" true. (Dawes, 1994, pp. 79–80)

Clinical prediction would seem to be a very useful addition to actuarial prediction. There is just one problem, however. Clinical prediction doesn't work.

For clinical prediction to be useful, the clinician's experience with the client and her or his use of information about the client would have to result in better predictions than we can get from simply coding information about the client and submitting it to statistical procedures that optimize the process of combining quantitative data in order to derive predictions. In short, the claim is that the experience of psychological practitioners allows them to go beyond the aggregate relationships that have been uncovered by research. The claim that clinical prediction is efficacious is, thus, easily testable. Unfortunately, the claim has been tested, and it has been falsified.

Research on the issue of clinical versus actuarial prediction has been consistent. Since the publication in 1954 of Paul Meehl's classic book *Clinical Versus Statistical Prediction*, five decades of research consisting of over a hundred research studies have shown that, in just about every clinical prediction domain that has ever been examined (psychotherapy outcome, parole behavior, college graduation rates, response to electroshock therapy, criminal recidivism, length of psychiatric hospitalization, and many more), actuarial prediction has been found to be superior to clinical prediction (Morera & Dawes, 2006; Ruscio, 2002; Swets et al., 2000; Tetlock, 2005).

In a variety of clinical domains, when a clinician is given information about a client and asked to predict the client's behavior, and when the same information is quantified and processed by a statistical equation that has been developed based on actuarial relationships that research has uncovered, invariably the equation wins. That is, the actuarial prediction is more accurate than the clinician's prediction. In fact, even when the clinician has more information available than is used in the actuarial method, the latter is superior. That is, when the clinician has information from personal contact and interviews with the client, in addition to the same information that goes into the actuarial equation, the clinical predictions still do not achieve an accuracy as great as the actuarial method: "Even when given an information edge, the clinical judge still fails to surpass the actuarial method; in fact, access to additional information often does nothing to close the gap between the two methods" (Dawes et al., 1989, p. 1670). The reason is of course that the equation integrates information accurately and consistently. This factor—consistency—can overcome any informational advantage the clinician has from information gleaned informally.

A final type of test in the clinical-actuarial prediction literature involves actually giving the clinician the predictions from the actuarial equation and asking the clinician to adjust the predictions based on his or her personal experience with the clients. When the clinician makes adjustments in the actuarial predictions, the adjustments actually decrease the accuracy of the predictions (see Dawes, 1994). Here we have an example of failing to "accept error in order to reduce error" that is directly analogous to the light prediction experiment previously described. Rather than relying on the actuarial information that the red light came on more often and predicting red each time (and getting 70 percent correct), the subjects tried to be correct on each trial by alternating red and blue predictions and ended up being 12 percent less accurate (they were correct on only 58 percent of the trials). Analogously the clinicians in these studies believed that their experience gave them "clinical insight" and allowed them to make better predictions than those that can be made from quantified information in the client's file. In fact, their "insight" is nonexistent and leads them to make predictions that are worse than those they would make if they relied only on the public, actuarial information. It should be noted, though, that the superiority of actuarial prediction is not confined to psychology but extends to many other clinical sciences as well—for example, to medicine (Groopman, 2007).

Regarding the research showing the superiority of actuarial prediction over clinical prediction, Paul Meehl (1986) said, "There is no controversy in social science which shows such a large body of qualitatively diverse studies coming out so uniformly in the same direction as this one" (pp. 373–374). Yet, embarrassingly, the field of psychology does not act on this knowledge. For example, the field continues to use personal interviews in the graduate admissions process and in the mental-health-training admissions process, even though voluminous evidence suggests that these interviews have virtually no validity. Instead, practitioners continue to use specious arguments to justify their reliance on "clinical intuition" rather than aggregate predictions that would work better. For example, Dawes et al. (1989) noted,

> A common anti-actuarial argument, or misconception, is that group statistics do not apply to single individuals or events. The argument abuses basic principles of probability. . . . An advocate of this anti-actuarial position would have to maintain, for the sake of logical consistency, that if one is forced to play Russian roulette a single time and is allowed to select a gun with one or five bullets in the chamber, the uniqueness of the event makes the choice arbitrary. (p. 1672)

An analogy to the last point would be to ask yourself how you react to the scientific findings that the probability of a successful kind of surgery is higher for surgeons that perform many of that particular type of surgical operation (Grady, 2009; Groopman, 2007). Would you rather have your operation done by a surgeon A, who is practiced in that type of surgery and has a low failure probability, or by surgeon B, who is unpracticed in that type of surgery and has a high failure probability? If you believe that "probabilities don't apply to the single case," you shouldn't mind having your surgery done by the unpracticed surgeon.

The field of psychology has little to lose in prestige by admitting the superiority of actuarial to clinical judgment in a domain such as predicting psychotherapeutic outcome because the same is true of professionals in numerous other domains as varied as medicine, business, criminology, accounting, and livestock judging. Although the field as a whole would have little to lose, individual practitioners who engage in activities in the role of "experts" (i.e., in courtroom testimony) and imply that they have unique clinical knowledge of individual cases would, of course, lose prestige and perhaps income. But as McFall and Treat (1999) warn in an article on the value of clinical assessment, "The events we are attempting to assess and predict are inherently probabilistic. This means that we cannot expect nature to be so well-behaved as to allow us to predict single events with certainty; instead, the best we can hope for is to identify an array of possible outcomes and to estimate the relative likelihood of each. From this probabilistic perspective, the idealized goal of traditional assessment predicting unique, remote events with precision is fanciful, reflecting our naivete and/or hubris" (p. 217).

In fact, the field, and society, would benefit if we developed the habit of "accepting error in order to reduce error." In attempting to find unique explanations of every single unusual case (unique explanations that simply may not be possible given the present state of our knowledge), we often lose predictive accuracy in the more mundane cases. Recall the red-blue light experiment again. The "100 percent red strategy" makes incorrect predictions of all of the minority or unusual events (when the blue lights flash). What if we focused more on those minority events by adopting the "70-percent-red-30-percent-blue strategy"? We would now be able to predict 9 of those 30 unusual events (30 times 0.30). But the cost is that we lose our ability to predict 21 of the majority events. Instead of 70 correct predictions of red, we now have only 49 correct predictions (70 times 0.70). Predictions of behavior in the clinical domain have the same logic. In concocting complicated explanations for every case, we may indeed catch a few more unusual cases—but at the cost of losing predictive accuracy in the majority of cases, where simple actuarial prediction would work better. Gawande (1998) points out that "accepting error in order to reduce error" is something that medicine needs to learn as well. He argues that the emphasis on an intuitive, personalized approach in medicine "is flawed—our attempt to acknowledge human complexity causes more mistakes than it prevents" (p. 80).

Wagenaar and Keren (1986) illustrated how overconfidence in personal knowledge and the discounting of statistical information can undermine safety campaigns advocating seat belt use because people think, "I am different, I drive safely." The problem is that over 85 percent of the population thinks that they are "better than the average driver" (Svenson, 1981)—obviously a patent absurdity.

The same fallacy of believing that "statistics don't apply to the single case" is an important factor in the thinking of individuals with chronic gambling problems. In his study of gambling behavior, Wagenaar (1988) concluded,

> From our discussions with gamblers it has become abundantly clear that gamblers are generally aware of the negative long-term result. They know that they have lost more than they have won, and that it will be the same in the future. But they fail to apply these statistical considerations to the next round, the next hour, or the next night. A rich repertoire of heuristics . . . gives them the suggestion that statistics do not apply in the next round, or the next hour. That they can predict the next outcome. (p. 117)

Wagenaar found that compulsive gamblers had a strong tendency not to "accept error in order to reduce error." For example, blackjack players had a tendency to reject a strategy called *basic* that is guaranteed to decrease the casino's advantage from 6 or 8 percent to less than 1 percent. Basic is a long-term statistical strategy, and the compulsive players tended to reject it because they believed that "an effective strategy ought to be effective in every single instance" (p. 110). The gamblers in Wagenaar's study "invariably said that the general prescriptions of such systems could not work, because they neglect the idiosyncrasies of each specific situation" (p. 110). Instead of using an actuarial strategy that was guaranteed to save them thousands of dollars, these gamblers were on a futile chase to find a way to make a clinical prediction based on the idiosyncrasies of each specific situation.

Of course, this discussion of the literature on clinical versus actuarial prediction is not meant to imply that there is not a role for the case study in psychology. Keep in mind that we have been speaking about the specific situation of the prediction of behavior. Recall the discussion of the role of the case study in Chapter 4. Case information is highly useful in drawing attention to variables that are important and that need to be mea-sured. What we have been saying in this section is that, once the relevant variables have been determined and we want to use them to predict behavior, measuring them and using a statistical equation to determine the predictions constitute the best procedure. First, we get more accurate predictions by using the actuarial approach. Second, the actuarial approach has an advantage over clinical prediction in that an actuarial equation is public knowledge—open for all to use, modify, criticize, or dispute. In contrast, the use of clinical prediction amounts to reliance on an authority whose assessments—precisely because these judgments are claimed to be singular and idiosyncratic—are not subject to public crit-icism. As Dawes (1994) noted,

> A professional psychologist who claims in court that a particularly devastating "clinical judgment" is based on years of experience and cannot be explicitly justified can be challenged only on irrelevant grounds—such as training, years of giving similar testimony, demeanor, and so on. In contrast, a statistical model may be challenged on rational grounds because it is public. (p. 104)

Summary

The role of chance in psychology is often misunderstood by the lay public and by clinical practitioners alike. People find it difficult to recognize that part of the variability in behavioral outcomes is determined by chance fac-tors. That is, variation in behavior is in part a function of random factors and, thus, psychologists should not claim to be able to predict behavior case by case. Instead, psychological predictions are probabilistic—predictions of aggregate trends.

The error of implying that psychological predictions can be made at the level of the individual is often made by clinical psychologists themselves, who sometimes mistakenly imply that clinical training confers an "intuitive" ability to predict an individual case. Instead, decades' worth of research has consistently indicated that actuarial prediction (prediction in terms of group statistical trends) is superior to clinical prediction in accounting for human behavior. There is no evidence of a clinical intuition that can predict whether a statistical trend will hold or not in a particular case. Thus, statistical information should never be set aside when one is predicting behavior. Statistical prediction also correctly signals that there will always be errors and uncertainties when one is predicting human behavior.

CHAPTER 12

The Rodney Dangerfield
of the Sciences

Although there is a great public fascination with psychological topics, most judgments about the field and its accomplishments are resoundingly negative. Psychologists are aware of this image problem, but most feel that there is little they can do about it, so they simply ignore it. This is a mistake. As the mass media become more and more influential in determining public perceptions (e.g., fictional TV "docudramas" become the true history for a public that does not read), ignoring psychology's image problem threatens to make it worse.

Rodney Dangerfield was a popular comedian for over three decades and whose trademark was the plaintive cry "I don't get no respect!" In a way, this is a fitting summary of psychology's status in the public mind. This chapter will touch on some of the reasons that psychology appears to be the Rodney Dangerfield of the sciences.

Psychology's Image Problem

Some of the reasons for psychology's image problem have already been discussed. For example, the Freud problem discussed in Chapter 1 undoubtedly contributes to the low esteem in which psychology is held. To the extent that the public knows about any reputable psychologists at all, Freud and B. F. Skinner are those psychologists (Overskeid, 2007). The distorted versions of their ideas that circulate among the public must contribute to the idea that psychology is a frivolous field indeed. There would appear to be little hope for a field when one of its most renowned scholars is said to have claimed that we have no minds and that we are just like rats. Of course, Skinner did not deny that we think (Gaynor, 2004), and many principles of operant conditioning that he developed from work with animals *have* been shown to generalize to human behavior. However, the public is little aware of any of these facts. Distorted ideas from Freudian doctrine also contribute to lowering the public esteem for psychology.

Psychology and Parapsychology

The layperson's knowledge of reputable psychological research, outside of the work of Freud or Skinner, is virtually nonexistent. One way to confirm this fact is to look in your local bookstore to see what material on psychology is available to the general public. Inspection will reveal that the material generally falls into three categories. First, there will be few classics (Freud, Skinner, Fromm, Erickson, Jung, etc.) heavily biased toward old-style psychoanalytic views that are totally unrepresentative of modern psychology. Frustratingly for psychologists, works of real worth in the field are often shelved in the science and/or biology sections of bookstores. For example, psychologist Steven Pinker's well-known and esteemed book *How the Mind Works* (1997) is often in the science section rather than the psychology section. Thus, the important work in cognitive science that he discusses becomes associated with biology, neurophysiology, or computer science rather than psychology.

The second class of material found in most stores might be called pseudoscience masquerading as psychology—that is, the seemingly never-ending list of so-called paranormal phenomena such as telepathy, clairvoyance, psychokinesis, precognition, reincarnation, biorhythms, astral projection, pyramid power, plant communication, and psychic surgery (Lilienfeld, Lohr, & Moirer, 2001). The presence of a great body of this material in the psychology sections of bookstores undoubtedly contributes to the widespread misconception that psychologists are the people who have confirmed the existence of such phenomena. There is a bitter irony for psychology in this misconception. In fact, the relationship between psychology and the paranormal is easily stated. These phenomena are simply not an area of active research interest in modern psychology. The reason, however, is a surprise to many people.

The statement that the study of ESP and other paranormal abilities is not accepted as part of the discipline of psychology will undoubtedly provoke the ire of many readers. Surveys have consistently shown that more than 40 percent of the general public believes in the existence of such phenomena and often holds these beliefs with considerable fervor (Farha & Steward, 2006; Kida, 2006; Musella, 2005; Rice, 2003). Historical studies and survey research have suggested why these beliefs are held so strongly (Begley, 2008b; Humphrey, 1996; Lilienfeld, 2005; Park, 2008; Stanovich, 2004). Like most religions, many of the so-called paranormal phenomena seem to promise things such as life after death, and for some people, they serve the same need for transcendence. It should not be surprising, then, that the bearer of the bad tidings that research in psychology does not validate ESP is usually not greeted with enthusiasm. The statement that psychology does not consider ESP a viable research area invariably upsets believers and often provokes charges that psychologists are dogmatic in banishing certain topics from their discipline. Psychologists do not contribute to public understanding when they throw up their hands and fail to deal seriously with these objections. Instead, psychologists should give a careful and clear explanation of why such objections are ill founded. Such an explanation would emphasize that scientists do not determine by edict which topics to investigate. No proclamation goes out declaring what can and cannot be studied. Areas of investigation arise and are expanded or terminated according to a natural selection process that operates on ideas and methods. Those that lead to fruitful theories and empirical discoveries are taken up by a large number of scientists. Those that lead to theoretical dead ends or that do not yield replicable or interesting observations are dropped. This natural selection of ideas and methods is what leads science closer to the truth.

The reason that ESP, for example, is not considered a viable topic in contemporary psychology is simply that its investigation has not proved fruitful. Therefore, very few psychologists are interested in it. It is important here to emphasize the word *contemporary*, because the topic of ESP was of greater interest to psychologists some years ago, before the current bulk of negative evidence had accumulated. As history shows, research areas are not declared invalid by governing authorities; they are merely winnowed out in the competing environment of ideas.

ESP was never declared an invalid topic in psychology. The evidence of this fact is clear and publicly available (Alcock, 1990; Hines, 2003; Hyman, 1992, 1996; Kelly, 2005; Marks, 2001; Milton & Wiseman, 1999; Park, 2008). Many papers investigating ESP have appeared in legitimate psychological journals over the years. Parapsychologists who thrive on media exposure like to give the impression that the area is somehow new, thus implying that startling new discoveries are just around the corner. The truth is much less exciting.

The study of ESP is actually as old as psychology itself. It is not a new area of investigation. It has been as well studied as many of the currently viable topics in the psychological literature. The results of the many studies that have appeared in legitimate psychological journals have been overwhelmingly negative. After more than 90 years of study, there still does not exist one example of an ESP phenomenon that is replicable under controlled conditions. This simple but basic scientific criterion has not been met despite dozens of studies conducted over many decades. Many parapsychologists and believers themselves are even in agreement on this point. In short, there is no demonstrated phenomenon that needs scientific explanation. For this reason alone, the topic is now of little interest to psychology.

And now the irony. Psychologists have played a prominent role in attempts to assess claims of paranormal abilities. The importance of their contribution is probably second only to that of the professional magicians, who have clearly done the most to expose the fraudulent nature of most purported demonstrations of paranormal abilities (Randi, 2005). Many of the most important books on the state of the evidence on paranormal abilities have been written by psychologists.

The irony, then, is obvious. Psychology, the discipline that has probably contributed most to the accurate assessment of ESP claims, is the field that is most closely associated with such pseudosciences in the public mind. Psychology suffers greatly from this guilt-by-association phenomenon. As will be discussed in greater detail later, psychology is often the victim of a "double whammy." Here is just one example. The assumption that anything goes in psychology, that it is a field without scientific mechanisms for deciding among knowledge claims, leads to its being associated with pseudosciences such as ESP. However, if psychologists ever become successful in getting the public to recognize these pseudosciences for what they really are, the pseudosciences' association with psychology will be seen as confirmation that psychology is indeed not a science!

The Self-Help Literature

The third category in the bookstore psychology section is the so-called self-help literature. There are, of course, many different genres within this category (see Fried & Schultis, 1995; Lilienfeld et al., 2003; Meyers, 2008; Paul, 2001; Santrock et al., 1994). Some books are spiritually uplifting tracts written with the purpose of generally increasing feelings of self-worth and competence. Others attempt to package familiar bromides about human behavior in new ways. A few (but all too few) are authored by responsible psychologists writing for the general public. Many that are not in the latter category vie for uniqueness by presenting new "therapies" that are usually designed not only to correct specific behavioral problems but also to help satisfy general human wants (making more money, losing more weight, and having better sex are the "big three"), thereby ensuring larger book sales. These so-called new therapies are rarely based on any type of controlled experimental investigation. They usually rest on personal experience or on a few case histories, if the author is a clinician. This is often true of the treatments of so-called "alternative medicine." Humorously, R. Barker Bausell, a biostatistician at the University of Maryland, calls the term alternative medicine "a scientific term for 'something you heard about from your hairdresser, who thinks she saw it on 'Oprah'" (Adler, 2007, p. 22).

The many behavioral and cognitive therapies that have emerged after painstaking psychological investigation as having demonstrated effectiveness are usually poorly represented on the bookshelves. The situation is even worse in the electronic media. Radio and TV carry virtually no reports of legitimate psychology and instead present purveyors of bogus "therapies" and publicity-seeking media personalities who have no connection to the actual field of psychology. The main reason is that the legitimate psychological therapies do not claim to provide an instant cure or improvement, nor do they guarantee success or claim a vast generality for their effects ("Not only will you quit smoking, but every aspect of your life will improve!").

It is similar in the case of the Internet. The lack of peer review ensures that the therapies and cures that one finds there are often bogus. Here is one example. In 2008 Paul Offit published an important book titled *Autism's False Prophets* in which he detailed the many treatments for autism that have been found to be bogus by actual scientific research but that have enjoyed popularity among parents desperate for a treatment to help their children. One, facilitated communication, I have discussed in Chapter 6. Offit describes many other pseudoscientific treatments that have falsely raised parents' hopes and have led them to spend thousands of dollars and to waste their time and energy chasing a bogus "cure." On January 2, 2009, I identified one of the bogus chemical "cures" for autism discussed in Offit's book (I will not name it in order not to add to its publicity) and typed it and the word "autism" into Google. Of the first ten links that appeared in the outcome of my search, four links were to websites that were *advocating* this totally bogus chemical "cure." Scientific accuracy is not guaranteed in a Web search because websites are not peer reviewed. They thus provide no consumer protection for the random searcher with no further knowledge of the scientific literature on the topic in question.

The self-help literature, which accounts for a substantial portion of the book market in the United States, has many unfortunate effects on the general perception of psychology. First, like the Freud problem, it creates confusion concerning the problems that dominate the attention of psychologists. For example, although a substantial number of psychologists are engaged in providing therapy for problems of obesity, of relationships, and of sexuality and also in researching these problems, the actual number is far less than that suggested by their representation in the self-help literature. This misrepresentation also contributes to the public's view that most psychologists are engaged in the treatment of and research on abnormal behavior. In fact, most psychological research is directed at nonpathological behavior that is typical of all humans. Ex-president of the American Psychological Association Martin Seligman (2002) has lamented that, to the public, psychology has become "almost synonymous with treating mental illness. Its historic mission of making the lives of untroubled people more productive and fulfilling takes a distant back seat to healing disorders" (p. 19).

Beyond the content confusion, the self-help literature creates an inaccurate impression of the methods and goals of psychology. As we showed in Chapter 4, the science of psychology does not consider a few case studies, testimonials, and personal experiences—which are the database for most of the self-help "therapies"—adequate empirical evidence to support the efficacy of a therapy. The self-help literature misleads the public by implying that this is the type of database on which most psychological conclusions rest. As illustrated in Chapter 8, the confirmation of a theory must rest on many different types of evidence, and case studies yield the weakest type of data. It is a fundamental mistake to view such data as definitive proof of a particular theory or therapy.

Recipe Knowledge

Finally, the self-help literature creates confusion about the goals of psychology and about the type of knowledge that most psychological investigations seek. Psychologist Leigh Shaffer (1981) suggested that this literature strongly implies that psychological researchers seek what has been termed *recipe knowledge*. Recipe knowledge is the knowledge of how to use something without knowledge of the fundamental principles that govern its functioning. For example, most people know many things about how to use a telephone. They know how to dial, how to get information, how to make long-distance connections, and so on. But many are completely ignorant of the physical principles on which the operation of the telephone is based. They do not know how it does what it does; they only know that they can make it work. This is recipe knowledge of the telephone. Our knowledge of many technological products in our society is also recipe knowledge.

Of course, this is not an entirely bad thing. Indeed, most technological products have been designed to be used without knowledge of all the principles that make them work. In fact, the idea of recipe knowledge provides one way of conceptualizing the difference between basic and applied research. The basic researcher seeks to uncover the fundamental principles of nature without necessarily worrying about whether they can be turned into recipe knowledge. The applied researcher is more interested in translating basic principles into a product that requires only recipe knowledge.

Most self-help literature provides only recipe knowledge about human behavior. It usually boils down to the form "Do X and you will become more Y," or "Do Z and person A will react more B." Now, there is nothing inherently wrong here, assuming, of course, that the recipes provided are correct (which is usually not a safe assumption). Many legitimate psychotherapies also provide much recipe knowledge. However, a problem arises when people mistakenly view recipe knowledge as the ultimate goal of all psychological research. Although a number of psychological researchers do work on turning basic behavioral principles into usable psychotherapeutic techniques, health-maintaining behavior programs, or models of efficient industrial organization, psychological research is largely basic research aimed at uncovering general facts and theories about behavior. Here we have another reason why psychological research may seem strange to the outsider.

Investigations of basic principles often look very different from studies focused on developing applications.

We would consider it silly to walk into a molecular biology laboratory and ask a researcher whether we should take two or three aspirins for a headache. The reason is not that molecular biology has nothing to do with pain relief. Future developments in pain relievers will probably involve knowledge from this area of science. It is silly to ask this question because the molecular biologist is simply not working at the recipe level that deals with whether to take two aspirins or three. The researcher is concerned with fundamental facts about the molecular level of biological substances. These facts could lead to recipe knowledge in any number of areas, but the transformation to recipe knowledge will probably not be accomplished by the same investigator who uncovered the basic facts at the molecular level, nor will it be accomplished by use of the same methods that led to the original discoveries.

Thus, because the self-help literature has led people to believe that most psychologists work at developing recipe knowledge, much of the basic research that psychologists conduct appears strange. What did Hecht's data (Chapter 7) about subjects looking at red lights in a dark room have to do with anything in the real world? Well, on the surface, nothing. Hecht was interested in uncovering basic laws about the way the visual system adapts to darkness. The basic principles were eventually translated into recipe knowledge of how to deal with some specific problems, such as night blindness due to vitamin deficiency. However, this translation was not done by Hecht himself, and it did not come until several years later.

Thus, the self-help literature has two unfortunate side effects on the public perception of psychology. The range of problems addressed in this literature does not necessarily represent the focus of contemporary psychology. Instead, it reflects, quite naturally, what people want to read about. The logic of television, radio, and web-based content is the same. However, the focus of science is not determined by polling the public. In all sciences, and in psychology in particular, there is usually a gap between the ideas that are productive for scientists and those that can be packaged to sell to the public. Consider the area of weight loss prescriptions. Scientists have slowly accumulated evidence for some mild prescriptions that help with weight control (Brody, 2008) but they are not breakthrough remedies. By contrast, consider the report of retired physician Harriet Hall (2008), who writes a science-based medicine blog. She describes one weight-loss product that "made the usual claims: eat all you want and still lose weight. But it had the best advertising slogan ever: 'We couldn't say it in print if it wasn't true!' I laughed out loud. Anyone can say anything in print until they get caught. These diet ads all say things that aren't true, and the Federal Trade Commission can't begin to catch them all" (p. 47). Hall's point is that there is a complete disconnect between good science and what the media (from television to print to websites) wants to publicize.

Journalists Barbara Kantrowitz and Claudia Kolb (2006) described the disconnect between science and the media in an article on the media reporting of the health effects of various foods. The subtitle of their article was "A new appetite for answers has put science on a collision course with the media." The "collision course" in the subtitle refers to the fact that the media want quick answers to questions that are of "public interest," whereas science produces slow answers to questions that are scientifically answerable—and all the questions that the public finds interesting might not be answerable.

Psychology and Other Disciplines

Psychology, of course, does not have a monopoly on studying behavior. Many other allied disciplines, using a variety of different techniques and theoretical perspectives, also contribute to our knowledge. Many problems concerning behavior call for an interdisciplinary approach. However, a frustrating fact that most psychologists must live with is that when work on an interdisciplinary problem is publicized, the contributions of psychologists are often usurped by other fields.

There are many examples of scientific contributions by psychologists that have been ignored, minimized, or partially attributed to other disciplines. For instance, the first major survey of the evidence on television's effects on children's behavior was conducted under the aegis of the U.S. Surgeon General, so it is not surprising that the American Medical Association (AMA) passed a resolution to reaffirm the survey's findings of a suggested causal link and to bring the conclusions more publicity. Again, there is nothing wrong here, but an unintended consequence of the repeated association of the findings on televised violence with the AMA is that it has undoubtedly created the impression that the medical profession conducted the scientific research that established the results. In fact, the vast majority of the research studies on the effects of television violence on children's behavior were conducted by psychologists.

One of the reasons that the work of psychologists is often ascribed to other disciplines is that the word *psychologist* has, over the years, become ambiguous. Many research psychologists commonly append their research specialty to the word *psychologist* when labeling themselves, calling themselves, for example, physiological psychologists, cognitive psychologists, industrial psychologists, evolutionary psychologists, or neuropsychologists. Some use a label that does not contain a derivative of the word *psychology* at all, for example, neuroscientist, cognitive scientist, artificial intelligence specialist, and ethologist. Both of these practices—in conjunction with the media's bias that "psychology isn't a science"—lead to the misattribution of the accomplishments of psychologists: The work of physiological psychologists is attributed to biology, the work of cognitive psychologists is attributed to computer science and neuroscience, the work of industrial psychologists is attributed to engineering and business, and so on. Psychology won't be helped by the fact that one of its most brilliant contemporary researchers, Daniel Kahneman, received the 2002 Nobel Prize in economics! Of course, no Nobel Prize is given in psychology (Benjamin, 2004; Kahneman, 2003; MacCoun, 2002).

In fact, here is how ridiculous the tendency to overlook psychology can get. In its April 17, 2008 issue, the *New York Review of Books* published the following correction on page 86: "In Sue Halperin's review of books about happiness [NYR, April 3], the field in which economist Daniel Kahneman has done pioneering research should have been referred to as hedonic psychology, not hedonistic psychology." At first we might give the magazine some points for accuracy—they corrected the mistaken use of the word hedonistic with the word hedonic. However, the editors did not notice, before printing this correction, that they had introduced *another* error—Daniel Kahneman is a cognitive psychologist, not an economist!

Psychologist Frederick King (1993), the director of the Yerkes Primate Research Center at Emory University, told of taking time to explain to a reporter the importance of animal models in the study of human neurological disorders. After listening to the long explanation by King, who had contributed for years to the research literature on the neurological and behavioral problems of epilepsy, the reporter asked, "How do you know anything about epilepsy? You're just a psychologist."

It is such thinking that leads many people to assume that the root of most medical errors lies in medical technology or in pharmaceutical products that do not work properly. In fact, most medical errors trace to defects in thinking—they are rooted in aspects of human psychology that are being studied so that medical practice might be improved (Groopman, 2007, 2008).

Consider another example. In the late 1970s, several cases involving the use of standardized tests were adjudicated in the courts. One such case, *PASE vs. Hannon*, involved the issue of cultural bias in intelligence tests. The judge in the case felt that the only way to arrive at a decision was to inspect each test item himself and to trust his own intuition. He had no reservations about his ability to make an accurate judgment and, in his legal opinion, cited his own view of each question on the tests involved (Bersoff, 1981, 1982). He concluded that eight items in one test and a single item in another may have been biased. The judge did not realize that the issue in question is an empirical one that can be answered by use of the scientific method. Personal opinion is not only irrelevant but may be extremely misleading. The determination of bias in test items involves complex statistical procedures and extensive data collection. Psychologists have been prominent in collecting the necessary data and developing the necessary statistical techniques for their evaluation.

Ironically, given the judge's action, research has in fact revealed that the layperson's intuitive judgment about which items are culturally biased is often markedly inaccurate. Many items that are judged to be fair are in fact biased in various ways, and many that are thought to be unfair are actually statistically unbiased (Sandoval & Miille, 1980). For example, the Wechsler Adult Intelligence Scale has been criticized in Canada because some of the items on one of its subscales (Information) clearly seem to be biased in favor of U.S. citizens. One item, for instance, asks the respondent to name four men who have been president of the United States since 1950. Thus, some of the items have been "Canadianized" for administration in Canada (Violato, 1984, 1986). The "presidents" item, for example, was changed to "Name four men who have been prime minister of Canada since 1900." However, there was one little problem with this obvious, "commonsense" change: Canadian citizens do better on the presidents version than on the prime ministers version!

Our Own Worst Enemies

Lest it appear that we are blaming everyone else for psychology's image problems, it is about time that we acknowledge the contribution of psychologists themselves to confusion about their field. There are very few rewards for the legitimate psychologist who tries to communicate actual psychology to the public. However, the APA and the APS are making more efforts to facilitate public communication. The APS has started a new journal for this purpose: *Psychological Science in the Public Interest*. The APS also sponsors a blog called "We're Only Human" for this purpose (http://www.psychologicalscience.org/onlyhuman/). Psychology needs to make much more of an effort in this area. Otherwise, we will have only ourselves to blame for the misunderstanding of our discipline (West, 2007).

Past APA president Ronald Fox (1996) spoke of psychology's communication problems in a recent presidential address and how we have brought some of these communication problems on ourselves:

> Some practitioners who are appearing in the mass media are behaving in ways that are unprofessional, marginally ethical at best, and downright embarrassing to a majority of their peers. . . . Our discipline lacks effective measures for responding to irresponsible and outrageous public claims. . . . Too often in today's world, the public is treated to the views and opinions of charlatans (as observed on a recent TV talk show in which a psychologist claimed to have helped dozens of patients remember traumas suffered in past lives), rather than rational practitioners. (pp. 779–780)

And, finally, there is the phenomenon of antiscientific attitudes within parts of psychology itself. For example, some groups of psychotherapists have traditionally resisted scientific evaluations of their treatments. Columnist and psychotherapist Charles Krauthammer (1985) wrote of how this attitude presents a serious threat to the integrity of psychotherapy. First, there is the proliferation of therapies that has occurred because of a reluctance to winnow out those that do not work. Such a proliferation not only removes a critical consumer protection but also promotes confusion in the field: "Psychotherapy has come upon this state of confusion because . . . it permits too few deaths among its schools. It is incapable of killing its own. Psychotherapy is dying of dilution." Krauthammer was here lamenting how the failure to use the falsification strategy prevents scientific progress.

Finally, Krauthammer pointed to the inconsistency of a therapeutic community that, on one hand, argues against scientific evaluation because it is "more art than science," in the common phrase, but is still greatly concerned about what he called the 800-pound gorilla: reimbursement for services by government and private health insurers. Krauthammer exposed the inconsistency of these attitudes within the psychotherapy community: "As long as psychotherapies resist pressure to produce scientific evidence that they work, the economic squeeze will tighten. After all, if psychotherapy is really an art, it should be supported by the National Endowment for the Humanities, not by Medicare." Consistent with this sentiment, in their review of psychotherapy outcome research, Kopta, Lueger, Saunders, and Howard (1999) argued, "The effectiveness of specific psychological treatments must be empirically validated to justify reimbursement by insurance and managed care companies and by government agencies that are demanding more accountability" (p. 442).

Some readers of the first few editions of this book commented that they thought I had "let psychologists get off too easily" by not emphasizing more strongly that unprofessional behavior and antiscientific attitudes among psychologists themselves contribute greatly to the discipline's image problem. My task of providing more balance on this point was made easier by the publication, in 1994, of Robyn Dawes's *House of Cards: Psychology and Psychotherapy Built on Myth*. If anyone doubts that psychologists themselves have contributed greatly to the field's dilemmas, they need only read this book. In this courageous work, Dawes did not hesitate to air psychology's dirty linen and, at the same time, to argue that the scientific attitude toward human problems that is at the heart of the true discipline of psychology is of great utility to society (although its potential is still largely untapped). For example, Dawes argued that "there really is a science of psychology that has been developed with much work by many people over many years, but it is being increasingly ignored, derogated, and contradicted by the behavior of professionals—who, of course, give lip service to its existence" (p. vii).

What Dawes, and others (Garb, 2005; Lilienfeld, Lynn, & Lohr, 2003; Lilienfeld, Ruscio, & Lynn, 2008; Mook, 2001; Wood, Nezworski, Lilienfeld, & Garb, 2003), are objecting to is that the field of psychology justifies licensure requirements based on the scientific status of psychology and then uses licensure to protect the unscientific behavior of psychological practitioners. For example, one thing that a well-trained psychologist should know is that we can be reasonably confident only in aggregate predictions. By contrast, predicting the behavior of particular individuals is fraught with uncertainty (see Chapters 10 and 11) and is something no competent psychologist should attempt without the strongest of caveats, if at all. As Dawes (1994) noted,

> A mental health expert who expresses a confident opinion about the probable future behavior of a single individual (for example, to engage in violent acts) is by definition incompetent, because the research has demonstrated that neither a mental health expert nor anyone else can make such a prediction with accuracy sufficient to warrant much confidence. (Professionals often state that their professional role "requires" them to make such judgments, however much they personally appreciate the uncertainty involved. No, they are not required—they volunteer.) (p. vii)

In short, the APA has fostered an ethos surrounding clinical psychology that suggests that psychologists can be trained to acquire an "intuitive insight" into the behavior of individual people that the research evidence does not support. When pushed to defend licensure requirements as anything more than restraint of trade, however, the organization uses its scientific credentials as a weapon (one president of the APA, defending the organization from attack, said "Our scientific base is what sets us apart from the social workers, the counselors, and the Gypsies"; Dawes, 1994, p. 21). But the very methods that the field holds up to justify its scientific status have revealed that the implication that licensed psychologists have a unique "clinical insight" is false. It is such intellectual duplicity on the part of the APA that spawned Dawes's book and that in part led to the formation of the APS in the 1980s by psychologists tired of an APA that was more concerned about Blue Cross payments than with science.

Scott Lilienfeld (1998), the winner of the David Shakow Award for early career contributions to clinical psychology, reiterated all of these points in his award acceptance speech, warning that "we in clinical psychology seem to have shown surprisingly little interest in doing much about the problem of pseudoscience that has been festering in our own backyards" (p. 3). Lilienfeld (1998) listed several categories of pseudosciences that have flourished in clinical psychology during the 1990s, including

1. Unvalidated and bizarre treatments for trauma
2. Demonstrably ineffective treatments for autism such as facilitated communication (see Chapter 6)
3. The continued use of inadequately validated assessment instruments (e.g., many projective tests)
4. Subliminal self-help tapes
5. Use of highly suggestive therapeutic techniques to unearth memories of child abuse.

Lilienfeld quoted noted clinical researcher Paul Meehl's (1993), "If we do not clean up our clinical act and provide our students with role models of scientific thinking, outsiders will do it for us" (p. 728; see also, Mahrer, 2000). Meehl was here referring to the tendency—discussed in Chapter 11—for clinicians to imply, contrary to the empirical evidence, that they have "special" knowledge of people that goes beyond general behavioral trends that are publicly available as replicable scientific knowledge. Arguing that the clinical psychologist must, if anything, be more concerned that knowledge be empirically and publicly verified, Meehl (1993) warns that "it is absurd, as well as arrogant, to pretend that acquiring a PhD somehow immunizes me from the errors of sampling, perception, recording, retention, retrieval, and inference to which the human mind is subject" (p. 728).

Questionable practices still plague the field of clinical psychology, however. For example, the critical-incident stress debriefing has, in many localities, become a standard procedure used to treat witnesses to catastrophic and traumatic events such as bombings, shootings, combat, terrorism, and earthquakes (Groopman, 2004; McNally, Bryant, & Ehlers, 2003). The debriefing procedure involves having the client "talk about the event and ventilate their emotions, especially in the company of peers who have experienced the same incident" (McNally et al., 2003, p. 56), and its purpose is to reduce the incidence of posttraumatic stress disorders (PTSDs). The majority of debriefed clients report that the experience was helpful. Of course, no one who has read this book will find that evidence convincing (recall the discussion of placebo effects in Chapter 4). A control group (who is not given the critical-incident stress debriefing) is obviously needed. In fact, "the vast majority trauma survivors recover from initial posttrauma reactions without professional help" (McNally et al., 2003, p. 45), so it clearly needs to be demonstrated that the recovery rate is higher when the critical-incident stress debriefing is used. Properly controlled studies have shown that this is not the case (Groopman, 2004; McNally et al., 2003), yet the procedure continues to be used.

Emery, Otto, and O'Donohue (2005), in a recent review of a large body of evidence, have shown that, likewise, the clinical psychology surrounding child custody evaluations is filled with pseudoscience (Novotney, 2008). For example, they describe several assessment instruments used by clinical psychologists purportedly to assess children's best interests in these custody disputes. After reviewing several of these instruments—for example, scales purporting to assess the perception of relationships and parental awareness skills—Emery et al. (2005) conclude that none of them have demonstrated reliability or validity. They note that "no study examining the properties of these measures has ever been published in a peer-reviewed journal—an essential criterion for science" (p. 8) and conclude that "our bottom-line evaluation of these measures is a harsh one: these measures assess ill-defined constructs, and they do so poorly, leaving no scientific justification for their use in child custody evaluations" (p. 7).

Emery et al. (2005) point out that it is not just the instruments in child custody evaluations that are often faulty, but the very concepts used by clinical psychologists. Emery et al. give as one example so-called "parental alienation syndrome." It is based on the "clinical experience" of just a single person and has no validation in convergent scientific research, but it is bandied about by clinical psychologists in custody evaluations as if it were a truly scientific construct. It is likewise with some well-known measures for assessing sex offenders. Clinical psychologists continue to use them in spite of their lack of predictive validity—the measures have no demonstrated ability to differentially predict the probability of re-offense (Ewing, 2006).

Cognitive psychologist Hal Arkes (2003) described his frustration when federal agencies did not use the information he provided them regarding how to make the grant review processes fairer. But, upon reflection, he had to admit that our profession presents an embarrassing face to the public. He recalls recently receiving a brochure from a conference at which professional psychologists would receive continuing education credit for sessions on communication with spirits and deceased ancestors. He admits that it is not surprising that federal agencies fail to be influenced by psychologists when "professional organizations grant continuing education credit for highly dubious 'workshops' [and when] I continue to have fully credentialled colleagues who embarrass the profession" (p. 6).

Psychoanalytically oriented clinical psychologists, as another example, have been guilty of many pseudoscientific practices. A historian of Freudian thought, Frank Sulloway, has argued that in response to critiques of Freud's ideas, psychoanalysis "reacted regressively by privatizing its training mechanisms, which means that it took itself out of the enormously successful tradition, which first emerged during the scientific revolution, of testing theories using formal methods of self-criticism. Instead, the discipline of psychoanalysis took a step back toward the medieval tradition that preceded the scientific revolution by founding small private institutes in which knowledge could be transmitted dogmatically and where students were taught how to overcome 'resistances' to the theory" (Dufresne, 2007, p. 65).

Things may be looking up, however. In 2002 a new journal was started: *The Scientific Review of Mental Health Practice* (Lilienfeld, 2002, 2007; see also, Lilienfeld, Ruscio, & Lynn, 2008). The journal is dedicated to research that tries to distinguish scientific from pseudoscientific treatments, and it has been endorsed by the Council for Scientific Mental Health Practice. Even more heartening are indications that at least some psychological organizations are showing the fortitude required to police clinical practice and to rid psychological practice of its ultimately destructive "anything goes" attitude. Lilienfeld and Lohr (2000) report on how the Arizona Board of Psychological Examiners sanctioned a psychologist who attempted to treat phobias with a pseudoscientific treatment that involved tapping body parts in a predetermined order. Needless to say, there are no controlled studies of the efficacy of this treatment, and the Arizona Board ordered the therapist to stop using it and put him on probation—an all too rare example of a psychological organization policing the pseudoscience that is practiced by its clinical members.

In short, psychology has a kind of Jekyll and Hyde personality. Extremely rigorous science exists right alongside pseudoscientific and antiscientific attitudes. This Jekyll and Hyde aspect of the discipline was clearly apparent in the recovered-memory–false-memory debate of the last two decades (Brainerd & Reyna, 2005; Gardner, 2006; Lilienfeld, 2007; Loftus & Guyer, 2002; McHugh, 2008). Many cases were reported of individuals who had claimed to remember instances of child abuse that had taken place decades earlier but had been forgotten. Many of these memories occurred in the context of therapeutic interventions. It is clear that some of these memories were induced by the therapy itself (Gardner, 2006; Lilienfeld, 2007; Loftus & Guyer, 2002; Lynn, Loftus, Lilienfeld, & Lock, 2003). Some people insisted that such memories were never to be trusted; others insisted that they were always to be trusted. In the emotionally charged atmosphere of such an explosive social issue, psychologists provided some of the more balanced commentary and, most important, some of the more dispassionate empirical evidence on the issue of recovered or false memories (Alexander et al., 2005; Brainerd & Reyna, 2005; Bremner, Shobe, & Kihlstrom, 2000; Goodman et al., 2003; McNally, 2003; Moore & Zoellner, 2007). Here we have the Jekyll and Hyde feature of psychology in full-blown form. Some of the cases of therapeutically induced false memories—and, hence, of the controversial phenomenon itself—were caused by incompetent and scientifically ignorant therapists who were psychologists. On the other hand, whatever uncertain partial resolution of the controversy we do have is in large part due to the painstaking efforts of research psychologists who studied the relevant phenomena empirically. Finally, I must make clear that I do not wish to imply that it is only psychology that is beset with such problems. Indeed, medicine has had to dragged—kicking and screaming—toward a fully evidence-based approach, and it is not there yet (Beane, Gingrich, & Kerry, 2008; Kenney, 2008).

I hope this section has helped to dispel the notion that I wish to "let psychology off the hook" with the use of my Rodney Dangerfield joke to title this chapter. In his book on research methods, psychologist Douglas Mook (2001) referred to my use of the Dangerfield joke and commented that "often indeed, psychology gets no respect; but sometimes, too, it is respected more than is warranted and for the wrong reasons" (p. 473). I agree completely with this sentiment. Mook is right that the student of psychology needs to understand the paradoxes that surround the discipline. As I have presented it in this book, as the science of human behavior, the discipline of psychology often gets too little respect. But the face that psychology often presents to the public—that of a clinician claiming "unique" insight into people that is not grounded in research evidence—often gets too much respect. The discipline is often represented to the public by segments of psychology that do not respect its unique defining feature—that it validates statements about human behavior by employing the methods of science.

Isn't Everyone a Psychologist? Implicit Theories of Behavior

We all have theories about human behavior. It is hard to see how we could get through life if we did not. In this sense, we are all psychologists. It is very important, though, to distinguish between this individual psychology and the type of knowledge produced by the science of psychology. The distinction is critical because the two are often deliberately confused in popular writings about psychology, as we shall see.

In what ways is our personal psychological knowledge different from the knowledge gained from a scientific study of behavior? We have already discussed several. Much of our personal psychological knowledge is recipe knowledge. We do certain things because we think they will lead others to behave in a certain way. We behave in particular ways because we think that certain behavior will help us achieve our goals. But it is not the mere presence of recipe knowledge that distinguishes personal psychology from scientific psychology (which also contains recipe knowledge). The main difference here is that the science of psychology seeks to validate its recipe knowledge empirically.

Scientific evaluation is systematic and controlled in ways that individual validation procedures can never be. Indeed, psychological research on decision making has indicated that humans have difficulty detecting correlations in their behavioral environment that run counter to their accepted beliefs (see Baron, 2008; Kida, 2006). We see what we want to see. Psychologists have uncovered many of the reasons why, but they need not concern us here. Even if we wanted to evaluate personal recipe knowledge on an individual basis, built-in biases that make us less than adequate observers of behavioral phenomena would make it extremely difficult. The scientific method has evolved to avoid the biases of any single human observer. The implication here is a simple one. The recipe knowledge generated by the science of psychology is more likely to be accurate because it has undergone validation procedures more stringent than those to which personal recipe knowledge is exposed.

As discussed throughout this book, the differences between personal and scientific psychologies go beyond the validation of recipe knowledge. Science always aspires to more than recipe knowledge of the natural world. Scientists seek more general, underlying principles that explain why the recipes work. However, the personal psychologies of some people *are* similar to scientific psychology in seeking more basic psychological principles and theories. These personal theories, though, often depart from scientific theories in important ways. We have already mentioned that they are often unfalsifiable. Rather than being coherently constructed, many people's personal psychological theories are merely a mixture of platitudes and clichés, often mutually contradictory, that are used on the appropriate occasion. They reassure people that an explanation does exist and, furthermore, that the danger of a seriously contradictory event—one that would deeply shake the foundations of a person's beliefs—is unlikely to occur. As discussed in Chapter 2, although these theories may indeed be comforting, comfort is all that theories constructed in this way provide. In explaining everything post hoc, these theories predict nothing. By making no predictions, they tell us nothing. Theories in the discipline of psychology must meet the falsifiability criterion, and in doing so, they depart from the personal psychological theories of many laypeople. Theories in psychology can be proved wrong, and, therefore, they contain a mechanism for growth and advancement that is missing from many personal theories.

The Source of Resistance to Scientific Psychology

For the reasons we just discussed, it is important not to confuse the idea of a personal psychological theory with the knowledge generated by the science of psychology. Such a confusion is often deliberately fostered to undermine the status of psychology in the public mind. The idea that "everyone's a psychologist" is true if it is understood to mean simply that we all have implicit psychological theories. But it is often subtly distorted to imply that psychology is not a science.

We discussed in Chapter 1 why the idea of a scientific psychology is threatening to some people. A maturing science of behavior will change the kinds of individuals, groups, and organizations that serve as sources of psychological information. It is natural that individuals who have long served as commentators on human psychology and behavior will resist any threatened reduction in their authoritative role. Chapter 1 described how the advance of science has continually usurped the authority of other groups to make claims about the nature of the world. The movement of the planets, the nature of matter, and the causes of disease were all once the provinces of theologians, philosophers, and generalist writers. Astronomy, physics, medicine, genetics, and other sciences have gradually wrested these topics away and placed them squarely within the domain of the scientific specialist.

Many religions, for example, have gradually evolved away from claiming special knowledge of the structure of the universe. The titanic battles between science and religion have passed into history, with the exception of some localized flare-ups such as the creationism issue. Scientists uncover the structure of the natural world. Many religions provide commentary on the implications of the uses of these discoveries, but they no longer contest with scientists for the right to determine what the discoveries are. The right to adjudicate claims about the nature of the world has unquestionably passed to scientists.

Writer Natalie Angier (2007) reminds us that many years ago when lightening would hit the wooden towers of churches and burn them down, the clergy and the populace would engage in an intense debate about whether this was a sign of "the vengeance of God." However, she reminds us that "in the eighteenth century, Benjamin Franklin determined that lightening was an electric rather than an ecclesiastic phenomenon. He recommended that conducting rods be installed on all spires and rooftops, and the debates over the lightening bolts vanished" (p. 26).

The issue, then, is the changing criteria of belief evaluation. Few newspaper editorials ever come out with strong stands on the composition of the rings of Saturn. Why? No censor would prevent such an editorial. Clearly the reason it is not written is that it would be futile. Society knows that scientists, not editorial writers, determine such things. Only a hundred years ago, newspapers and preachers in the pulpit did comment vociferously on the origins of species in the animal kingdom. These comments have largely disappeared because science has destroyed the conditions that would allow them to be believed by rational thinkers. Psychology threatens to destroy those conditions in another large domain of nature.

Some people find it difficult to accept such a state of affairs when it comes to psychology. They cling tenaciously to their right to declare their own opinions about human behavior even when these opinions contradict the facts. Of course, the correct term here is really not "right," because, obviously, in a free society, everyone has the *right* to voice opinions, regardless of their accuracy. It is important to understand that what many people want is much *more* than simply the right to declare their opinions about human behavior. What they really want is *the conditions that are necessary for what they say to be believed.* When they make a statement about human psychology, they want the environment to be conducive to the acceptance of their beliefs. This is the reason that there are always proponents of the "anything-goes" view of psychology, that is, the idea that psychological claims cannot be decided by empirical means and are simply a matter of opinion. But science is always a threat to the "anything-goes" view, because it has a set of strict requirements for determining whether a knowledge claim is to be believed. Anything does not go in science. This ability to rule out false theories and facts accounts for scientific progress.

In short, a lot of the resistance to scientific psychology is due to what might be termed *conflict of interest.* As discussed in earlier chapters, many pseudosciences are multimillion-dollar industries that thrive on the fact that the public is unaware that statements about behavior can be empirically tested (there are 20 times more astrologers in the United States than astronomers; Gilovich, 1991, p. 2). The public is also unaware that many of the claims that are the basis of these industries (such as astrological prediction, subliminal weight loss, biorhythms, the administration of laetrile, and psychic surgery) have been tested and found to be false. A subcommittee of the U.S. Congress has estimated that $10 billion is spent annually on medical quackery, an amount that dwarfs the sum that is spent on legitimate medical research (Eisenberg et al., 1993; U.S. Congress, 1984).

How do we recognize pseudoscientific claims? Clinical psychologist Scott Lilienfeld (2005, p. 40) gives us a list of things to watch for that could serve as a summary of many of the things that have covered in this book. Pseudoscientific claims tend to be characterized by

- A tendency to invoke ad hoc hypotheses as a means of immunizing claims from falsification
- An emphasis on confirmation rather than refutation
- A tendency to place the burden of proof on skeptics, not proponents, of claims
- Excessive reliance on anecdotal and testimonial evidence to substantiate claims
- Evasion of the scrutiny afforded by peer review
- Failure to build on existing scientific knowledge (lack of connectivity).

True scientists are at pains to emphasize these criteria rather than to avoid them. For example, three of the scientists who had major roles in introducing the concept of emotional intelligence (EI) into psychology became worried about the media, clinicians, and even other researchers at times using the concept in unscientific ways. They wrote an article specifically directing others to invoke the types of scientific criteria listed above and discussed in this book: "In our opinion, the journalistic popularizations of EI frequently employ inadequate and overly broad definitions of EI, implausible claims, and misunderstandings of the concepts and research more generally. We urge researchers and practitioners alike to refer to the scientific literature on emotions, intelligence, and emotional intelligence to guide their thinking. Simply put, researchers need to cite the research literature rather than journalistic renderings of scientific concepts, which serve a different purpose" (Mayer, Salovey, & Caruso, 2008, pp. 513–514).

By contrast, many purveyors of pseudosciences and bogus therapies depend on an atmosphere of "anything goes" surrounding psychology. It provides a perfect environment for feeding on public gullibility, because the public has no consumer protection if anything goes. As attorney Peter Huber (1990) argued, "[At] the fringes of science and beyond . . . assorted believers in homeopathic medicine and the curative powers of crystals and pyramids . . . must discredit orthodox science to build their own cases for unorthodox nostrums" (p. 97). Those selling pseudoscience have a vested interest in obscuring the fact that there are mechanisms for testing behavioral claims. As biologist Michael Ghiselin (1989) warned, "What is going on here is quite straightforward. People are trying to sell a given point of view. Those who know how to evaluate the product are not the same as those to whom it is being marketed" (p. 139). In the domain of behavioral claims and therapies, psychologists are the ones who "know how to evaluate the product." This is why the pseudoscience industry continues to oppose the authority of scientific psychology to pass judgment on behavioral claims. However, the purveyors of pseudoscience often do not need to do direct battle with psychology. They simply do an end run around psychology and go straight to the media with their claims. The media make it very easy for cranks, quacks, and pseudoscientists to do an end run around scientific psychology. The talk shows that have inundated the airwaves do not ask the guests to produce their bibliographies of scientific research. If these guests are "interesting," they are simply put on the show.

Folk wisdom often contains a lot of wishful thinking: People want to believe that the world is the way they wish it to be rather than the way it is. Science often has the unenviable task of having to tell the public that the nature of the world is somewhat different from how they wish it to be ("No, that fast-food lunch is *not* good for your health"). The media, which could help in this situation (by telling people what is true rather than what they want to hear), only make it worse with their focus on what will "entertain" rather than on what will inform.

Science, then, does rule out the special-knowledge claims of those proposing statements that do not meet the necessary tests. The courts rule out claims of special knowledge too. In ruling on a famous case known as *Daubert vs. Merrell Dow,* the Supreme Court established when expert testimony could be presented in court—that is, what makes expert testimony *expert!* The Court identified four factors that judges could consider when deliberating about whether to allow expert testimony: (a) the "testability" of the theoretical basis for the opinion; (b) the error rates associated with the approach, if known; (c) whether the technique or approach on which the opinion is based has been subjected to peer review; and (d) whether the technique or approach is generally accepted in the relevant scientific community (Emery, Otto, & O'Donohue, 2005; Michaels, 2008). The four criteria map into major topics in this book: (a) falsifiability; (b) probabilistic prediction; (c) public knowledge subjected to peer review; and (d) scientific knowledge based on convergence and consensus. The courts are like science in ruling out claims of special knowledge, intuition, and testimonials as adequate evidence.

In this book, we have briefly touched on what are considered adequate and inadequate tests in science. Introspection, personal experience, and testimonials are all considered inadequate tests of claims about the nature of human behavior. Thus, it should not be surprising that conflict arises because these are precisely the types of evidence that nonpsychologist commentators have been using to support their statements about human behavior since long before a discipline of psychology existed.

However, it should not be thought that I am recommending a sour, spoilsport role for the science of psychology. Quite the contrary. The actual findings of legitimate psychology are vastly more interesting and exciting than the repetitious gee-whiz pseudoscience of the media. Furthermore, it should not be thought that scientists are against fantasy and imagination. Again, on the contrary, scientists have nothing against fantasy, imagination, and flights of fancy—in their proper contexts. Peter Medawar (1990) addressed this point,

> I am quite a believer in hot air in its proper place. I believe that most people psychologically need to be what Paul Jennings calls "bunkrapt." (You may remember Paul Jennings' typewriter when he was trying to write "bankrupt" wrote "bunkrapt.") Everybody needs to be bunkrapt, and I prefer to be bunkrapt by listening to Wagner's music dramas or reading Tolkien's novels. But it must not spill over into science (p. 5).

If we stop and think for a minute, most of us would agree with Medawar's point. We want fancy and fantasy when we go to the movies or the theater—but not when we go to the doctor's office, buy insurance, register our children for child care, fly in an airplane, or have our car serviced. We could add to this list going to a psychotherapist, having our learning-disabled child tested by a school psychologist, or taking a friend to suicide-prevention counseling at the university psychology clinic. Psychology, like other sciences, must remove fantasy, unfounded opinion, "common sense," commercial advertising claims, the advice of gurus, testimonials, and wishful thinking from its search for the truth.

It is difficult for a science to have to tell parts of society that their thoughts and opinions are needed—but not here. Psychology is the latest of the sciences to be in this delicate position. The difference in time period for psychology, however, is relevant. Most sciences came of age during periods of elite control of the structures of society, when the opinion of the ordinary person made no difference. Psychology, on the other hand, is emerging in a media age of democracy and ignores public opinion at its own peril. Many psychologists are now taking greater pains to remedy the discipline's lamentable record in public communication. As more psychologists take on a public communication role, the conflicts with those who confuse a personal psychology with scientific psychology are bound to increase.

Not everyone is a physicist, even though we all hold intuitive physical theories. But in giving up the claim that our personal physical theories must usurp scientific physics, we make way for a true science of the physical universe whose theories, because science is public, will be available to us all. Likewise, everyone is not a psychologist. But the facts and theories uncovered by the science of psychology are available to be put to practical ends and to enrich the understanding of all of us.

The Final Word

We are now at the end of our sketch of how to think straight about psychology. It is a rough sketch, but it can be of considerable help in comprehending how the discipline of psychology works and in evaluating new psychological claims. Our sketch has revealed that

1. Psychology progresses by investigating solvable empirical problems. This progress is uneven because psychology is composed of many different subareas, and the problems in some areas are more difficult than in others.
2. Psychologists propose falsifiable theories to explain the findings that they uncover.
3. The concepts in the theories are operationally defined, and these definitions evolve as evidence accumulates.
4. These theories are tested by means of systematic empiricism, and the data obtained are in the public domain, in the sense that they are presented in a manner that allows replication and criticism by other scientists.
5. The data and theories of psychologists are in the public domain only after publication in peer-reviewed scientific journals.
6. What makes empiricism systematic is that it strives for the logic of control and manipulation that characterizes a true experiment.
7. Psychologists use many different methods to arrive at their conclusions, and the strengths and weaknesses of these methods vary.
8. The behavioral principles that are eventually uncovered are almost always probabilistic relationships.
9. Most often, knowledge is acquired only after a slow accumulation of data from many experiments each containing flaws but nonetheless converging on a common conclusion.

The most exciting endeavor in science today is the quest to understand the nature of human behavior. By learning the concepts in this book you become able to follow this quest and perhaps, indeed, become a part of it.

References

Abrami, P., Bernard, R., Borokhovski, E., Wade, A., Surkes, M., Tamim, R., & Zhang, D. (2008). Instructional interventions affecting critical thinking skills and dispositions: A stage 1 meta-analysis. *Review of Educational Research, 78*, 1102–1134.

Adler, J. (2006, November 6). Plotting Pluto's comeback. *Newsweek,* pp. 60–61.

Adler, J. (2007, December 10). A big dose of skepticism. *Newsweek, 22.*

Adler, J. E., & Rips, L. J. (Eds.). (2008). *Reasoning: Studies of human inference and its foundations.* New York: Cambridge University Press.

Alcock, J. E. (1984). Parapsychology's past eight years: A lack-of-progress report. *Skeptical Inquirer, 8,* 312–320.

Alcock, J. E. (1990). *Science and supernature: A critical appraisal of parapsychology.* Buffalo, NY: Prometheus Books.

Alexander, K. W., Quas, J. A., Goodman, G. S., Ghetti, S., Edelstein, R. S., Redlich, A. D., Cordon, I. M., & Jones, D. P. H. (2005). Traumatic impact predicts long-term memory for documented child sexual abuse. *Psychological Science, 16,* 33–40.

Ali, L. (2008, July 7). True or false? Having kids makes you happy. *Newsweek,* 62–63.

American Psychiatric Association. (2000). *Diagnostic and statistical manual of mental disorders* (4th ed.; Text Revision). Washington, DC: Author.

Anderson, C. A., & Anderson, K. B. (1996). Violent crime rate studies in philosophical context: A destructive testing approach to heat and Southern culture of violence effects. *Journal of Personality and Social Psychology, 70,* 740–756.

Anderson, C. A., Berkowitz, L., Donnerstein, E., Huesmann, L. R., Johnson, J., Linz, D., Malamuth, N. M., & Wartella, E. (2003). The influence of media violence on youth. *Psychological Science in the Public Interest, 4,* 81–110.

Anderson, C. A., & Bushman, B. J. (2001). Effects of violent video games on aggressive behavior, aggressive cognition, aggressive affect, physiological arousal, and prosocial behavior: A meta-analytic review of the scientific literature. *Psychological Science, 12,* 353–357.

Anderson, C. A., & Huesmann, L. R. (2005). The evidence that media violence stimulates aggression in young viewers remains 'unequivocal.' *APS Observer, 18*(10), 7.

Anderson, C. A., Lindsay, J. J., & Bushman, B. J. (1999). Research in the psychological laboratory: Truth or triviality? *Current Directions in Psychological Science, 8,* 3–9.

Angell, M., & Kassirer, J. P. (1998). Alternative medicine: The risks of untested and unregulated remedies. *The New England Journal of Medicine, 339*(12), 839–841.

Angier, N. (2007). *The canon: A whirligig tour of the beautiful basics of science.* New York: Mariner Books.

Angier, N. (2008, November 11). Scientists and philosophers find that 'gene' has a multitude of meanings. *New York Times,* p. D2.

Ariely, D. (2008). *Predictably irrational.* New York: HarperCollins.

Arkes, H. R. (2003). The nonuse of psychological research at two federal agencies. *Psychological Science, 14,* 5–6.

Asimov, I. (1989). The relativity of wrong. *Skeptical Inquirer, 14,* 35–44.

Associated Press. (2007, April 24). *Can aspirin prevent cancer? The answer is not clear.*

Auletta, K. (1992). *Three blind mice: How the TV networks lost their way.* New York: Vintage Books.

Ayres, I. (2007). *Super crunchers: Why thinking by numbers is the new way to be smart.* New York: Bantam Books.

Azar, B. (1999, November). Crowder mixes theories with humility. *APA Monitor,* p. 18.

Baron, J. (1998). *Judgment misguided: Intuition and error in public decision making.* New York: Oxford University Press.

Baron, J. (2008). *Thinking and deciding* (4th ed.). Cambridge, MA: Cambridge University Press.

Baron-Cohen, S. (2005). *Autism: The facts.* Oxford: Oxford University Press.

Barrett, L., Dunbar, R., & Lycett, J. (2002). *Human evolutionary psychology.* Princeton, NJ: Princeton University Press.

Bartels, L. M. (2008). *Unequal democracy: The political economy of the new gilded age.* Princeton, NJ: Princeton University Press.

Baumeister, R. F., Bushman, B. J., & Campbell, K. W. (2000). Self-esteem, narcissism, and aggression: Does violence result from low self-esteem or from threatened egotism? *Current Directions in Psychological Science, 9,* 26–29.

Baumeister, R. F., Campbell, J. D., Krueger, J. I., & Vohs, K. D. (2003). Does high self-esteem cause better performance, interpersonal success, happiness, or healthier lifestyles? *Psychological Science in the Public Interest, 4,* 1–44.

Baumeister, R. F., Campbell, J. D., Krueger, J. I., & Vohs, K. D. (2005). Exploding the self-esteem myth. *Scientific American, 292*(1), 84–91.

Baumeister, R. F., Vohs, K. D., & Funder, D. C. (2007). Psychology as the science of self-reports and finger movements. *Perspectives on Psychological Science, 2,* 396–403.

Bausell, R. B. (2007). *Snake oil science: The truth about complimentary medicine and alternative medicine.* New York: Oxford University Press.

Bazerman, M. (2001). Consumer research for consumers. *Journal of Consumer Research, 27,* 499–504.

Beane, B., Gingrich, N., & Kerry, J. (2008, October 24). How to take American health care from worst to first. *New York Times,* A27.

Beck, M. (2008, November 4). And you thought the debate over fluoridation was settled. *Wall Street Journal,* D1.

Begley, S. (2007, August 13). The truth about denial. *Newsweek,* 20–29.

Begley, S. (2008a, March 17). Placebo nation: Just believe. *Newsweek,* 46.

Begley, S. (2008b, November 3). Why we believe. *Newsweek*, 56–60.

Benjamin, L. T. (2001). American psychology's struggles with its curriculum: Should a thousand flowers bloom? *American Psychologist, 56,* 735–742.

Benjamin, L. T. (2004). Behavioral science and the Nobel Prize: A history. *American Psychologist, 58,* 731–741.

Benson, E. S. (2006a, June). All that's gold does not glitter: How the Golden Fleece tarnished psychological science. *APS Observer, 19,* 12–19.

Benson, E. S. (2006b, January). Emotion, perception, cognition—it's all part of really intelligent design. *APS Observer, 19,* 22–24.

Berkowitz, L., & Donnerstein, E. (1982). External validity is more than skin deep. *American Psychologist, 37,* 245–257.

Berliner, D. C., & Biddle, B. (1995). *The manufactured crisis: Myths, fraud, and the attack on America's public schools.* Reading, MA: Addison-Wesley.

Bersoff, D. (1981). Testing and the law. *American Psychologist, 36,* 1047–1056.

Bersoff, D. (1982). Larry P. and PASE: Judicial report cards on the validity of intelligence tests. In T. R. Kratochwill (Ed.), *Advances in school psychology* (pp. 145–162). Hillsdale, NJ: Erlbaum.

Beyerstein, B. L. (1999). Whence cometh the myth that we use only 10% of our brains? In S. Della Sala (Ed.), *Mind myths: Exploring popular assumptions about the mind and brain* (pp. 3–24). Chichester, England: John Wiley & Sons.

Bilmes, L. J., & Stiglitz, J. E. (2009, January). The $10 trillion hangover. *Harper's Magazine, 318,* 31–35.

Birnbaum, M. H. (1999). Testing critical properties of decision making on the Internet. *Psychological Science, 10,* 399–407.

Birnbaum, M. H. (2004). Human research and data collection via the internet. *Annual Review of Psychology, 55,* 803–832.

Bjorklund, D. F. (2004). *Children's thinking: Cognitive development and individual differences.* Stamford, CT: Wadsworth.

Blass, T. (2004). *The man who shocked the world: The life and legacy of Stanley Milgram.* New York: Basic Books.

Boden, M. A. (2003). *The creative mind: Myths and mechanisms.* London: Routledge.

Boneau, C. A. (1990). Psychological literacy: A first approximation. *American Psychologist, 45,* 891–900.

Borenstein, M., Hedges, L. V., Higgins, J., & Rothstein, H. (2009). *Introduction to meta-analysis* (Vol. 1). Hoboken, NJ: Wiley.

Bower, B. (1996, August 24). New pitch for placebo power. *Science News, 150,* 123.

Boyd, R. (2008, February 7). Do people only use 10 percent of their brains? Scientific American, retrieved from http://www.sciam.com/article.cfm?id=people-only-use-10-percent-of-brain on November 17, 2009.

Brainerd, C. J., & Reyna, V. F. (2005). *The science of false memory.* Oxford: Oxford University Press.

Breitmeyer, B. J., & Ramey, C. T. (1986). Biological nonoptimality and quality of postnatal environment as codeterminants of intellectual development. *Child Development, 57,* 1151–1165.

Bremner, J. D., Shobe, K. K., & Kihlstrom, J. F. (2000). False memories in women with self-reported childhood sexual abuse: An empirical study. *Psychological Science, 11,* 333–337.

Broadbent, D. E. (1958). *Perception and communication.* New York: Pergamon Press.

Broadbent, D. (1973). *In defense of empirical psychology.* London: Methuen.

Brody, J. E. (2008, December 10). Weight-loss guides without gimmicks. *New York Times,* D7.

Bronfenbrenner, U., & Mahoney, M. (1975). The structure and verification of hypotheses. In U. Bronfenbrenner & M. Mahoney (Eds.), *Influence on human development.* Hinsdale, IL: Dryden.

Bronowski, J. (1956). *Science and human values.* New York: Harper & Row.

Bronowski, J. (1973). *The ascent of man.* Boston: Little, Brown.

Bronowski, J. (1974). Science, poetry, and human specificity. *American Scholar, 43,* 386–404.

Bronowski, J. (1977). *A sense of the future.* Cambridge, MA: MIT Press.

Bronowski, J. (1978a). *The common sense of science.* Cambridge, MA: Harvard University Press.

Bronowski, J. (1978b). *Magic, science, and civilization.* New York: Columbia University Press.

Brooks, A. C. (2008). *Gross national happiness.* New York: Basic Books.

Bruck, M., & Ceci, S. (2004). Forensic developmental psychology: Unveiling four common misconceptions. *Current Directions in Psychological Science, 13,* 229–232.

Buchtel, E. E., & Norenzayan, A. (2009). Thinking across cultures: Implications for dual processes. In J. S. B. T. Evans & K. Frankish (Eds.), *In two minds: Dual processes and beyond.* Oxford: Oxford University Press.

Burton, R. (2008). *On being certain.* New York: St. Martin's Press.

Bushman, B. J., & Anderson, C. A. (2002). Violent video games and hostile expectations: A test of the general aggression model. *Personality and Social Psychology Bulletin, 28,* 1679–1686.

Buss, D. M. (Ed.). (2005). *The handbook of evolutionary psychology.* Hoboken, NJ: John Wiley.

Buss, D. M. (2007). *Evolutionary psychology: The new science of the mind* (3rd ed.). Boston: Allyn and Bacon.

Byrnes, G., & Kelly, I. (1992). Crisis calls and lunar cycles: A twenty-year review. *Psychological Reports, 71,* 779–795.

Cacioppo, J. T. (2007a). Psychology is a hub science. *APS Observer, 20,* 5, 42.

Cacioppo, J. T. (2007b). The structure of psychology. *APS Observer, 20,* 3, 50.

Carnagey, N. L., Anderson, C. A., & Bartholow, B. D. (2007). Media violence and social neuroscience: New questions and new opportunities. *Current Directions in Psychological Science, 16,* 178–182.

Carnoy, M., Jacobsen, R., Mishel, L., & Rothstein, R. (2005). *The charter school dust-up: Examining the evidence on enrollment and achievement.* New York: Teachers College Press.

Carpenter, S. (1999, August 21). Kansas cuts evolution from curriculum. *Science News, 156,* 117.

Carroll, S. B. (2005). Endless forms most beautiful: A new revolution in biology. *Skeptical Inquirer, 29*(6), 51–52.

Cartwright, J. (2008). *Evolution and human behavior* (2nd ed.). Cambridge, MA: MIT Press.

Casscells, W., Schoenberger, A., & Graboys, T. (1978). Interpretation by physicians of clinical laboratory results. *New England Journal of Medicine, 299,* 999–1001.

Cassidy, J. (1995, October 15). Who killed the middle class? *New Yorker,* pp. 113–124.

Catrambone, R., Jones, C. M., Jonides, J., & Seifert, C. (1995). Reasoning about curvilinear motion: Using principles or analogy. *Memory and Cognition, 23,* 368–373.

Cheng, C. (2001). Assessing coping flexibility in real-life and laboratory settings: A multimethod approach.

Journal of Personality and Social Psychology, 80, 814–833.

Chida, Y., & Hamer, M. (2008). Chronic psychosocial factors and acute physiological responses to laboratory-induced stress in healthy populations: A quantitative review of 30 years of investigations. *Psychological Bulletin, 134,* 829–885.

Cho, H. J., Hotopf, M., & Wessely, S. (2005). The placebo response in the treatment of chronic fatigue syndrome: A systematic review and meta-analysis. *Psychosomatic Medicine, 67,* 301–313.

Churchland, P. M. (1988). *Matter and consciousness* (rev. ed.). Cambridge, MA: MIT Press.

Clark, A. (2001). *Mindware: An introduction to the philosophy of cognitive science.* New York: Oxford University Press.

Clay, R. A. (2008, June). Science vs. ideology: Psychologists fight back against misuse of research. *APA Monitor,* 41–43.

Claypool, H., Hall, C., Mackie, D., & Garcia-Marques, T. (2008). Positive mood, attribution, and the illusion of familiarity. *Journal of Experimental Social Psychology, 44,* 721–728.

Clotfelter, C., & Cook, P. (1989). *Selling hope: State lotteries in America.* Cambridge, MA: Harvard University Press.

Clotfelter, C., & Cook, P. (1993). The "gambler's fallacy" in lottery play. *Management Science, 39,* 1521–1525.

CNN.com (2004, May 1). Nightline airs war dead amid controversy. Retrieved December 30, 2005 from http://www.cnn.com/2004/SHOW BIZ/TV/05/01/abc.nightline/

Cohen, A. (2008, December 29). Four decades after Milgram, we're still willing to inflict pain. *New York Times,* A22.

Cohen, R. (1985, December 17). Despair: America's double standard. *Detroit Free Press,* p. 11.

Cole, K. C. (1998). Calculated risks. *Skeptical Inquirer, 22*(5), 32–36.

Conkle, A., & West, C. (2008, June). Psychology on the road. *APS Observer, 21,* 18–23.

Cozby, P. C. (2008). *Methods in behavioral research* (10th ed.). New York: McGraw-Hill.

Crews, F. (1993, November 18). The unknown Freud. *New York Review of Books,* pp. 55–66.

Crews, F. (2004, July 15). Out, damned blot! *New York Review of Books, 51,* 22–25.

Cummins, R. A., & Prior, M. P. (1992). Autism and assisted communication: A response to Bilken. *Harvard Educational Review, 62,* 228–241.

Currier, J. M., Neimeyer, R., & Berman, J. (2008). The effectiveness of psychotherapeutic interventions for berearved persons: A comprehensive quantitative review. *Psychological Bulletin, 134,* 648–661.

Curtis, B. M., & O'Keefe, J. H. (2002). Autonomic tone as a cardiovascular risk factor: The dangers of chronic fight or flight. *Mayo Clinic Proceedings, 77,* 45–54.

Dacey, A. (2008). *The secular conscience.* Amherst, NY: Prometheus Books.

Dawes, R. M. (1988). *Rational choice in an uncertain world.* San Diego: Harcourt Brace & Jovanovich.

Dawes, R. M. (1991). Probabilistic versus causal thinking. In D. Cicchetti & W. Grove (Eds.), *Thinking clearly about psychology: Essays in honor of Paul E. Meehl* (Vol. 1, pp. 235–264). Minneapolis: University of Minnesota Press.

Dawes, R. M. (1994). *House of cards: Psychology and psychotherapy built on myth.* New York: Free Press.

Dawes, R. M., Faust, D., & Meehl, P. E. (1989). Clinical versus actuarial judgment. *Science, 243,* 1668–1673.

Dawkins, R. (1998). *Unweaving the rainbow.* Boston: Houghton Mifflin.

Day, S. X., & Rounds, J. (1998). Universality of vocational interest structure among racial minorities. *American Psychologist, 53,* 728–736.

Deary, I. J. (2001). Human intelligence differences: Towards a combined experimental-differential approach. *Trends in Cognitive Sciences, 5*(4), 164–170.

Deary, I. J., Batty, G. D., & Gale, C. R. (2008). Bright children become enlightened adults. *Psychological Science, 19,* 1–6.

deCharms, R. C., Maeda, F., Glover, G., Ludlow, D., Pauly, J., Soneji, D., Gabrieli, J., & Mackey, S. (2005). Control over brain activation and pain learned by using real-time functional MRI. *Proceedings of the National Academy of Sciences, 102,* 18626–18631.

de la Cruz, D. (2007, January 5). FTC fines diet-drug marketers. *The Oregonian* (from Associated Press), p. A10.

Demetriou, A., Kui, Z. X., Spanoudis, G., Christou, C., Kyriakides, L., & Platsidou, M. (2005). The architecture, dynamics, and development of mental processing: Greek, Chinese, or universal? *Intelligence, 33,* 109–141.

Dennett, D. C. (1995). *Darwin's dangerous idea: Evolution and the meanings of life.* New York: Simon & Schuster.

Dennett, D. C. (1998). *Brainchildren: Essays on designing minds.* Cambridge, MA: MIT Press.

Dennett, D. C. (2000). Why getting it right matters: Postmodernism and truth. *Free Inquiry, 20*(1), 40–43.

Dickinson, D. K., & Neuman, S. B. (Eds.). (2005). *Handbook of early literacy research* (Vol. 2). New York: Guilford Press.

Dickson, D. H., & Kelly, I. W. (1985). The "Barnum effect" in personality assessment: A review of the literature. *Psychological Reports, 57,* 367–382.

Diener, E. (2006, June). Why Robert Kraut smiles. *APS Observer, 19,* 15.

Dingfelder, S. F. (2006, December). Nix the tics. *APA Monitor,* 18–20.

Dixon, R., & Backman, L. (Eds.). (1995). *Compensating for psychological deficits and declines: Managing losses and promoting gain.* Mahwah, NJ: Erlbaum.

Dobzhansky, T. (1973). Nothing in biology makes sense except in the light of evolution. *American Biology Teacher, 35,* 125–129.

Dodes, J. E. (1997). The mysterious placebo. *Skeptical Inquirer, 21*(1), 44–45.

Dokoupil, T. (2007, July 16). Trouble in a black box: Did effort to reduce teen suicides backfire? *Newsweek,* 48.

Domjan, M., & Purdy, J. E. (1995). Animal research in psychology: More than meets the eye of the general psychology student. *American Psychologist, 50,* 496–503.

Dos Passos, J. (1964). *Occasions and protests.* New York: Henry Regnery.

Dufresne, T. (Ed.). (2007). *Against freud: Critics talk back.* Stanford, CA: Stanford University Press.

Duncan, J., Parr, A., Woolgar, A., Thompson, R., Bright, P., Cox, S., Bishop, S., & Nimmo-Smith, I. (2008). Goal neglect and Spearman's g: Competing parts of a complex task. *Journal of Experimental Psychology: General, 137,* 131–148.

Durso, F. T., Nickerson, R. S., Dumais, S., Lewandowsky, S., & Perfect, T. (2007). *Handbook of applied cognition.* Hoboken, NJ: Wiley.

Dvoskin, R. (2008, December). Abortion risk reviewed. *Scientific American Mind, 19*(6), 10.

Egan, J. (2005, December 18). Start with a stock index—Now try to turbocharge it. *New York Times,* p. BU7.

Ehrenberg, R. G., Brewer, D. J., Gamoran, A., & Williams, J. D. (2001). Class size and student achievement.

Psychological Science in the Public Interest, 2, 1–27.

Ehri, L. C., Nunes, S., Stahl, S., & Willows, D. (2001). Systematic phonics instruction helps students learn to read: Evidence from the national reading Panel's meta-analysis. *Review of Educational Research, 71,* 393–447.

Einhorn, H. J. (1986). Accepting error to make less error. *Journal of Personality Assessment, 50,* 387–395.

Eisenberg, L. (1977). The social imperatives of medical research. *Science, 198,* 1105–1110.

Eisenberg, D. M., Kessler, R., Foster, C., Norlock, F., Calkins, D., & Delbanco, T. (1993). Unconventional medicine in the United States. *The New England Journal of Medicine, 328*(4), 246–252.

Ellis, B. J., & Bjorklund, D. F. (Eds.). (2005). *Origins of the social mind: Evolutionary psychology and child development.* New York: Guilford.

Emery, R. E., Otto, R. K., & O'Donohue, W. T. (2005). A critical assessment of child custody evaluations. *Psychological Science in the Public Interest, 6*(1), 1–29.

Epstein, A. S. (2008). An early start on thinking. *Educational Leadership, 65*(5), 38–42.

Ernst, E., & Abbot, N. C. (1999). I shall please: The mysterious power of placebos. In S. Della Sala (Ed.), *Mind myths: Exploring popular assumptions about the mind and brain* (pp. 209–213). Chichester, England: John Wiley & Sons.

Estes, W. (1979). Experimental psychology: An overview. In E. Hearst (Eds.), *The first century of experimental psychology* (pp. 12–38). Hillsdale, NJ: Erlbaum.

Evans, J. P. (2008, July 1). A conversation with James P. Evans. *New York Times,* D2.

Evans, J. St. B. T. (2005). *How to do research: A psychologist's guide.* Hove, England: Psychology Press.

Ewing, C. P. (2006, January). Testing tool in question. *APA Monitor,* 61.

Fackelman, K. (1996, November 9). Gastrointestinal blues. *Science News, 150,* 302–303.

Fancher, R. (1985). *The intelligence men.* New York: W. W. Norton.

Farber, I. B., & Churchland, P. S. (1995). Consciousness and the neurosciences: Philosophical and theoretical issues. In M. S. Gazzaniga (Ed.), *The cognitive neurosciences* (pp. 1295–1306). Cambridge, MA: MIT Press.

Farha, B. (2007). *Paranormal claims: A critical analysis.* Lanham, MD: University Press of America.

Farha, B., & Steward, G. (2006). Paranormal beliefs: An analysis of college students. *Skeptical Inquirer, 30*(1), 37–40.

Fernald, D. (1984). *The Hans legacy.* Hillsdale, NJ: Erlbaum.

Feshbach, S., & Tangney, J. (2008). Television viewing and aggression. *Perspectives on Psychological Science, 3,* 387–389.

Fiedler, K., & Freytag, P. (2004). Pseudocontingencies. *Journal of Personality and Social Psychology, 87,* 453–467.

Finkel, A. M. (1996, May). Who's exaggerating? *Discover, 17*(5), 48–54.

Flynn, J. R. (2007). *What is intelligence?* Cambridge: Cambridge University Press.

Forrest, B., & Gross, P. R. (2004). *Creationism's Trojan horse: The wedge of intelligent design.* Oxford: Oxford University Press.

Foster, E. A., Jobling, M. A., Taylor, P. G., Donnelly, P., Deknijff, P., Renemieremet, J., Zerjal, T., & Tyler-Smith, C. (1998). Jefferson fathered slave's last child. *Nature, 396,* 27–28.

Foster, K. R., & Huber, P. W. (1999). *Judging science: Scientific knowledge and the federal courts.* Cambridge, MA: MIT Press.

Foster, R. G., & Roenneberg, T. (2008). Human responses to the geophysical daily, annual and lunar cycles. *Current Biology, 18,* R784–R794.

Fountain, H. (2006, January 15). On not wanting to know what hurts you. *New York Times,* p. WK14.

Fox, R. E. (1996). Charlatanism, scientism, and psychology's social contract. *American Psychologist, 51,* 777–784.

Fried, S. B., & Schultis, G. A. (1995). *The best self-help and self awareness books.* Chicago: American Library Association.

Friedrich, J., Buday, E., & Kerr, D. (2000). Statistical training in psychology: A national survey and commentary on undergraduate programs. *Teaching of Psychology, 27,* 248–257.

Frith, U. (2003). *Autism: Explaining the enigma* (2nd ed.). Oxford: Basil Blackwell.

Gage, N. L. (1996). Confronting counsels of despair for the behavioral sciences. *Educational Researcher, 25*(3), 5–15.

Galovski, T. E., Malta, L. S., & Blanchard, E. B. (2006). *Road rage: Assessment and treatment of the angry, aggressive driver.* Washington, DC: American Psychological Association.

Garb, H. N. (2005). Clinical judgment and decision making. *Annual Review of Clinical Psychology, 1,* 67–89.

Gardner, M. (1972, April). Mathematical games: Why the long arm of coincidence is usually not as long as it seems. *Scientific American, 227*(4), 110–112.

Gardner, M. (2001). Facilitated communication: A cruel farce. *Skeptical Inquirer, 25*(1), 17–19.

Gardner, M. (2006). The memory wars. *Skeptical Inquirer, 30*(1), 28–31.

Gaunt, R. (2006). Couple similarity and marital satisfaction: Are similar

spouses happier? *Journal of Personality, 74,* 1401–1420.

Gawande, A. (1998, February 8). No mistake. *The New Yorker,* pp. 74–81.

Gawande, A. (1999, February 9). The cancer-cluster myth. *The New Yorker,* pp. 35–37.

Gaynor, S. T. (2004). Skepticism and caricatures: B. F. Skinner turns 100. *Skeptical Inquirer, 28*(1), 26–29.

Gazzaniga, M. S. (2008). *Cognitive neuroscience* (3rd ed.). New York: Norton.

Geary, D. C. (2005). *The origin of the mind: Evolution of brain, cognition, and general intelligence.* Washington, DC: American Psychological Association.

Geary, D. C. (2008). An evolutionarily informed education science. *Educational Psychologist, 28,* 179–195.

Geertz, C. (2000). *Available light: Anthropological reflections on philosophical topics.* Princeton, NJ: Princeton University Press.

Gelman, A. (2008). *Red state, blue state, rich state, poor state.* Princeton, NJ: Princeton University Press.

Gernsbacher, M. A. (2007, May). The value of undergraduate training in psychological science. *APS Observer, 20,* 5–6.

Ghiselin, M. T. (1989). *Intellectual compromise.* New York: Paragon House.

Gigerenzer, G. (2002). *Calculated risks: How to know when numbers deceive you.* New York: Simon & Schuster.

Gigerenzer, G. (2004). Dread risk, September 11, and fatal traffic accidents. *Psychological Science, 15,* 286–287.

Gigerenzer, G. (2006). Out of the frying pan into the fire: Behavioral reactions to terrorist attacks. *Risk Analysis, 26,* 347–351.

Gigerenzer, G., Gaissmaier, W., Kurz-Milcke, E., Schwartz, L. M., & Woloshin, S. (2007). Helping doctors and patients make sense of health statistics. *Psychological Science in the Public Interest, 8,* 53–96.

Gilbert, D. (2006). *Stumbling on happiness.* New York: Alfred A. Knopf.

Gilovich, T. (1991). *How we know what isn't so: The fallibility of human reason in everyday life.* New York: Free Press.

Gilovich, T., Griffin, D., & Kahneman, D. (Eds.). (2002). *Heuristics and biases: The psychology of intuitive judgment.* New York: Cambridge University Press.

Gladwell, M. (1996, July 8). Conquering the coma. *The New Yorker,* pp. 34–40.

Gladwell, M. (2004, December 13). The picture problem. *The New Yorker,* 74–81.

Gleitman, H. (1981). *Psychology.* New York: W. W. Norton.

Goldacre, B. (2008). *Bad science.* London: Fourth Estate.

Goodman, G. S., Ghetti, S., Quas, J. A., Edelstein, R. S., Alexander, K. W., Redlich, A. D., Cordon, I. M., & Jones, D. P. H. (2003). A prospective study of memory for child sexual abuse: New findings relevant to the repressed-memory controversy. *Psychological Science, 14,* 113–118.

Gorchoff, S., John, O. P., & Helson, R. (2008). Contextualizing change in marital satisfaction during middle age. *Psychological Science, 19,* 1194–1200.

Gosling, S. D. (2001). From mice to men: What can we learn about personality from animal research? *Psychological Bulletin, 127,* 45–86.

Gosling, S. D., Simine, V., Srivastava, S., & John, O. P. (2004). Should we trust web-based studies? A comparative analysis of six preconceptions about Internet questionnaires. *American Psychologist, 59,* 93–104.

Goswami, U. (Ed.). (2008). *Cognitive development: The learning brain.* London: Psychology Press.

Grady, D. (2008, June 24). From a prominent death, some painful truths. *New York Times,* D5.

Grady, D. (2009, January 6). Should patients be told of better care elsewhere? *New York Times,* D1.

Gray, P. (2008). The value of Psychology 101 in liberal arts education: A psychocentric theory of the university. *APS Observer, 21,* 29–32.

Gould, S. J. (1987). Justice Scalia's misunderstanding. *Natural History, 96,* 14–21.

Grice, G. (2001, July 30). Slice of life: How a convicted killer's corpse brought anatomy into the digital age. *The New Yorker,* pp. 36–41.

Griffin, S., Regnier, E., Griffin, P., & Huntley, V. (2007). Effectiveness of fluoride in preventing cares in adults. *Journal of Dental Research, 86,* 410–415.

Griggs, R. A., Proctor, D. L., & Bujak-Johnson, A. (2002). The nonexistent common core. *American Psychologist, 57,* 452–453.

Groopman, J. (2004, January 26). The grief industry: How much does crisis counselling help—or hurt? *The New Yorker,* pp. 30–38.

Groopman, J. (2007). *How doctors think.* Boston: Houghton Mifflin.

Groopman, J. (2008, September). Why doctors make mistakes. *AARP Magazine,* 34–36.

Gutkin, T. B., & Reynolds, C. R. (Eds.). (2008). *The handbook of school psychology* (4th ed.). Hoboken, NJ: Wiley.

Haack, S. (2007). *Defending science—within reason: Between scientism and cynicism.* Buffalo, NY: Prometheus Books.

Hacking, I. (1990). *The taming of chance.* Cambridge: Cambridge University Press.

Hacohen, M. C. (2000). *Karl Popper: The formative years, 1902–1945.* Cambridge, England: Cambridge University Press.

Hafer, C. L., & Begue, L. (2005). Experimental research on just-world theory: Problems, developments, and future challenges. *Psychological Bulletin, 131,* 128–167.

Hagen, M. A. (2001). Damaged goods? What, if anything, does science tell us about the long-term effects of childhood sexual abuse? *Skeptical Inquirer, 25*(1), 54–59.

Haggbloom, S. J., Warnick, R., Warnick, J. E., Jones, V. K., Yarbrough, G. L., Russell, T. M., Borecky, C. M., McGahhey, R., Powell, J. L., Beavers, J., & Monte, E. (2002). The 100 most eminent psychologists of the 20th century. *Review of General Psychology, 6,* 139–152.

Haidt, J. (2006). *The happiness hypothesis.* New York: Basic Books.

Hammond, K. R., Harvey, L. O., & Hastie, R. (1992). Making better use of scientific knowledge: Separating truth from justice. *Psychological Science, 3,* 80–87.

Hariri, A. R., & Holmes, A. (2006). Genetics of emotional regulation: The role of the serotonin transporter in neural function. *Trends in Cognitive Sciences, 10,* 182–191.

Harlow, H. F. (1958). The nature of love. *American Psychologist, 13,* 673–685.

Harlow, H. F., & Suomi, S. J. (1970). The nature of love—Simplified. *American Psychologist, 25,* 161–168.

Harriet, H. (2008, September/October). 'We couldn't say it in print if it wasn't true'. *Skeptical Inquirer, 32,* 46–49.

Harrington, A. (2008). *The cure within.* New York: Norton.

Hastie, R., & Dawes, R. M. (2001). *Rational choice in an uncertain world.* Thousand Oaks, CA: Sage.

Hauser, R. M. (1998). Trends in black-white test score differentials: Uses and misuses of NAEP/SAT data. In U. Neisser (Ed.), *The rising curve: Long-term gains in IQ and related measures* (pp. 219–249). Washington, DC: American Psychological Association.

Hearst, E. (1979). *The first century of experimental psychology.* Hillsdale, NJ: Erlbaum.

Hendrie, C. (2005). Book faults achievement in charter schools. *Education Week,* p. 3.

Henrich, J., Boyd, R., Bowles, S., Camerer, C., Fehr, E., & Gintis, H. (2004). *Foundations of human sociality: Economic experiments and ethnographic evidence from fifteen small-scale societies.* Oxford: Oxford University Press.

Henriques, G. (2004). Psychology defined. *Journal of Clinical Psychology, 60,* 1207–1221.

Henriques, G. (2005). Toward a useful mass movement. *Journal of Clinical Psychology, 61,* 121–139.

Higbee, K. L., & Clay, S. L. (1998). College students' beliefs in the ten-percent myth. *The Journal of Psychology, 132,* 469–476.

Hilton, D. J. (2003). Psychology and the financial markets: Applications to understanding and remedying irrational decision-making. In I. Brocas & J. D. Carrillo (Eds.), *The psychology of economic decisions: Rationality and well-being* (Vol. 1, pp. 273–297). Oxford: Oxford University Press.

Hines, T. M. (1998). Comprehensive review of biorhythm theory. *Psychological Reports, 83,* 19–64.

Hines, T. M. (2003). *Pseudoscience and the paranormal* (2nd ed.). Buffalo, NY: Prometheus Books.

Hollon, S. D., Thase, M. E., & Markowitz, J. C. (2002). Treatment and prevention of depression. *Psychological Science in the Public Interest, 3,* 39–77.

Holton, G. (1996). *Einstein, history, and other passions: The rebellion against science at the end of the twentieth century.* Reading, MA: Addison-Wesley.

Holton, G., & Roller, D. (1958). *Foundations of modern physical science.* Reading, MA: Addison-Wesley.

Honda, H., Shimizu, Y., & Rutter, M. (2005). No effect of MMR withdrawal on the incidence of autism: A total population study. *Journal of Child Psychology and Psychiatry, 46,* 572–579.

Huber, P. W. (1990). Pathological science in court. *Daedalus, 119,* 97–118.

Hudson, A., Melita, B., & Arnold, N. (1993). A case study assessing the validity of facilitated communication. *Journal of Autism and Developmental Disorders, 23,* 165–173.

Hulbert, M. (2006, January 15). Positive ratings for a ratings makeover. *New York Times,* p. BU6.

Humes, E. (2007). *Monkey girl: Evolution, education, religion, and the battle for America's soul.* New York: Ecco Press.

Humphrey, N. (1996). *Leaps of faith.* New York: Copernicus.

Hunt, E., & Carlson, J. (2007). Considerations relating to the study of group differences in intelligence. *Perspectives on Psychological Science, 2,* 194–213.

Hunt, M. (1999). *The new know-nothings: The political foes of the scientific study of human nature.* New Brunswick, NJ: Transaction Publishers.

Hyman, R. (1992). What does Goodfellow's classic analysis tell researchers today? *Journal of Experimental Psychology: General, 121,* 128–129.

Hyman, R. (1996). Evaluation of the military's twenty-year program on psychic spying. *Skeptical Inquirer, 20*(2), 21–26.

If it sounds just ducky, it probably quacks. (1990, March 23). *Detroit Free Press.*

Immen, W. (1996, August 8). Could you repeat that in Klingon? *Globe & Mail (Toronto).*

Insurance Institute for Highway Safety (2005, July 16). If you drive while phoning you're far more likely to get into a crash in which you'll be injured. *Status Report, 40*(6), 1–3.

Ioannidis, J. (2004). Contradicted and initially stronger effects in highly cited clinical research. *JAMA, 294,* 218–228.

Jacobson, J. W., Foxx, R. M., & Mulick, J. A. (Eds.). (2004). *Controversial therapies for developmental disabilities: Fads, fashion, and science in professional practice.* Mahwah, NJ: Erlbaum.

Jaffe, E. (2005). How random is that? Students are convenient research subjects but they're not a simple sample. *APS Observer, 18*(9), 20–30.

Johnson, E. J. (2001). Digitizing consumer research. *Journal of Consumer Research, 28,* 331–338.

Johnson, H. (1991). *Sleepwalking through history: America in the Reagan years.* New York: Anchor Books.

Johnson, S. (2007). *The ghost map.* New York: Riverhead Books.

Jordan, S. D. (2007, May). Global climate change triggered by global warming. *Skeptical Inquirer, 31,* 32–45.

Judelsohn, R. G. (2007, November/December). Vaccine safety: Vaccines are one of public health's great accomplishments. *Skeptical Inquirer, 31*(6), 32–35.

Kagan, J. (2006). *An argument for mind.* New Haven, CT: Yale University Press.

Kahneman, D. (1973). *Attention and effort.* Englewood Cliffs, NJ: Prentice Hall.

Kahneman, D. (2003). A perspective on judgment and choice: Mapping bounded rationality. *American Psychologist, 58,* 697–720.

Kahneman, D., & Frederick, S. (2005). A model of heuristic judgment. In K. J. Holyoak & R. G. Morrison (Eds.), *The Cambridge handbook of thinking and reasoning* (pp. 267–293). New York: Cambridge University Press.

Kahneman, D., & Tversky, A. (Eds.). (2000). *Choices, values, and frames.* Cambridge, England: Cambridge University Press.

Kalat, J. W. (2007). *Biological psychology* (9th ed.). Belmont, CA: Wadsworth.

Kantrowitz, B., & Kalb, C. (2006, March 13). Food news blues. *Newsweek,* 44–54.

Karger, H. (2005). *Shortchanged: Life and debt in the fringe economy.* San Francisco: Berrett-Koehler.

Kassin, S. M., Tubb, V. A., Hosch, H. M., & Memon, A. (2001). On the "general acceptance" of eyewitness testimony research. *American Psychologist, 56,* 405–416.

Keating, D. P. (2007). Understanding adolescent development: Implications for driving safety. *Journal of Safety Research, 38,* 147–157.

Keith, K. D., & Beins, B. C. (2008, August). *My students believe what? Psychological myths and sound science in the undergraduate classroom.* Paper presented at the meeting of the American Psychological Association, Boston, MA.

Keizer, K., Lindenberg, S., & Steg, L. (2008, November 20). The spreading of disorder. *Science, 321.*

Kelly, I. W. (1997). Modern astrology: A critique. *Psychological Reports, 81,* 931–962.

Kelly, I. W. (1998). Why astrology doesn't work. *Psychological Reports, 82,* 527–546.

Kelly, I., Rotton, J., & Culver, R. (1985). The moon was full and nothing happened: A review of studies on the moon and human behavior and lunar beliefs. *Skeptical Inquirer, 10,* 129–143.

Kelly, L. (2005). *The skeptic's guide to the paranormal.* New York: Thunder's Mouth Press.

Kenney, C. (2008). *The best practice: How the new quality movement is transforming medicine.* New York: PublicAffairs Books.

Kenrick, D. T. (2001). Evolutionary psychology, cognitive science, and dynamical systems: Building an integrative paradigm. *Current Directions in Psychological Science, 10*(1), 13–17.

Kershaw, A. (1991, July 21). The psychic guide to hiring and firing. *London Independent.*

Kety, S. (1974). Preface. In J. Swazey, *Chlorpromazine in psychiatry: A study of therapeutic intervention.* Cambridge, MA: MIT Press.

Kida, T. (2006). *Don't believe everything you think: The 6 basic mistakes we make in thinking.* Amherst, NY: Prometheus Books.

King, F. (1993, March). Science literacy and public support of science. *APS Observer, 6*(2), 2–11.

King, R. N., & Koehler, D. J. (2000). Illusory correlations in graphological inference. *Journal of Experimental Psychology: Applied, 6,* 336–348.

Kirsch, I., Deacon, B. J., Huedo-Medino, T., Scoboria, A., Moore, T. E., & Johnson, B. (2008). Initial severity and antidepressant benefits: A meta-analysis of data submitted to the Food and Drug Administration. *PLoS Medicine, 5*(2), e45. doi:10.1371/journal.pmed.0050045.

Knight, G. P., Johnson, L., Carlo, G., & Eisenberg, N. (1994). A multiplicative model of the dispositional antecedents of a prosocial behavior: Predicting more of the people more of the time. *Journal of Personality and Social Psychology, 66,* 178–183.

Koehler, J. J., & Thompson, W. C. (2006). Mock juror's reactions to selective presentation of evidence from multiple-opportunity searches. *Law and Human Behavior, 30,* 455–468.

Kolbert, E. (2005, September 19). Storm warnings. *The New Yorker,* 35–36.

Koocher, G. P. (2006, October). Psychological science is not politically correct. *APA Monitor, 5.*

Kopta, S. M., Lueger, R. J., Saunders, S. M., & Howard, K. I. (1999). Individual psychotherapy outcome and process research. *Annual Review of Psychology, 50,* 441–469.

Kozhevnikov, M., & Hegarty, M. (2001). Impetus beliefs as default heuristics: Dissociation between explicit and implicit knowledge about motion. *Psychonomic Bulletin and Review, 8,* 439–453.

Kramer, S. P. (1987). *How to think like a scientist: Answering questions by the scientific method.* New York: Thomas Y. Crowell Junior Books.

Krauthammer, C. (1985, December 29). The twilight of psychotherapy? *Detroit News.*

Krauss, L. M. (2008, October 28). McCain's science earmark error. *Los Angeles Times.* Retrieved November 5, 2008 from http://genesis1.asu.edu/ ~krauss/latimesoct28.html

Krueger, J. I., Vohs, K. D., & Baumeister, R. F. (2008). Is the allure of self-esteem a mirage after all? *American Psychologist, 63,* 64–65.

Kunar, M. A., Carter, R., Cohen, M., & Horowitz, T. S. (2008). Telephone conversation impairs sustained visual attention via a central bottleneck. *Psychonomic Bulletin & Review, 15,* 1135–1140.

Kushner, H. I. (1999). *A cursing brain? The histories of Tourette Syndrome.* Cambridge, MA: Harvard University Press.

Laden, G. (2008). Likely voters prefer evolution over creationism. *Skeptical Inquirer, 32*(4), 13–14.

Langer, E. J. (1975). The illusion of control. *Journal of Personality and Social Psychology, 32,* 311–328.

Langewiesche, W. (1993, December). The turn. *The Atlantic Monthly,* pp. 115–122.

Lassiter, G. D., Geers, A. L., Munhall, P. J., Ploutz-Snyder, R. J., & Breitenbecher, D. L. (2002). Illusory causation: Why it occurs. *Psychological Science, 13,* 299–305.

Latane, B., & Darley, J. (1970). *The unresponsive bystander: Why doesn't he help?* New York: Appleton-Century-Crofts.

Lazar, I., Darlington, R., Murray, H., Royce, J., & Sniper, A. (1982). Lasting effects of early education: A report from the consortium of longitudinal studies. *Monographs of the Society for Research in Child Development, 47* (Serial No. 195).

Leary, D. E. (2001). One big idea, one ultimate concern. *American Psychologist, 56,* 425–432.

Leavy, J. (1992). Our spooky presidential coincidences contest. *Skeptical Inquirer, 16,* 316–319.

Lee, V., Brooks-Gunn, J., Schnur, E., & Liaw, F. (1990). Are Head Start's effects sustained? A longitudinal follow-up comparison of disadvantaged children attending Head Start, no preschool, and other preschool programs. *Child Development, 61,* 495–507.

Leibowitz, H. W. (1996). The symbiosis between basic and applied research. *American Psychologist, 51,* 366–370.

Lerner, L. S. (2005). What should we think about Americans' beliefs regarding evolution? *Skeptical Inquirer, 29*(6), 59–60.

Levin, J. R., & O'Donnell, A. M. (2000). What to do about educational research's credibility gaps? *Issues in Education: Contributions from Educational Psychology, 5,* 1–87.

Levy, J., Pashler, H., & Boer, E. (2006). Central interference in driving: Is there any stopping the psychological refractory period? *Psychological Science, 17,* 228–235.

Levy, S. (2005, January 31). Does your iPod play favorites? *Newsweek,* p. 10.

Lewis, M. (1997). *Trail fever.* New York: Knopf.

Li, C. (1975). *Path analysis: A primer.* Pacific Grove, CA: Boxwood Press.

Lilienfeld, S. O. (1998). Pseudoscience in contemporary clinical psychology: What it is and what we can do about it. *The Clinical Psychologist, 51*(4), 3–9.

Lilienfeld, S. O. (2002). New journal dedicated to distinguishing science from pseudoscience in mental health. *Skeptical Inquirer, 26*(3), 7–8.

Lilienfeld, S. O. (2005). The 10 commandments of helping students distinguish science from pseudoscience in psychology. *APS Observer, 18*(9), 39–51.

Lilienfeld, S. O. (2006, February). Correlation still isn't causation. *APS Observer, 19*, 9.

Lilienfeld, S. O. (2007). Psychological treatments that cause harm. *Perspectives on Psychological Science, 2*, 53–70.

Lilienfeld, S. O., & Lohr, J. M. (2000). Thought field therapy practitioners and educators sanctioned. *Skeptical Inquirer, 24*(2), 5.

Lilienfeld, S. O., Lohr, J. M., & Moirer, D. (2001). The teaching of courses in the science and pseudoscience of psychology: Useful resources. *Teaching of Psychology, 28*(3), 182–191.

Lilienfeld, S. O., Lynn, S. J., & Lohr, J. M. (Eds.). (2003). *Science and pseudoscience in clinical psychology.* New York: Guilford Press.

Lilienfeld, S. O., Ruscio, J., & Lynn, S. J. (Eds.). (2008). *Navigating the mindfield: A guide to separating science from pseudoscience in mental health.* Buffalo, NY: Prometheus Books.

Lilienfeld, S. O., Wood, J. M., & Garb, H. N. (2000). The scientific status of projective techniques. *Psychological Science in the Public Interest, 1*, 27–66.

Lipsey, M. W., & Wilson, D. B. (1993). The efficacy of psychological, educational, and behavioral treatment: Confirmation from meta-analysis. *American Psychologist, 48*, 1181–1209.

Loftus, E. F., & Guyer, M. J. (2002, May/June). Who abused Jane Doe: The hazards of the single case history. *Skeptical Inquirer, 26*(3), 24–32.

Lubinski, D. (2004). Introduction to the special section on cognitive abilities: 100 years after Spearman's (1904) "General Intelligence, Objectively Determined and Measured." *Journal of Personality and Social Psychology, 86*, 96–111.

Lutsky, N. (2006, March). Teaching quantitative reasoning. *APS Observer, 19*, 35–36.

Lynn, S. J., Loftus, E. F., Lilienfeld, S. O., & Lock, T. (2003). Memory recovery techniques in psychotherapy: Problems and pitfalls. *Skeptical Inquirer, 27*(4), 40–46.

MacCoun, R. (2002, December). Why a psychologist won the Nobel Prize in economics. *APS Observer, 15*(10), 1–8.

Macmillan, M. (1997). *Freud evaluated.* Cambridge, MA: MIT Press.

Madrick, J. (2006, January 12). The way to a fair deal. *New York Review of Books*, pp. 37–40.

Magee, B. (1985). *Philosophy and the real world: An introduction to Karl Popper.* LaSalle, IL: Open Court.

Mahrer, A. R. (2000). Philosophy of science and the foundations of psychotherapy. *American Psychologist, 55*, 1117–1125.

Maizels, M. (2005). Why should physicians care about behavioral research? *Headache, 45*, 411–413.

Malkiel, B. G. (2008). *A random walk down Wall Street* (9th ed.). New York: Norton.

Manjoo, F. (2008). *True enough: Learning to live in a post-fact society.* Hoboken, NJ: John Wiley.

Margolis, H. (1996). *Dealing with risk.* Chicago: University of Chicago Press.

Marks, D., & Kammann, R. (1980). *The psychology of the psychic.* Buffalo, NY: Prometheus Books.

Marks, D. F. (2001). *The psychology of the psychic.* Buffalo, NY: Prometheus Books.

Marshall, E. (1980). Police science and psychics. *Science, 210*, 994–995.

Martin, B. (1998). Coincidences: Remarkable or random? *Skeptical Inquirer, 22*(5), 23–28.

Martin, R., & Hull, R. (2006). The case study perspective on psychological research. In R. J. Sternberg, H. L. Roediger & D. F. Halpern (Eds.), *Critical thinking in psychology* (pp. 90–109). New York: Cambridge University Press.

Matthews, K. A. (2005). Psychological perspectives on the development of coronary heart disease. *American Psychologist, 60,* 783–796.

Mayer, J. D., Salovey, P., & Caruso, D. R. (2008). Emotional intelligence: New ability or eclectic traits? *American Psychologist, 63,* 503–517.

Maynard Smith, J. (1998). *Evolutionary genetics* (2nd ed.). Oxford: Oxford University Press.

McBride-Chang, C., & Kail, R. V. (2002). Cross-cultural similarities in the predictors of reading acquisition. *Child Development, 73,* 1392–1407.

McCabe, D. P., & Castel, A. D. (2008). Seeing is believing: The effect of brain images on judgments of scientific reasoning. *Cognition, 107,* 343–352.

McCloskey, M. (1983, April). Intuitive physics. *Scientific American, 248*(4), 122–130.

McCorduck, P. (2004). *Machines who think: A personal inquiry into the history and prospects of artificial intelligence.* Wellesley, MA: AK Peters.

McCullough, M. L. (2001). Freud's seduction theory and its rehabilitation: A saga of one mistake after another. *Review of General Psychology, 5,* 3–22.

McEvoy, S. P., Stevenson, M. R., McCartt, A. T., Woodword, M., Haworth, C., Palamara, P., & Cercarelli, R. (2005, August 20). Role of mobile phones in motor vehicle crashes resulting in hospital attendance: A case-crossover study. *British Medical Journal, 331*(7514), 428.

McFall, R. M., & Treat, T. A. (1999). Quantifying the information value of clinical assessments with signal detection theory. *Annual Review of Psychology, 50,* 215–241.

McGraw, K. O., Tew, M. D., & Williams, J. E. (2000). The integrity of web-delivered experiments: Can you trust the data? *Psychological Science, 11,* 502–506.

McHugh, P. (2008). *The memory wars: Psychiatry's clash over meaning, memory, and mind.* Washington, DC: The Dana Foundation.

McNally, R. J. (2003). Recovering memories of trauma: A view from the laboratory. *Current Directions in Psychological Science, 12,* 32–35.

McNally, R. J., Bryant, R. A., & Ehlers, A. (2003). Does early psychological intervention promote recovery from posttraumatic stress? *Psychological Science in the Public Interest, 4*(2), 45–79.

Medawar, P. B. (1967). *The art of the soluble.* London: Methuen.

Medawar, P. B. (1979). *Advice to a young scientist.* New York: Harper & Row.

Medawar, P. B. (1984). *The limits of science.* New York: Harper & Row.

Medawar, P. B. (1990). *The threat and the glory.* New York: HarperCollins.

Medawar, P. B., & Medawar, J. S. (1983). *Aristotle to zoos: A philosophical dictionary of biology.* Cambridge, MA: Harvard University Press.

Medin, D. L., & Atran, S. (2004). The native mind: Biological categorization and reasoning in development and across cultures. *Psychological Review, 111,* 960–983.

Meehl, P. E. (1954). *Clinical versus statistical prediction: A theoretical analysis and review of the literature.* Minneapolis: University of Minnesota Press.

Meehl, P. E. (1986). Causes and effects of my disturbing little book. *Journal of Personality Assessment, 50,* 370–375.

Meehl, P. E. (1993). Philosophy of science: Help or hindrance? *Psychological Reports, 72,* 707–733.

Meier, B., Robinson, M., & Wilkowski, B. (2007). Aggressive primes activate hostile information in memory: Who is most susceptible? *Basic and Applied Social Psychology, 29,* 23–34.

Meyers, L. (2008, January). Recommended reading: Psychologists share the contents of their self-help shelves. *APA Monitor,* 26–27.

Michaels, D. (2008). *Doubt is their product: How industry's assault on science threatens your health.* New York: Oxford University Press.

Miller, K. R. (2008). *Only a theory: Evolution and the battle for America's soul.* New York: Viking.

Miller, N. E. (1985a). Rx: Biofeedback. *Psychology Today, 19,* 54–59.

Miller, N. E. (1985b). The value of behavioral research on animals. *American Psychologist, 40,* 423–440.

Milton, J., & Wiseman, R. (1999). Does psi exist? Lack of replication of an anomalous process of information transfer. *Psychological Bulletin, 125,* 387–391.

Mineka, S., & Zinbarg, R. (2006). A contemporary learning theory perspective on the etiology of anxiety disorders. *American Psychologist, 61,* 10–26.

Mischel, W. (2008, December). The toothbrush problem. *APS Observer, 21.*

Mlodinow, L. (2008). *The drunkard's walk: How randomness rules our lives.* New York: Pantheon.

Moerman, D., & Harrington, A. (2005). Making space for the placebo effect in pain medicine. *Seminars in Pain Medicine, 3,* 2–6.

Monk, R. (1990). *Ludwig Wittgenstein: The duty of genius.* New York: Free Press.

Mook, D. G. (1982). *Psychological research: Strategies and tactics.* New York: Harper & Row.

Mook, D. G. (1983). In defense of external invalidity. *American Psychologist, 38,* 379–387.

Mook, D. G. (1989). The myth of external validity. In L. W. Poon, D. C. Rubin, & B. A. Wilson (Eds.), *Everyday cognition in adulthood and late life* (pp. 25–43). Cambridge, England: Cambridge University Press.

Mook, D. G. (2001). *Psychological research: The ideas behind the methods.* New York: Norton.

Moore, S. A., & Zoellner, L. (2007). Overgeneral autobiographical memory and traumatic events: An evaluative *Psychological Bulletin, 133,* 419–437.

Moore, T. E. (1995). Subliminal self-help auditory tapes: An empirical test of perceptual consequences. *Canadian Journal of Behavioural Science, 27,* 9–20.

Morera, O. F., & Dawes, R. M. (2006). Clinical and statistical prediction after 50 years: A dedication to Paul Meehl. *Journal of Behavioral Decision Making, 19,* 409–412.

Mostert, M. P. (2001). Facilitated communication since 1995: A review of published studies. *Journal of Autism and Developmental Disorders, 31*(3), 287–313.

Mulick, J., Jacobson, J., & Kobe, F. (1993, Spring). Anguished silence and helping hands: Autism and facilitated communication. *Skeptical Inquirer, 17,* 270–280.

Murchison, C. (1934). *Handbook of general experimental psychology.* Worcester, MA: Clark University Press.

Musella, D. P. (2005). Gallup Poll shows that Americans' belief in the paranormal persists. *Skeptical Inquirer, 29*(5), 5.

Myers, D. G. (2006). *Social psychology.* Columbus, OH: McGraw-Hill.

Nathan, P. E., & Gorman, J. M. (Ed.). (1998). *A guide to treatments that work.* New York: Oxford University Press.

National Highway Traffic Safety Administration (2004). *Traffic safety facts, 2004.* Washington, DC: Author.

National Reading Panel: Reports of the Subgroups. (2000). Teaching children to read: An evidence-based assessment of the scientific research literature on reading and its implications for reading instruction. Washington, DC.

National Safety Council (2001). *Report on Injuries in America, 2001.* Retrieved March 29, 2002, from www.nsc.org/library/rept2000.htm

Nickerson, R. S. (1998). Confirmation bias: A ubiquitous phenomenon in many guises. *Review of General Psychology, 2,* 175–220.

Nickerson, R. S. (1999). Basic versus applied research. In R. J. Sternberg (Ed.), *The nature of cognition* (pp. 409–423). Cambridge, MA: MIT Press.

Nickerson, R. S. (2002). The production and perception of randomness. *Psychological Review, 109,* 330–357.

Nickerson, R. S. (2004). *Cognition and chance: The psychology of probabilistic reasoning.* Mahwah, NJ: Erlbaum.

Nijhuis, M. (2008, June/July). The doubt makers. *Miller-McCune, 26*–35.

Nisbett, R. E. (2003). *The geography of thought.* New York: Free Press.

Nisbett, R. E., & Ross, L. (1980). *Human inference: Strategies and shortcomings of social judgment.* Englewood Cliffs, NJ: Prentice Hall.

Nolen-Hoeksema, S., Wisco, B., & Lyubomirsky, S. (2008). Rethinking rumination. *Perspectives on Psychological Science, 3,* 400–424.

Novacek, M. J. (2006, April 17). Darwin would have loved it. *Time Magazine,* p. 60.

Novella, S. (2007, November/December). The anti-vaccine movement. *Skeptical Inquirer, 31*(6), 25–31.

Novick, L. R., & Cheng, P. W. (2004). Assessing interactive causal influence. *Psychological Review, 111,* 455–485.

Novotney, A. (2008, July). Custody collaborations. *APA Monitor,* 49–51.

Nye, B., Hedges, L. V., & Konstantopoulos, S. (2000). The effects of small classes on academic achievement: The results of the Tennessee class size experiment. *American Educational Research Journal, 37,* 123–151.

Oberman, L. M., & Ramachandran, V. S. (2007). The simulating social mind: The role of the mirror neuron system and simulation in the social and communicative deficits of autism spectrum disorders. *Psychological Bulletin, 133,* 310–327.

Offit, P. A. (2008). *Autism's false prophets.* New York: Columbia University Press.

Olivola, C. Y., & Oppenheimer, D. M. (2008). Randomness in retrospect: Exploring the interactions between memory and randomness cognition. *Psychonomic Bulletin & Review, 15,* 991–996.

Olson, R. K. (2004). SSSR, environment, and genes. *Scientific Studies of Reading, 8,* 111–124.

Oreskes, N. (2004). Beyond the ivory tower: The scientific consensus on climate change. *Science, 306,* 1686.

Overskeid, G. (2007). Looking for Skinner and finding Freud. *American Psychologist, 62,* 590–595.

Page, E., & Keith, T. (1981). Effects of U.S. private schools: A technical analysis of two recent claims. *Educational Researcher, 10,* 7–17.

Paloutzian, R. F., & Park, C. L. (Eds.). (2005). *Handbook of the psychology of religion and spirituality.* New York: Guilford Press.

Park, R. L. (2008). *Supersition: Belief in the age of science.* Princeton, NJ: Princeton University Press.

Parker-Pope, T. (2009, January 13). A problem of the brain, not the hands. *New York Times,* D5.

Parris, M. (2007, May 12). Nothing ventured nothing gained—although it's better to be safe than sorry. *The Spectator*, p. 28.

Paul, A. M. (2001, March/April 2001). Self-help: Shattering the myths. *Psychology Today*, pp. 62–68.

Paul, G. L. (1966). *Insight vs. desensitization in psychotherapy*. Stanford, CA: Stanford University Press.

Paul, G. L. (1967). Insight vs. desensitization in psychotherapy two years after termination. *Journal of Consulting Psychology, 31*, 333–348.

Paulos, J. A. (2001). *Innumeracy: Mathematical illiteracy and its consequences*. New York: Hill and Wang.

Pennington, B. F., & Olson, R. K. (2005). Genetics of dyslexia. In M. J. Snowling & C. Hulme (Eds.), *The science of reading: A handbook* (pp. 453–472). Malden, MA: Blackwell.

Peterson, R. A. (2001). On the use of college students in social science research: Insights from a second-order meta-analysis. *Journal of Consumer Research, 28*, 450–461.

Petry, N. M. (2005). *Pathological gambling: Etiology, comorbidity, and treatment*. Washington, DC: American Psychological Association.

Pinker, S. (1997). *How the mind works*. NewYork: W. W. Norton.

Pinker, S. (2002). *The blank slate: The modern denial of human nature*. New York: Viking.

Plotkin, D. (1996, June). Good news and bad news about breast cancer. *Atlantic Monthly*, 53–82.

Pohl, R. (Ed.). (2004). *Cognitive illusions: A handbook on fallacies and biases in thinking, judgment and memory*. Hove, England: Psychology Press.

Popper, K. R. (1959). *The logic of scientific discovery*. New York: Harper & Row.

Popper, K. R. (1963). *Conjectures and refutations*. New York: Harper & Row.

Popper, K. R. (1972). *Objective knowledge*. Oxford, England: Oxford University Press.

Popper, K. R. (1976). *Unended quest: An intellectual biography*. La Salle, IL: Open Court.

Postman, N. (1988). *Conscientious Objections*. New York: Vintage Books.

Powell, B. (1993, December). Sloppy reasoning, misused data. *Phi Delta Kappan, 75*(4), 283, 352.

Powell, B., & Steelman, L. C. (1996). Bewitched, bothered, and bewildering: The use and misuse of state SAT and ACT scores. *Harvard Educational Review, 66*, 27–59.

Pressley, M. (2005). *Reading instruction that works: The case for balanced teaching* (3rd ed.). New York: Guilford Press.

Price, C. J., & McCrory, E. (2005). Functional brain imaging studies of skilled reading and developmental dyslexia. In M. J. Snowling & C. Hulme (Eds.), *The science of reading: A handbook* (pp. 473–496). Malden, MA: Blackwell.

Radford, B. (1999). The ten-percent myth. *Skeptical Inquirer, 23*(2), 52–53.

Radford, B. (2005). Ringing false alarms: Skepticism and media scares. *Skeptical Inquirer, 29*(2), 34–39.

Radford, B. (2006). Geller revisited. *Skeptical Inquirer, 30*(1), 27.

Raine, A. (2008). From genes to brain to antisocial behavior. *Current Directions in Psychological Science, 17*, 323–328.

Rajendran, G., & Mitchell, P. (2007). Cognitive theories of autism. *Developmental Review, 27*, 224–260.

Ramey, S. L. (1999). Head Start and preschool education. *American Psychologist, 54*, 344–346.

Randall, L. (2005, September 18). Dangling particles. *New York Times*, p. WK13.

Randi, J. (1983). The project alpha experiment: 1. The first two years. *Skeptical Inquirer, 7*, 24–33.

Randi, J. (1995). *An encyclopedia of claims, frauds, and hoaxes of the occult and supernatural exposed by*

James Randi. New York: St. Martin's Press.

Randi, J. (2005). Fakers and innocents: The one million dollar challenge and those who try for it. *Skeptical Inquirer, 29*(4), 45–50.

Raymo, C. (1999). *Skeptics and true believers.* Toronto: Doubleday Canada.

Redelmeier, D. A., & Tibshirani, R. J. (1997). Association between cellular-telephone calls and motor vehicle collisions. *The New England Journal of Medicine, 336*(7), 453–458.

Redelmeier, D. A., & Tibshirani, R. J. (2001). Car phones and car crashes: Some popular misconceptions. *Canadian Medical Association Journal, 164*(11), 1581–1582.

Rice, T. W. (2003). Believe it or not: Religious and other paranormal beliefs in the United States. *Journal for the Scientific Study of Religion, 42,* 95–106.

Ridley, M. (2004). *Evolution.* New York: Oxford University Press.

Riener, C., Proffitt, D. R., & Salthouse, T. (2005). A psychometric approach to intuitive physics. *Psychonomic Bulletin and Review, 12,* 740–745.

Rind, B. (2008). The Bailey affair: Political correctness and attacks on sex research. *Archives of Sexual Behavior, 37,* 481–484.

Rind, B., Tromovitch, P., & Bauserman, R. (2001). The validity and appropriateness of methods, analyses, and conclusions in Rind et al. (1998): A rebuttal of victimological critique from Ondersma et al. (2001) and Dallam et al. (2001). *Psychological Bulletin, 127,* 734–758.

Robins, R. W., Gosling, S. D., & Craik, K. H. (1999). An empirical analysis of trends in psychology. *American Psychologist, 54,* 117–128.

Robins, R. W., Gosling, S. D., & Craik, K. H. (2000). Trends in psychology: An empirical issue. *American Psychologist, 55,* 276–277.

Robinson, D. N. (2001). Sigmund Koch—Philosophically speaking. *American Psychologist, 56,* 420–424.

Rosa, L., Rosa, E., Sarner, L., & Barrett, S. (1998). A close look at therapeutic touch. *JAMA, 279,* 1005–1010.

Rosenthal, R. (1990). How are we doing in soft psychology? *American Psychologist, 46,* 775–776.

Rosnow, R. L., & Rosenthal, R. (2003). Effect sizes for experimenting psychologists. *Canadian Journal of Experimental Psychology, 57,* 221–237.

Ross, L., & Nisbett, R. E. (1991). *The person and the situation: Perspectives of social psychology.* Philadelphia: Temple University Press.

Rowe, W. (1993). Psychic detectives: A critical examination. *Skeptical Inquirer, 17,* 159–165.

Rozin, P. (2006). Domain denigration and process preference in academic psychology. *Perspectives on Psychological Science, 1,* 365–376.

Rozin, P. (2007). Exploring the landscape of modern academic psychology: Finding and filling the holes. *American Psychologist, 62,* 754–765.

Rozin, P., Lowery, L., Imada, S., & Haidt, J. (1999). The CAD Triad Hypothesis: A mapping between three moral emotions (contempt, anger, disgust) and three moral codes (community, autonomy, divinity). *Journal of Personality and Social Psychology, 76,* 574–586.

Ruscio, J. (2000). Risky business: Vividness, availability, and the media paradox. *Skeptical Inquirer, 24*(2), 22–26.

Ruscio, J. (2002, March). The emptiness of holism. *Skeptical Inquirer, 26*(2), 46–50.

Ruse, M. (1999). *Mystery of mysteries: Is evolution a social construction?* Cambridge, MA: Harvard University Press.

Ruse, M. (2008). *Darwinism and its discontents.* New York: Cambridge University Press.

Russo, F. (1999, May). The clinical-trials bottleneck. *The Atlantic Monthly*, pp. 30–36.

Rutter, M. (1979). Maternal deprivation, 1972–1978: New findings, new concepts, and new approaches. *Child Development, 50*, 283–305.

Rutter, M. (2007). Proceeding from observed correlation to causal inference: The use of natural experiments. *Perspectives on Psychological Science, 2*, 377–395.

Rzewnicki, R., & Forgays, D. G. (1987). Recidivism and self-cure of smoking and obesity: An attempt to replicate. *American Psychologist, 42*, 97–100.

Sagan, C. (1996). *The demon-haunted world: Science as a candle in the dark.* New York: Random House.

Salthouse, T. A. (2004). What and when of cognitive aging. *Current Directions in Psychological Science, 13*, 140–144.

Sandoval, J., & Miille, M. (1980). Accuracy of judgments of WISC-R item difficulty for minority groups. *Journal of Consulting and Clinical Psychology, 48*, 249–253.

Santrock, J. W., Minnett, A. M., & Campbell, B. D. (1994). *The authoritative guide to self-help books.* New York: Guilford Press.

Scahill, L., et al. (2006). Contemporary assessment and pharmacotherapy of Tourette syndrome. *NeuroRx 3*, 192–206.

Schachter, S. (1982). Recidivism and self-cure of smoking and obesity. *American Psychologist, 37*, 436–444.

Schwartz, M. (2008, December). The golden touch. *Harper's Magazine, 317*, 71–78.

Scott, E. C. (2005). *Evolution vs. creationism.* Berkeley, CA: University of California Press.

Scott, S. (1999, January 2). Risking all on alternative cancer therapies. *National Post (Toronto)*, p. B1.

See, J. (2006, May). When 007 meets Ph.D. *APS Observer, 19*(5), 15.

Seligman, M. E. P. (2002). *Authentic happiness.* New York: Free Press.

Senechal, M. (2006). Testing the home literacy model: Parent involvement in kindergarten is differentially related to Grade 4 reading comprehension, fluency, spelling, and reading for pleasure. *Scientific Studies of Reading, 10*, 59–88.

Seppa, N. (2006, January 14). Put down that fork: Studies document hazards of obesity. *Science News, 169*, 21.

Shadish, W. R., & Baldwin, S. A. (2005). Effects of behavioral marital therapy: A meta-analysis of randomized controlled trials. *Journal of Consulting and Clinical Psychology, 73*, 6–14.

Shaffer, L. (1981). The growth and limits of recipe knowledge. *Journal of Mind and Behavior, 2*, 71–83.

Shane, H. (1993, June). FC: Facilitated or "factitious" communication. *Communicating Together, 11*(2), 11–13.

Shapin, S. (2006, November 6). Sick city: Maps and mortality in the time of cholera. *The New Yorker*, 110–115.

Shapiro, A., Shapiro, E., Bruun, R., & Sweet, R. (1978). *Gilles de la Tourette syndrome.* New York: Raven Press.

Shaywitz, S. E., & Shaywitz, B. A. (2004). Neurobiologic basis for reading and reading disability. In P. McCardle & V. Chhabra (Eds.), *The voice of evidence in reading research* (pp. 417–442). Baltimore: Paul Brookes.

Sheese, B. E., & Graziano, W. G. (2005). Deciding to defect: The effects of video-game violence on cooperative behavior. *Psychological Science, 16*, 354–357.

Shepard, R. (1983). "Idealized" figures in textbooks versus psychology as an empirical science. *American Psychologist, 38*, 855.

Shermer, M. (1997). *Why people believe weird things.* New York: W. H. Freeman.

Shermer, M. (2005). *Science friction: Where the known meets the unknown.* New York: Times Books.

Shermer, M. (2006). *Why Darwin matters: The case against intelligent design.* New York: Times Books.

Shtulman, A. (2006). Qualitative differences between naive and scientific theories of evolution. *Cognitive Psychology, 52,* 170–194.

Siegert, R. J., & Ward, T. (2002). Clinical psychology and evolutionary psychology: Toward a dialogue. *Review of General Psychology, 6,* 235–259.

Simmons, R., Burgeson, R., Carlton-Ford, S., & Blyth, D. (1987). The impact of cumulative change in early adolescence. *Child Development, 58,* 1220–1234.

Simonton, D. K. (2004). Psychology's status as a scientific discipline: Its empirical placement within an implicit hierarchy of the sciences. *Review of General Psychology, 8,* 59–67.

Sinaceur, M., Heath, C., & Cole, S. (2005). Emotional and deliberative reactions to a public crisis: Mad cow disease in France. *Psychological Science, 16,* 247–254.

Singh, K., Spencer, A., & Brennan, D. (2007). Effects of water fluoride exposure at crown completion and maturation on caries of permanent first molars. *Caries Research, 41,* 34–42.

Sivak, M., & Flannagan, M. J. (2003). Flying and driving after the September 11 attacks. *American Scientist, 91,* 6–7.

Slovic, P. (2007). "If I look at the mass I will never act": Psychic numbing and genocide. *Judgment and Decision Making, 2,* 79–95.

Smith, D. (2003). Angry thoughts, at-risk hearts. *APA Monitor, 34*(3), 46–48.

Smith, M., & Belcher, R. (1993). Facilitated communication with adults with autism. *Journal of Autism and Developmental Disorders, 23,* 175–183.

Smith, R. E., Wheeler, G., & Diener, E. (1975). Faith without works. *Journal of Applied Social Psychology, 5,* 320–330.

Smith, T., Polloway, E., Patton, J., & Dowdy, C. (2008). *Teaching students with special needs in inclusive settings* (5th ed.). Boston: Allyn & Bacon.

Snowling, M. J., & Hulme, C. (Eds.). (2005). *The science of reading: A handbook.* Malden, MA: Blackwell.

Spitz, H. H. (1997). *Nonconscious movements: From mystical messages to facilitated communication.* Mahwah, NJ: Erlbaum.

Standing, L. G., & Huber, H. (2003). Do psychology courses reduce belief in psychological myths? *Social Behavior and Personality, 31,* 585–592.

Stanovich, K. E. (2000). *Progress in understanding reading.* New York: Guilford Press.

Stanovich, K. E. (2004). *The robot's rebellion: Finding meaning in the age of Darwin.* Chicago: University of Chicago Press.

Stanovich, K. E. (2009). *What intelligence tests miss: The psychology of rational thought.* New Haven, CT: Yale University Press.

Sternberg, R. J. (Ed.). (2002). *Why smart people can be so stupid.* New Haven, CT: Yale University Press.

Sternberg, R. J. (Ed.). (2005). *Unity in psychology: Possibility or pipedream?* Washington, DC: American Psychological Association.

Sternberg, R. J., & Grigorenko, E. L. (Eds.). (2002). *The general factor of intelligence: How general is it?* Mahwah, NJ: Lawrence Erlbaum Associates.

Sternberg, R. J., Roediger, H. L., & Halpern, D. F. (Eds.). (2006). *Critical thinking in psychology.* New York: Cambridge University Press.

Stevenson, H., Stigler, J., Lee, S., Lucker, G., Kitamura, S., & Hsu, C. (1985). Cognitive performance and academic achievement of Japanese, Chinese, and American children. *Child Development, 56,* 718–734.

Stewart-Williams, S., & Podd, J. (2004). The placebo effect: Dissolving the expectancy versus conditioning debate. *Psychological Bulletin, 130,* 324–340.

Stout, M. (2000). *The feel-good curriculum: The dumbing down of America's kids in the name of self-esteem.* Cambridge, MA: Perseus Publishing.

Strayer, D. L., & Drews, F. A. (2007). Cell-phone-induced driver distraction. *Current Directions in Psychological Science, 16,* 128–131.

Strayer, D. L., & Johnston, W. A. (2001). Driven to distraction: Dual-task studies of simulated driving and conversing on a cellular telephone. *Pschological Science, 12,* 462–466.

Suls, J., & Bunde, J. (2005). Anger, anxiety, and depression as risk factors for cardiovascular disease: The problems and implications of overlapping affective dispositions. *Psychological Bulletin, 131,* 260–300.

Sunstein, C. R. (2002). *Risk and reason: Safety, law, and the environment.* Cambridge: Cambridge University Press.

Sutherland, S. (1992). *Irrationality: The enemy within.* London: Constable.

Svenson, O. (1981). Are we all less risky and more skillful than our fellow drivers? *Acta Psychologica, 47,* 143–148.

Swanson, D. (2001). *Nibbling on Einstein's brain: The good, the bad & the bogus in science.* Toronto: Annick Press.

Swanson, D. (2004). *Turn it loose: The scientist in absolutely everybody.* Toronto: Annick Press.

Swets, J. A., Dawes, R. M., & Monahan, J. (2000). Psychological science can improve diagnostic decisions. *Psychological Science in the Public Interest, 1,* 1–26.

Tager-Flusberg, H. (2007). Evaluating the theory-of-mind hypothesis of autism. *Current Directions in Psychological Science, 16,* 311–315.

Talbot, M. (2005, December 5). Darwin in the dock. *The New Yorker,* pp. 66–77.

Taleb, N. (2007). *The black swan: The impact of the highly improbable.* New York: Random House.

Taube, K. T., & Linden, K. W. (1989). State mean SAT score as a function of participation rate and other educational and demographic variables. *Applied Measurement in Education, 2,* 143–159.

Taylor, A. K., & Kowalski, P. (2004). Naive psychological science: The prevalence, strength, and sources of misconceptions. *Psychological Record, 54,* 15–25.

Taylor, B. (2006). Vaccines and the changing epidemiology of autism. *Child Care, Health, and Development, 32,* 511–519.

Tetlock, P. E. (2005). *Expert political judgment.* Princeton, NJ: Princeton University Press.

Thaler, R. H. (1992). *The winner's curse: Paradoxes and anomalies of economic life.* New York: Free Press.

Thaler, R. H., & Sunstein, C. R. (2008). *Nudge: Improving decisions about health, wealth, and happiness.* New Haven, CT: Yale University Press.

Thomas, G., Alexander, K., & Eckland, B. (1979). Access to higher education: The importance of race, sex, social class, and academic credentials. *School Review, 87,* 133–156.

Thornton, E. (1986). *The Freudian fallacy.* London: Paladin Books.

Tilburt, J. C., Emanuel, E. J., Kaptchuk, T. J., Curlin, F. A., & Miller, F. G. (2008, October 23). Prescribing placebo treatments: Results of national survey of US internists and rheumatologists. *BMJ 337,* a1938 (doi:10.1136/bmj.a1938)

Tooby, J. (2002, October 6). The greatest Englishman since Newton. *New York Times Book Review,* p. 12.

Toplak, M., Liu, E., Macpherson, R., Toneatto, T., & Stanovich, K. E.

(2007). The reasoning skills and thinking dispositions of problem gamblers: A dual-process taxonomy. *Journal of Behavioral Decision Making, 20,* 103–124.

Trout, J. D. (2008). Seduction without cause: Uncovering explanatory necrophilia. *Trends in Cognitive Science, 12,* 281–282.

Tufte, E. R. (1997). *Visual and statistical thinking: Displays of evidence for making decisions.* Cheshire, CT: Graphics Press.

Turing, A. (1950). Computing machinery and intelligence. *Mind, 59,* 433–460.

Turner, C., Simons, L., Berkowitz, L., & Frodi, A. (1977). The stimulating and inhibiting effects of weapons on aggressive behavior. *Aggressive Behavior, 3,* 355–378.

Tversky, A., & Kahneman, D. (1974). Judgment under uncertainty: Heuristics and biases. *Science, 185,* 1124–1131.

Twachtman-Cullen, D. (1997). *A passion to believe.* Boulder, CO: Westview.

U. S. Congress House Select Committee on Aging. (1984, May 31). *Quackery: A $10 billion scandal.* Washington, DC: U. S. Government Printing Office.

University of California, Berkeley. (1991, January). The 18-year gap. *Berkeley Wellness Letter,* p. 2.

Unsworth, N., & Engle, R. W. (2005). Working memory capacity and fluid abilities: Examining the correlation between Operation Span and Raven. *Intelligence, 33,* 67–81.

Vazire, S., & Gosling, S. D. (2003). Bridging psychology and biology with animal research. *American Psychologist, 58,* 407–408.

Vellutino, F., Fletcher, J. M., Snowling, M., & Scanlon, D. M. (2004). Specific reading disability (dyslexia): What have we learned in the past four decades? *Journal of Child Psychology and Psychiatry, 45,* 2–40.

Violato, C. (1984). Effects of Canadianization of American-biased items on the WAIS and WAIS-R information subtests. *Canadian Journal of Behavioral Science, 16,* 36–41.

Violato, C. (1986). Canadian versions of the information subtests of the Wechsler tests of intelligence. *Canadian Psychology, 27,* 69–74.

Waber, R., Shiv, B., Carmon, Z., & Ariely, D. (2008). Commercial features of placebo and therapeutic efficacy. *JAMA, 299,* 1016–1017.

Wachs, T. D. (2000). *Necessary but not sufficient: The respective roles of single and multiple influences on individual development.* Washington, DC: American Psychological Association.

Wade, C., & Tavris, C. (2008). *Psychology* (9th ed.). Upper Saddle River, NJ: Pearson Education.

Wagenaar, W. A. (1988). *Paradoxes of gambling behavior.* Hove, England: Erlbaum.

Wagenaar, W. A., & Keren, G. (1986). The seat belt paradox: Effect of adopted roles on information seeking. *Organizational Behavior and Human Decision Processes, 38,* 1–6.

Wainer, H. (1993). Does spending money on education help? A reaction to the Heritage Foundation and the Wall Street Journal. *Educational Researcher, 22*(9), 22–24.

Wainer, H. (1999). The most dangerous profession: A note on nonsampling error. *Psychological Methods, 4,* 250–256.

Wargo, E. (2007). Aiming at happiness and shooting ourselves in the foot. *APS Observer, 20,* 13–15.

Wargo, E. (2008, October). The many lives of superstition. *APS Observer, 21,* 18–24.

Wegner, D. M., Fuller, V. A., & Sparrow, B. (2003). Clever hands: Uncontrolled intelligence in facilitated communication. *Journal of Personality and Social Psychology, 85,* 5–19.

Weisberg, D. S., Keil, F. C., Goodstein, J., Rawson, E., & Gray, J. R. (2008). The seductive allure of neuroscience explanations. *Journal of Cognitive Neuroscience, 20,* 470–477.

Wellman, H., Cross, D., & Watson, J. (2001). Meta-analysis of theory-of-mind development: The truth about false belief. *Child Development, 72,* 655–684.

Wells, G. L., Memon, A., & Penrod, S. D. (2006). Eyewitness evidence: Improving its probative value. *Psychological Science in the Public Interest, 7,* 45–75.

West, C. (2007, May). From findings to front page: APS engages the public in psychological science. *APS Observer, 20,* 15–19.

Wheeler, D. L., Jacobson, J. W., Paglieri, R. A., & Schwartz, A. A. (1993). An experimental assessment of facilitated communication. *Mental Retardation, 31,* 49–60.

Wickens, C. D., Lee, J., Liu, Y., & Gordon-Becker, S. (2003). *Introduction to human factors engineering* (2nd ed.). Upper Saddle River, NJ: Prentice Hall.

Wilkinson, L. (1999). Statistical methods in psychology journals: Guidelines and explanations. *American Psychologist, 54,* 595–604.

Wilkowski, B., & Robinson, M. (2008). The cognitive basis of trait anger and reactive aggression: An integrative analysis. *Personality and Social Psychology Review, 12,* 3–21.

Wilson, D. S. (2007). *Evolution for everyone: How Darwin's theory can change the way we think about our lives.* New York: Delacorte Press.

Wilson, T. D., & Brekke, N. (1994). Mental contamination and mental correction: Unwanted influences on judgments and evaluations. *Psychological Bulletin, 116,* 117–142.

Wintre, M. G., North, C., & Sugar, L. A. (2001). Psychologists' response to criticisms about research based on undergraduate participants: A developmental perspective. *Canadian Psychology, 42,* 216–225.

Wolf, M. (2007). *Proust and the squid.* New York: Harper.

Wood, J. M., Nezworski, M. T., Lilienfeld, S. O., & Garb, H. N. (2003). *What's wrong with the Rorschach?* San Francisco: Jossey-Bass.

Woodcock, R. W. (1998). *Woodcock Reading Mastery Tests, Revised-Normative Update.* Shoreview, MN: American Guidance Service.

Woolley, B. (2000). *The bride of science: Romance, reason, and Byron's daughter.* New York: McGraw-Hill.

Wright, R. (1988). *Three scientists and their gods.* New York: Harper & Row.

Wright, R. (1999, December 13). The accidental creationist. *The New Yorker,* pp. 56–65.

Zebrowitz, L. A., White, B., & Wieneke, K. (2008). Mere exposure and racial prejudice: Exposure to other-race faces increases liking for strangers of that race. *Social Cognition, 26,* 259–275.

Zill, N., & Winglee, M. (1990). *Who reads literature?* Cabin John, MD: Seven Locks Press.

Zimbardo, P. G. (2004). Does psychology make a significant difference in our lives? *American Psychologist, 59,* 339–351.

Zimmer, C. (2008, October). The search for intelligence. *Scientific American,* 68–75.

Zweig, M. (2008). *Your money and your brain.* New York: Simon & Schuster.

Name Index

Subject Index